CATEGORIES OF THE IMPOLITICAL

FORDHAM UNIVERSITY PRESS NEW YORK 2015

COMMONALITIES
Timothy C. Campbell, series editor

CATEGORIES OF THE IMPOLITICAL

ROBERTO ESPOSITO

Translated by Connal Parsley

This book was originally published in Italian as Roberto Esposito, *Categorie dell'impolitico*, © 1988 by Società editrice il Mulino, Bologna, new edition 1999.

The translation of this work has been funded by SEPS
SEGRETARIATO EUROPEO PER LE PUBBLICAZIONI SCIENTIFICHE

Via Val d'Aposa 7 - 40123 Bologna - Italy
seps@seps.it - www.seps.it

Library of Congress Cataloging-in-Publication Data

Esposito, Roberto, 1950–
[Categorie dell'impolitico. English]
Categories of the impolitical / Roberto Esposito ; translated by Connal Parsley. — First edition.
pages cm. — (Commonalities)
ISBN 978-0-8232-6420-9 (hardback) — ISBN 978-0-8232-6421-6 (paper)
1. Political science—Philosophy. I. Title.
JA71.E6813 2015
320.01—dc23

2014045388

Printed in the United States of America

17 16 15 5 4 3 2 1

First edition

This book—and the hard work it required—is dedicated to my father.

CONTENTS

TRANSLATOR'S NOTE

Existing English translations have been used wherever possible, and where a modification has been made in order to maintain the consistency of the text, this has been noted. In all other cases, the references provided are to original sources and the translation is my own, made in sympathy with the author's Italian. In consultation with the author, some of the reference material in the original work has been omitted from this translation. An earlier version of this translation of the Preface to the Italian Edition of 1999 appeared in the journal *diacritics*.

I would like to express my thanks to Roberto Esposito, Donatella Alessandrini, Riccardo Baldissone, Lorenzo Corsini, Diane Brown, Charles Devellennes, Benoît Dillet, Maria Drakopoulou, Peter Goodrich, Nicholas Heron, Kent Law School's research support fund (particularly Didi Herman, Sally Sheldon and Kate Bedford), Thomas Lay, Gregory McNamee and the staff at Fordham University Press, Shaun McVeigh, Timothy Neale, Marco Piasentier, Walter Rech, Flora Renz, Peter Rush and Ben Watson, for their various kinds of important help and support toward the preparation of this translation. I extend particularly deep gratitude to Timothy Campbell and Rossella Buono.

PREFACE TO THE ITALIAN EDITION OF 1999

When I submitted *Categories of the Impolitical* to the printers exactly ten years ago, my expectations for its success were certainly not high. Those of my editor were even less so, I suppose, even though the faith he placed in the book (thanks largely to friends like Carlo Galli and teachers Nicola Matteucci and Ezio Raimondi) later proved to have been decisive. How could we have imagined that political philosophy, having been conquered by the absolute certainties of "political science" and the normative stance adopted by the various forms of public ethics, might be willing to concern itself with a notion like the "impolitical"? Faced with an intellectual debate almost entirely devoted to raising methodological barriers between political science, political theory, and political philosophy, how could we present authors with no real disciplinary statute at all—authors who are in fact decidedly undisciplined—such as those examined in this volume? These authors are not only resolutely "undecided" between politics, philosophy, theology, and literature; they are positively allergic in principle to any descriptive or normative model. It is true that some more sophisticated research perspectives were then in play, particularly a new attention to the history of political concepts (descending essentially from the German *Begriffsgeschichte*). But although these approaches certainly constituted an improvement on the traditional "history of ideas," they remained within a direct and frontal hermeneutics of *political* categories. For this reason, they were incapable of even coming at those categories laterally, much less of returning to a place prior to their imagination. It was as if political philosophy remained immune or insufficiently attentive to the deconstructive vortex that had already radically called into question the "positive" sayability of every other object of twentieth-century knowledge. From critical theory to anthropology and from psychoanalysis to aesthetics, twentieth-century thought was suspended by the articulation of its "non"—both the shadowy place from which it first emerged, and the margin of difference that crossed it, as its irreducible alterity.

It was as though political philosophy had not yet fully realized the heuristic productivity of thinking its lexicon's long words and grand concepts not as self-contained entities, but rather as "terms," or border markers, and thus as places where various different languages overlapped and even conflicted. Or it was as though the search for the ultimate sense of every concept, one that would move beyond the epochal stratum to include also the tension that connects it antinomically to its opposite, had been neglected. Certainly, not all Italian political philosophy suffered from this lack of complexity. In the same period important and innovative books on power, modernity, and sovereignty appeared, along with the first attempts at genealogical reconstruction and topological inquiry in the field of political semantics. These, however, represented more the preferences of individual authors than a leap in the quality of research as a whole. It goes without saying that in this slightly stagnant environment, to "risk" a book on the impolitical may have appeared somewhat reckless.

In an unexpected combination of circumstances, however, things were to unfold otherwise. The "Atlantic wave," having reached its peak at the end of the 1980s, began to ebb away—in part because of the obvious unworkability of the models, parameters, and dilemmas it had so painstakingly constructed. At the same time, the most radical continental thought regained currency. In the 1970s, Carl Schmitt managed to defend the positions he had already conquered, albeit amid some ideological misapprehensions from the right just as much as the left. Heidegger survived the ultimate political trial (though not without difficulty), and through this extreme ordeal confirmed his unquestionable centrality to the twentieth century. Wittgenstein revealed himself to be completely incompatible with the neopositivist methodology to which he had been hastily assimilated, reinstating the problem of the limit or the undecidable foundation of language at the center of debate. Meanwhile, the first translations of Leo Strauss were suddenly widespread, and these were soon flanked by others that had the effect of at least calling into question his image as a literal reactionary—an identity foisted upon him by the guardians of local historicism. An even more sudden and sweeping fortune was to befall Hannah Arendt, precisely because her work was unclassifiable within traditional political-philosophical typologies. At the same time, another even more acute window of attention opened for that radical segment of interwar French philosophical writing that has, at its extremes, the thought—but it might be better to say the experience—of Simone Weil and Georges Bataille. Without undervaluing other favorable influences that might have been equally decisive—for example, the rupture (or at least complication) of the ideological split between right and left, the strong surge of feminist philosophies of difference, and the arrival of Derrida *in parte infedelium* across the Atlantic—I hope it is not too presumptuous to claim some small measure of the credit for this general shift of interests by attributing it to this book, now returning to print. It could perhaps more accurately be said that this book intuited the shift slightly ahead of time: in the past decade, all of the authors considered in the volume have consolidated and even increased their specific bearing on culture, both Italian and otherwise.

The decisive factor in this book's return to print was that this fortune extended not only to the individual authors it discusses, but even more so to the very "category" that in some way unites them into a common arc: the impolitical. This term, which emerged gradually from the set of concerns that are examined in this book, and before that from an essay on Nietzsche by Massimo Cacciari,[1] came to cover a wide and often varied range of referents. At the conclusion of the book's publication cycle, and on this wave of semantic proliferation (when Adelphi rightly decided to lose no more time in reprinting Thomas Mann's *Reflections*[2]), the adjective "impolitical" was already circulating not only in publishing networks (thanks to an ever-growing number of philosophers and writers[3]) but also in the editorial offices of newspapers, in commentaries by prestigious columnists, and even in political headlines. Of course, all this had only a minimal bearing on the book's circulation, which was limited to a much smaller group of readers. But it does speak to the sociocultural dynamics sparked by the events marking our most recent history, and particularly the extraordinary acceleration of the crisis—it might be better to say storm—that has struck all the political institutions of this country: not only the political parties, but also its so-called movements, not to mention ideologies as such. Without being able to expand on all the potentialities and ambiguities of the matter here, we can at least say that it remains an open question as to how far the proliferation of the term "impolitical" was driven by politics' general loss of traction on society, culture, and the collective language. What is clear is that this powerful external factor (which is not altogether irrelevant to the question posed by this book) resulted in an excess of complications and indeed confusions about a category whose meaning was already uncertain.[4] If we consider these confusions in combination with the series of misunderstandings, analytical obstacles, and defensive prejudices shown toward it by even its most properly scientific interpreters (not to mention the numerous discussions, contestations, and problematizations that this volume has itself provoked over the years), then the need for an initial and necessarily provisional orientation to the term "impolitical" is obvious.

This orientation could proceed by following the line traced out by the sequence of scholarly objections, or at least interrogations, that the book incited (not altogether independently of the more general situation I have just evoked). I would say that these, or at least the most relevant among them, can be classified into four distinct if not completely unrelated kinds of argument: (1) the impolitical is a relative of the "antipolitical" that is dominant today, albeit a fairly sophisticated one; (2) the impolitical is a kind of gnostic negative political theology, and as such is bound to a presupposed dualism that severely limits its hermeneutic potential; (3) the impolitical is a category internal to modernity, and more precisely to the extreme phase of its crisis, which limits the impolitical to reflecting that crisis in an inverse form; and (4) precisely because of its withdrawal from the political, impolitical philosophy inherits the highest political will to power by claiming a monopoly of judgment on it.

Before attempting a response to these arguments, I will make one final caveat. I might have limited myself to arranging these and other criticisms in such a way as to reveal them as conflictual, thus allowing them to neutralize each other's force—but I prefer simply to discuss each on its own merits. I will say further that the following discussion does not change the fact that each of these criticisms contains a dimension of at least legitimacy, if not "truth," that I do not intend to deny, and for which I have accounted in the work undertaken since they have been made—deepening, redefining, and even modifying the initial framework of the book. Any thought that wishes to do justice to itself, as well as to its object, must also and above all be prepared to listen to the objections it provokes: perhaps to confirm its original convictions, but also to redefine its course.

The first criticism, which assimilates the impolitical to the antipolitical, has not been overtly formulated but is rather presupposed by a wide range of articles—and not only from within the academy.[5] In responding to it I will not repeat the relevant points made in the introduction to the volume; points that are also reaffirmed on multiple occasions in each of the chapters, and which, taken together, make clear the fundamental difference in orientation between an impolitical perspective and any stance that could be termed apolitical (or even more so antipolitical). The impolitical implies neither weakening nor abandoning a focus on the political, but on the contrary it entails a focus that is even more radical and intense—as the work (but also the lives) of all the authors associated with it unmistakably attest: from Hannah Arendt to Simone Weil, from Hermann Broch to Georges Bataille and finally René Char.[6] But this declaration of intention is always at risk of remaining exactly that: a subjective intention that is not borne out in the objective outcome of its discourse. Although it is programmatically distinct from and opposed to the antipolitical, the impolitical paradigm could in fact bring us to the same conclusions, running aground on the same aporetic short circuit.

In order to respond to this objection—a fairly captious task, since there is no way to disprove a theory except to begin with its premises—I will reverse its order and begin with a definition not of the impolitical but of the antipolitical, in order to demonstrate not only that it has nothing to do with the former term but that it amounts to its perfect negation. In fact, I will go so far as to outline the conclusion of this reasoning first, and in no uncertain terms: The antipolitical cannot be the same thing as the impolitical because it already the same thing as the political. It descends from the political, and it reproposes the political in the very act of negating it. The antipolitical is not something contrary to the political, but simply its mirror image: a manner of *doing politics* that consists in setting itself against politics. That is, it works by putting to use the same enmity that characterizes the political in its essential form. This is so well attested historically as to require no further demonstration. Every time an antipolitical argument, rhetoric, or symbology is adopted, this is always done—and it could not be done otherwise—using the very presuppositions, instruments, and finality as the politics to which it declares itself in opposition (albeit, evidently, in the service of other interests, which are themselves in turn politicized or available for politicization). It is no accident that both recent and not-so-recent champions of the antipolitical always end up "getting in the ring" sooner or later, as the unfortunate expression goes, thus attesting to the thoroughly political nature of their claimed opposition to the political universe.

This is especially true of that form of unwitting (or perhaps all too witting) antipoliticality that attempts to reduce or eliminate all conflict—thus naturally and inevitably conflicting with it,[7] as even the most cogent pacifism realizes when it cannot defend the peace, its *own* peace, except by declaring war on war, combatting war always and again by means of war. What matters in the *political* constitution of every antipolitical stance, in short, are not the contents, values, or ideals it rises to defend—thus offending the politics or the politicians who seem to oppose them—so much as the polemic (and polemicizing) *form* implicit in its own prefix: an "anti," understood from the very beginning as being "against" in the strong sense. This presupposition was perfectly clear to the most celebrated of "impolitical" scholars, who wrote in his eponymous *Reflections of a Nonpolitical Man* that "antipolitics is also politics, for politics is a terrible force: if one only *knows* about it, one has already succumbed to it. One has lost one's innocence."[8] But this fact seems entirely lost on those who subject the antipolitical to an axiological valuation. This valuation is itself unwittingly deduced by contrast with a value assigned to the political,[9] such that the antipolitical is valued positively where the political has been connoted in terms of dominion and violence,[10] or negatively where it is acknowledged as a democratic and emancipatory potentiality.[11] What each of these possibilities risks losing is precisely the structural connection—being its conflictual intention—that morphologically binds the political to its *double*, the antipolitical, in a single, indissoluble knot.

The political fate that befalls the antipolitical does not escape the impolitical gaze. On the contrary, it can be said that this destiny comes to full visibility only when viewed through the specific angle of refraction opened up by the impolitical. This is because only the impolitical defines the whole of reality in political terms. As this book attempts to argue through its chosen authors, for the impolitical there is no entity, no force, and no power that is capable of contesting the political from within its own language. But nor from outside of this language—since such an "outside" could exist only as an ideological, mythical, self-legitimating projection of that same politics that has descended into a "civil war" with its antipolitical "twin." This dialectic of identification-by-opposition is clear as far as the oppositional semantics of the prefix "anti" is concerned. But it is just as applicable to those who declare themselves merely "apolitical." That "a–," too, which signals externality, indifference, or disinterest in the political, assumes a significance only in relation to the reality from which it attempts to take its distance; a reality that is still, and always, political. This reality may be depoliticized, like the one modernization has been producing for some decades (or, it could be said, for some centuries) through the immunization from every form of community—that is, through the supremacy of society, the economy, and technology over the elemental fact of relation. But this distance is always taken with a logic that is, in the final analysis, political, in the sense that it is decided by (or at least functions for) certain vested interests. This well-established fact can be demonstrated both historically and categorically. Historically, in the sense that modern depoliticization—of Hobbesian origin—is born only within the shell of an "absolute politics"[12] and sovereign obligation. And categorically because, as is shown by the "anormative," exceptional, and decisionist origin of every normative order, the neutralization of political conflict can always also be interpreted as the political neutralization of conflict: a politics of neutralization. Was modern politics not born precisely in order to neutralize conflict? Was it not always, in that sense, "antipolitical"? From this point of view, the antipolitical is only the extreme, posthumous, and completed form of a modern politics understood as the inevitably conflictual means of neutralizing an even more unsustainable conflict.

This neutralization is precisely what the impolitical does not attempt. Far from conflicting with political conflict and negating the political *as* conflict, the impolitical considers the political the *only* reality and the *entirety* of reality, adding, however, that it is *only reality*. Not in the sense that outside of this reality there exists another space, time, or possibility, much less an "anti" that could oppose it (thus inevitably confirming and reinforcing it). Rather in the sense that its nonopposition is precisely a "non": neither an apologetic assumption of the political, nor an impossible withdrawal from it.[13] This "non" is the limit that defines the political, circumscribing it within its specific, finite terms. The political's terms are finite not as opposed to something else that is infinite, but rather in the sense of being complete in themselves, and for that reason not susceptible to being taken to an end other than the one that inheres originarily within them, and which has never ceased to characterize them. The political is not always aware of its constitutive finitude—on the contrary, it is constitutively inclined to forget it. So the impolitical does nothing but "remind" the political of its finitude, returning it to the very heart of the political so that finitude dwells not only at its margins, but at its very center. And at the center of the political lies a heart that is impolitical because it is neither produced by nor productive of politics. To be political—or to produce any kind of politics—it would need to detach itself, recognizing itself in a relationship of alterity with the very element that is presupposed within it as its only dimension. From this point of view, then, just as we have seen with the antipolitical, it may certainly be said that the impolitical too coincides with the political. But it may be said only on the condition that we acknowledge the radical difference between an impolitical and an antipolitical coincision. Whereas the antipolitical coincides with the political because in renouncing it, it reproduces and reemphasizes it, the impolitical coincides with the political precisely because it does *not* renounce it. On the basis of this distinction, the paradoxically affirmative character of the impolitical "negation" begins to emerge. What does the impolitical affirm? That there is no political but the political. But also, that precisely for this reason the political is closed—or, more accurately, determined—by this identity with itself. It is nothing other than itself. Its potential [*potenza*] is only such as it is. It cannot transcend itself toward any end or completion beyond its own bare being-such. The impolitical is the end of every "end of the political."[14]

This means that neither is it possible to understand the impolitical as a form of eschatology, whether positive or negative, Christian or gnostic. This is the second objection leveled at the impolitical: that it opposes every form of political theology, but from a point of view that in the end, in being nonpolitical, paradoxically takes on a theological inflection (albeit a negative one).[15] Let us proceed through this notion logically. It seems to me that there can be no doubt as to the anti–political-theological intention of the impolitical. If there exists one clear point of commonality between the various "impolitical" authors, at least starting with Benjamin, it can be found precisely in their rejection of *any* kind of conjunction—immediate, delayed, or providential—between the Good and power. For these authors, power is neither a representation of the Good nor an emanation from it, and still less a dialectical mechanism capable of recuperating Good out of evil, thus converting the latter into the former.[16] The difference between these two terms is so clear that it severs the impolitical's ties with any possible political-theological perspective. Such a perspective is at work in the ancient "political religions" that Eric Voegelin critically revisited,[17] the Roman imperial monotheism that Erik Peterson interpreted as a self-legitimating superimposition of the religious lexicon onto that of the political,[18] and the specifically Catholic concern with restoring the representative connection between political decision and transcendental order, a connection severed by the knife of modernity (treated in varying but convergent manners by Jacques Maritain, Romano Guardini, and Hans Urs von Balthasar). But the impolitical is also foreign to any political theology understood as a genealogical theory of sovereignty (seen above all in Schmitt). Such a political theology coincides, in the end, with the very secularization of theological language into the juridico-political.[19] But the reason that the impolitical remains foreign to this political theology is not that it refuses to go along with the notion of an originary void of substance, a lacuna, a lack: on the contrary, that is precisely its own perspective. Rather it is because, unlike Schmitt, it does not propose the transformation of that void toward a new order, however precarious and contingent. It postulates no coercive order capable of transposing that lack of substance into another, more powerful representative form.

If the impolitical *were* to give itself the task (or ascribe to itself the destiny) of bestowing this originary lack with a "form," it would lapse into precisely that political-theological stance from which it withdraws—and all the more powerfully for being conscious of its own secularized nature. But the impolitical instead declares itself unavailable as the host of this intersection of theology and secularization, of myth and technology, of representation and decision. It is not only unavailable to aid the consecration of power by ancient legitimating practices, but it also refuses to recognize that within its own modern desacralization there should be any new normative mechanism (which would itself inevitably abound with sacral elements). It is unavailable, in short, to uphold either the law of power or the power of Law, and it is this antinomy—in the literal sense of a withdrawal from *nomos*—that shelters the impolitical from becoming a positive political theology. But, it could be asked, in doing so does this antinomy not end up reducing the impolitical to a *negative* political theology? This is the second of the objections with which we began. This is precisely how Jacob Taubes interpreted Saint Paul's antinomianism[20]—in terms of a negative political theology. Paul did not intend to counter Roman *nomos* with another power [*potere*]: He limits himself to denying the law any capacity to order the political. Rather, in arriving at the point where he equiparates law with sin, Paul effects the law's greatest possible delegitimation. But, paradoxically, for Taubes it is precisely this delegitimation that contains the political potential [*potenza*] of Paul's message of salvation, rightly considered by the Romans to be more dangerous than any counterproposition of an alternative power. This is what gives rise to his conviction that Paul's remains a *political* theology, albeit a negative one. It is true that through the desired "contamination" by the pagans, the "Jewish people" to whom Paul speaks loses every nationalist inflection and tends to assume a universal significance. But nothing could be more *politically* subversive of the Roman order than this universalism.

Without being able to enter into the merits of Taubes's interpretation of Paul here—which is quite different from Karl Barth's, for example, which I personally prefer—the point I would like to emphasize is the difference between even a negative political theology and the horizon of the impolitical. Their heterogeneity derives, it could be said, from the "place" that the impolitical assigns to the negative. In what sense? Why does an impolitical critique of political theology correspond not at all to a negative political theology? Because while the latter situates the bar of the "non" between the political and theology, denying that theology could be politics and politics theology, the impolitical places it also *within* each of the two terms themselves. The distinction—or better, the contradiction—thus passes not only between theology and politics but also within them. We have already seen how the political, when defined by its own finite terms, cannot be "theologized." But the same is true of theology, which, seen from an "impolitical" point of view, can no longer be *fully* such: a theo-logy. It too is destined to experience its own logical indigence, as the early Barth well knew; or its own internal lacuna, as Dietrich Bonhoeffer had recognized even more radically.[21] Is it not Simone Weil who brings this depropriating line to a kind of completion, depropriating the "theological" and the political alike, when she places absence at the very core of divine creation, inverting it so that it becomes "decreation"? And how else should we understand Georges Bataille's explicitly "atheological" texts, if not in the sense of a deconstruction of theology that pushes it to the point where theology is inverted and becomes its exact opposite?

It is true that this twin reference to Weil and Bataille (whom this book distinguishes analytically partly by assigning to each a different register of the impolitical, ascetic and ecstatic respectively)[22] exposes another flank that has felt the critical barbs of more than one commentator.[23] I refer to the accusation of Gnosticism, which, on this reasoning, might threaten to engulf the entire impolitical perspective. I must concede that this is a real possibility, especially since both Weil and Bataille certainly absorbed influences from gnostic texts (we could include at least Hermann Broch here, too). Their thought as a whole, furthermore, remains susceptible to an oscillation that at times seems to push it in a gnostic direction. This is not always the case, as both this book and my subsequent works have attempted to argue. But how can we fail to see a gnostic streak in Weil's conception of creation as the withdrawal of the Good? Or, perhaps even more clearly, in Bataille's conclusion (which is also Weil's, albeit in a different way), that the only sure means of escape from the idolatrous travesty of an evil disguised as the Good is to maintain that it is necessary to practice evil? And how can we not see that this same negative definition of reality—whether created or decreated—brings with it a dualistic consequence or presupposition?

Certainly, the gnostic risk is real. Yet all of the thought arising from this book in the past decade has been characterized by the very attempt to rid itself of this association. I would even go further and say that the text represented here initiated a discursive path that is essentially opposed to any such dualistic tendency. This intention is already visible throughout the book, for example in its constant concern to deny the existence of any reality, whether conceived as secondary or more primary, besides that which can be experienced [*sperimentabile*]. As I have said, the impolitical is not something other than the political, but only the political itself as seen from a point of view that "measures" it against something that it neither *is* nor can *ever be*: the political's impossibility. In this sense there is not really a duality, only difference. And this difference is a question of the perspective of the gaze, not the object that is gazed upon—and even less its subject. But, particularly in the final chapter of the book, this impolitical "self-scrutiny" is heightened to such a degree that it arrives at an *affirmative* invocation of what it otherwise negates. This is what happens when an impolitical deconstruction of the political's categories is directed also at the impolitical itself. It is as if the category of the impolitical were excavated from within, until it loses any kind of identity—even a negative one. As if it could not manifest itself except by cancelling itself out in the pure "taking place" [*aver luogo*] of the political, in its simple "dwelling." But not—as has also been authoritatively suggested—in a form of "supreme, sovereign indifference" to the regime of difference.[24] If that were so, the impolitical would not only lose all of its deconstructive charge, but it would be dissolved altogether. The operation involved here is instead an intensification of the limit that distinguishes, but at the same time its conversion into the other thing that division implies: it is a division, but at the same time a union, of what it divides. The gnostic-dualistic hypothesis can arise only if we allow the accent to fall wholly on the first sense of this limit: separation. If we recognize in that limit only a "power of separation," we inevitably produce two separate and opposing spheres. Things change, however, if we also emphasize this limit's other facet, one that is complementary to and deconstructive of the first: its connectivity, which unifies no less than it separates (or rather, connects precisely that which it separates). At this moment the impolitical becomes not only the limit of the political, but also the limit of its own being-limit. There is a term that renders perfectly a sense of the limit as a copresencing of separation and connection: "sharing" [*condivisione*] (or, in Bataille's French, *partage*). From this point of view, we would have to say that the impolitical is not divided from the political, but that it shares the political space. It is the sharing of the political—or better still, the political *as* sharing. Here, at the extreme opposite of the gnostic risk, there opens a space for the thought of community.

Before arriving at that space, however, a discussion of the third objection is necessary. In truth, this objection does not challenge the impolitical in itself, but rather seeks to constrain its hermeneutic relevance to the limited sphere of modernity, and late modernity in particular. Carlo Galli has formulated this objection most clearly. Galli acknowledges that the impolitical is the ultimate and perhaps *only* radically critical horizon of modernity, but suggests that for this very reason it is also internal to modernity and categorically "encompassed" by it. If it is true that the impolitical breaks ground [*sfondare*] for a critique of the logic of the modern, it can do so only *on* the ground [*fondo*] of the modern. This means that its "breakthrough" is gripped by the very same terms it believes itself to define: "Even where it is exposed to the most radical critique, modernity is affirmed as the positively insuperable horizon of thought. The impolitical and the modern *simul stabunt, simul cadent*."[25] Whereas for Galli the impolitical offers the only nonideological deconstruction of the modern precisely because it is the other side of the modern coin (that is, a deconstruction that is not reactive, recuperative, or utopian), Biagio de Giovanni circumscribes its application to an even smaller sphere. Here the delimitation of the impolitical assumes the quality of a true and proper "reduction," and for that reason effectively also its neutralization. For de Giovanni, the impolitical fails to apprehend the conceptual movement of modernity as a whole (which is much more variegated and contradictory than the impolitical makes out), because it is an expression of a specific and peculiar moment centering on our century: "In the whole of twentieth-century thought . . . the impolitical inheres as a counterpoint to the elements of violence, multitude, and war that make the short century the century of totalitarianism."[26] There is thus a double confine "constricting" the impolitical between a *terminus a quo* situated at the beginning of the 1920s and a *terminus ad quem* marked by the crumbling of the final wall: if impolitical philosophy constituted a response at the level of the great "European civil war," it "is nevertheless exhausted with the death of the century."[27] The impolitical is not an immanent critique of modernity, suggests this objection, but only of its concluding crisis—to which it remains riveted in an indissoluble relation of cause and effect. What else is *critique*, if not the historical and conceptual emergence of a *crisis*?

What can be said in response to this reading? There is no doubt some truth to this idea that there is a nexus between the concept and its historical moment, especially if we reject a historicist inflection in favor of a much more convincing "epochal" perspective. There is even empirical support for its plausibility: Is it not true that the most intensely impolitical texts were written in the period from before the First World War to after the Second—a stretch of just a few years? And is that same period not the one we regard as the "critical" era of modern times par excellence? A fundamental difficulty lies, however, in the use and the relevance of this category "criticality." The problem is that the term is not symmetrical with the space of reflection that is opened by the impolitical. That space, as we have seen, does not coincide with the one commonly assigned to a critical stance, because the impolitical does not "critique" reality in the name of something other than reality—some different ideal, value, or interest. If it were to do so, it would remain bound from within by the tradition it aims to critique; the tradition that already accommodates the many critiques of religion, economics, politics, and so on.[28] But there is an even more inherent reason that the impolitical is freed from any traditionally critical perspective: the difference between its own point of view and the very idea of "crisis" from which critique derives (and not only etymologically).

Although a detailed consideration of the matter is not possible here, we can say that the use of "crisis" as a point of reference is an integral part of any philosophy of history ordered as a chronological succession both between epochs and within them. Certainly, this succession could be understood as being either of progress or decline. It might leave room for discontinuity and contradiction, or provide for ruptures, interruptions, or recurrences. It may position historical periods asymmetrically, or arrange them along an irregular plane. But what it cannot do, because it is beyond its reach, is conceptualize the ahistorical element of history—which is precisely what the impolitical does in interrogating its border with the political (the limit from which it arises, and which it bears "eternally" within itself as its immanent transcendental). If, in short, languages are modified historically (as *Begriffsgeschichte* rightly reminds us) then so too is history determined linguistically, resulting in a dialectic whose origin cannot be grasped by discourse. Not because that origin is too distant from any given epoch, but rather because it is too *close* to them all—or rather copresent within them.[29] It is precisely this copresence that dissolves the historical succession of epochs into the fundamental unity that crosses and disorders them: the problem of the un/originary nature of the origin (or the an/archic nature of the *arché*).[30] What might this expression mean? How should such a bar separating the origin from itself be understood? Unusual caution is called for here. It is not that the philosophy of crisis makes no reference to the problem of the origin—on the contrary, it is precisely by reference to the origin that it can define a certain moment as critical. Rather, the problem is that the origin to which this philosophy refers is always conceived as a beginning that is full, whole, and substantial, and for this very reason inherently precritical. It is precisely in relation (and in contrast) to this kind of origin that crisis becomes possible: crisis, in this case, is indeed the rupture of the origin through a divisive process that destroys its originarily unitary character, therefore betraying, distorting, and perverting it (but in such a way as to always leave it open to the possibility of becoming whole once more). Looking beyond their various therapeutic strategies (restorative, recompositional, or regenerative), this is the presupposition that unites all European philosophies of crisis into a common diagnosis: If a crisis has emerged, it is logically necessary that there must have been a *more* originary time, one which was *truly* originary, in which the crisis did not exist. There must be a moment, moreover, beyond the crisis that makes it resolvable, or at least makes it impossible to exclude altogether the possibility of a resolution.

It is precisely this line of reasoning that the impolitical contests. Not because of its supposed division within the origin—which it too radically assumes—but for the idea that this division could be dated to a subsequent (or at least nonoriginary) phase of historical progression, generally identified with the advent of technology. Leaving aside all of their considerable differences of diagnosis and prognosis, this is exactly the point of convergence among Max Weber, Schmitt, and Arendt (though not the impolitical Arendt), and also many "critics of civilization." At some specific moment, the political gets away from itself, betrays its true essence, and falls prey to technology. But this essentialist-degenerative reading comes at the cost of a kind of narrowing of perspective whose effect is to circumscribe to modernity something that is actually much more originary—something that in fact coincides with the origin. There has never existed a *polis*, understood as a unitary cosmos, that was subsequently shattered—just as there has never existed a natural order that was then violated, uprooted, and destroyed by the violence of technology. On the contrary, from the very beginning the *nomoi* of the *polis* were in conflict with each other, just as nature has forever been "denatured" by and in the supplementary logic of the artificial. Is this not what Plato meant when he excluded the ideal city from the range of historical possibilities? Or Aristotle, when he located the specific nature of practical politics precisely in the disjuncture that separates it from its "truth"? Is it not necessary to assume that the political has neither determinate properties nor an essence—that what is most proper to it lies in the absence of propriety, as its essence lies in an irreparable inessentiality?

This is precisely the originary problem—the problem of the origin—that the modern neither discovers nor produces but, since Machiavelli, is limited to conceptualizing in an ever more conscious way: the constitutively "demonic" nature of the political,[31] meaning its inability to be reduced to a single "symbol." From this point of view, it can be said that it is not the history of political thought, and even less so its modern phase, that "explains" the impolitical perspective. If anything, it is the latter that sheds light on the former, and at the same time deconstructs it. What it deconstructs, precisely, is the succession of oppositional phases that casts the political as a history of either emancipation or degeneration (or both, each in compensation for the other). Against this pattern—or better, beyond it—the impolitical recognizes the perfectly co-originary nature of technology and politics; recognizing, too, that contrary to the teachings of a long tradition there is no *praxis* that is prior to *techne*, nor qualitatively different from it.[32] As one of Plato's myths tells us, politics does not come first, to be followed by technology: if anything, it is the opposite (*Protagoras* 322c). This means that technology is not the end of the political but its origin. But if this is true, if—as Nietzsche well knew—the political originates *together with* and *within* technology, if—as Simone Weil emphasized—the origin does not "fall" down the precipice of the "post" because the fall and the precipice are already originary;[33] if—as Heidegger's preferred expression has it—the origin is given only in the form of its withdrawal; then this implies that the most primary origin is always secondary to something else, from which it emerges as its originary defect. Or, the origin coincides with its own fault. Or, it is at the same time both origin and nonorigin—its trace, as Jacques Derrida would have said: it is difference from itself and therefore the un/originary articulation of that which originates. If the origin is a continual "coming to presence"—which is always contemporaneous to us—then it can never be fully present to itself. It is properly unrepresentable. The impolitical is nothing other than the enunciation of this unrepresentability. It is the "with-drawal" [*ritratto*] of the originary trace (in the dual sense of to "withdraw itself" [*ritirarsi*], and to "re-mark" itself [*rimarcare*]).[34]

The final reservation against the impolitical focuses on the nature of this *retrait* (as the French say),[35] and it does so in a way that in a certain sense connects and recapitulates all of the others. This very trait (claims this objection)—its inclination to withdraw from action—assigns to the impolitical the tremendous power of judgment on action. It exercises the sovereign faculty of separating good from evil, just from unjust, true from false. "The work of the impolitical," as we can read in a recent summing up for the prosecution, "coincides with the issuing of a judgment, a verdict, that separates truth and good from the political, thereby posing itself as the guardian of this division."[36] Precisely because it proclaims itself the bearer of "a knowledge more originary and radical than any historical and empirical knowledge,"[37] the impolitical claims dominance over real, impredicable events, and the "emancipatory" practices to which they give rise. Is this really the result—if not the intention—of an impolitical stance? Or is this criticism actually the fruit of an analysis that clings obstinately, prejudicially, to a simplified and reductive picture of a dialectic that is in reality much more complex? This dialectic is primarily a dialectic between "inside" and "outside," and if the impolitical were simply situated outside the political—or if it were limited to tracing the political's outer limit—that argument would certainly hit its mark. But that is not the case. The reason, to be clear, is because the "outside"—or more accurately, the void of substance to which the impolitical refers—is located squarely within the political. One could say, perhaps, that it is that very same "political," but without the operation of its mythical "fullness."

This point requires clarification. I do not wish to deny that in various formulations of impolitical thought, and above all the earliest ones, the emphasis fell on its exteriority. And even more so on the limit, the border, the margin that the political cannot determine precisely because it is in turn determined by it—just as the voice is by silence. But silence is not another voice; nor is it the voice of the other. It is not even the foundation or the presupposition of the voice (although I cannot deny having sometimes interpreted it as such; as the "non" that opens the possibility of "saying," or more precisely in this case, of "doing"). Rather, that silence must increasingly be understood as the caesura, or the articulation, within language itself: making possible not only that which remains unsaid in language, but also what it pronounces clearly. In short, the entire elaboration of the category of the impolitical in recent years has tended ever more explicitly to interiorize its exteriority, its being-outside, its limit—just as Bataille called his passion for the "outside" precisely *inner experience*, thereby alluding to a perfect overlapping of immanence and transcendence. As discussed at length in the final chapter of this book, transcendence is not the opposite of immanence but rather its interruption, or its exposure to its *own* "outside." It is the transcendence *of* immanence, not *from* immanence.

It could be said that this journey within the self-analysis of the impolitical is marked, or more precisely constituted, by the thought of community. Initiated in the chapter of this book that concerns Bataille, this thought finds a more mature form in a later book that continues the work of this one (but also displaces its semantic center of gravity).[38] I could define this lexical transition—which developed above all through exposure to the thought of Jean-Luc Nancy—as moving from a logic of presupposition toward one of exposition,[39] or (and this is really the same thing), from an analytical plane to an ontological one. Community is not something that puts into relation what is; it is being itself as a relation. This clarification is significant, because this is what radically distinguishes the impolitical from all contemporary philosophies, ethics, and anthropologies of community. But it also separates it from every "politics of friendship," to recall the title of a recent work by Derrida.[40] My impression on this matter—an impression shared by Derrida himself, despite his opposing point of departure—is that notwithstanding all the possible interweavings, affinities, and references between the lexicon of friendship and that of community, an insuperable disjuncture lingers between them. The difference is between on one hand a linguistic code that can be political only through reference to its subjects (subjects of friendship, or inversely, of enmity), and on the other hand one that concerns being "in common" as such. That is, this code registers a shared existence that splits and decentralizes the dimension of subjectivity, in the sense that the relation—being *in* relation and being *as* relation—cannot be thought except through the "withdrawal" of its subjective terms.

These remarks help to avoid a possible misunderstanding that Bataille's thought has not always escaped; famously oriented, as it was, especially at the end of the 1930s, toward a "community of death" (which was not always distinct from the rather more disquieting prospect of the death of community). It is said that *The Categories of the Impolitical* does not distance itself explicitly enough from the sacrificial (or self-sacrificial) tendency that was lived, in a peculiar way, through the striking and disastrous adventure that was *Acéphale*.[41] And it is said moreover that in its final pages, devoted to the mass suicide at Numantia, the book seems to share *Acéphale*'s tendency to degeneration, thus apparently warranting one of the most acute criticisms of the impolitical advanced by Maurizio Ferraris: just as the *noluntas* is but the mirror-image of the *voluntas*, "it does not seem difficult to see in the community as being-toward-death the simple reverse of the community of life."[42] After all, like the impolitical, *Acéphale* offers a relief from a philosophy of the subject (if not also of action) through its sovereign self-decapitation, such that "in that death by consent, the archetype of the death of Socrates reappears: a consciousness that knows itself to be worth more than life and limb, because it is the living spirit that triumphs over death."[43] This observation is not unfounded, even if it brings me to conclusions that are distinctly different from those reached by Ferraris. But it relies on an idea of the community of sacrifice that, even if it did constitute one of the possible outcomes of Bataille's experience (certainly not the only one), is entirely excluded from the horizon of meaning of *communitas* because of the way this term has since been configured. Indeed, according to its old etymology, *communitas* can no longer be conceived as the product of a shared will, nor as the line of death that subjects join in a kind of sacrificial ecstasy, because it precedes every will and every subject as the originary *munus* from which they arise as an uninterrupted expropriation. The void [*nulla*], in short, cannot be the *telos* of community, nor its presupposition. It is rather the community itself, if it is thought not as a subjective bond (and even less so an objective one), but rather as the space [*spaziamento*] outlined by the impossibility of its operation. In this sense, it can be said that this impossibility is nothing other than that un/originary origin to which we have already referred—the absent origin, or an origin withdrawn from itself by a lack that is irreparable because it coincides with its own constitution. Every tale of the founding crime at the origin of society merely translates this crime's "commission," this originary lack, into an anthropological register.

The impolitical perspective has known intimately, from the very beginning, that community can never coincide with itself, and can never appear historically without being distorted. This is community's constitutive conflict, and it cannot be resolved except by falling into political theology, or, to the contrary, being neutralized along the more dominant lines of the modern project. But I would like to insist that it is now necessary that this originary void [*vuoto*] not be inflected only negatively, nor in a simply deconstructive sense. Insofar as it is *munus*, it can also be understood as "munificent": that is, as a "nothing in common" that even whilst dwelling in the dimension of conflict and violence, also bears within it the dimension of donativity.[44] It is not by chance that the void is always also the custodian, or the heart, of the communal entity. The donativity alluded to here certainly has nothing to do with the ingenuous repropositions of the paradigm of the gift attempted by the social sciences. All too often these rehabilitations forget the constitutively ambivalent character—both offer and threat—that is implicit in the donative dynamic. Rather, this donativity recalls the risk and the danger that the originary *munus* presents to those who choose to share it, lacerating their own subjective identities in the process. But what appears to us as a choice here is, in truth, only the awareness of a reality to which we belong without ever *wholly* belonging. What else could the impolitical be, if not this imperceptible disjuncture?

ACKNOWLEDGMENTS

The parts of this book concerning Romano Guardini, Hannah Arendt, and Hermann Broch were published in a partial and provisional form in the journals *il Centauro*, *Il Mulino*, and *Filosofia Politica*. I would like to thank the managing editors of these journals, Biagio de Giovanni and Nicola Matteucci, for permitting the republication of this material, and for years of lively collaboration.

CATEGORIES OF THE IMPOLITICAL

INTRODUCTION

An Impolitical Departure

It was with some hesitation that I gave this book a title positioned halfway between two great twentieth-century texts: Thomas Mann's *Reflections of a Nonpolitical Man* and Carl Schmitt's *Categories of the Political*, the translated collection that determined Schmitt's fortune in Italy. Establishing a close connection with these works and their particular heritage might have been misleading. Quite clearly so in Mann's case, because the book proposes to radically depart from his sense of the word "nonpolitical," as we will see in a few pages. In the case of Schmitt, no less so: Although he occupies a place in the first part of the volume, Schmitt is more a point of departure than an internal point of reference. It could be said that the book begins where Schmitt's discourse ends, taking up what lies "beyond" it—despite the fact that it takes for granted a whole host of his considerable analytical achievements. Chief among these are the insights contained in the perennially undervalued fragment *Roman Catholicism and Political Form*, which functions as what the French call a *mise en abyme* for certain parts of this book; a kind of pre-text or explanatory key. But then, it should not surprise us if a book dedicated to an investigation of the impolitical might seek elaboration *outside itself* (in a text that constitutes perhaps the last great defense of the political, no less). The impolitical is a negative notion, and it must remain bound to that negativity or suffer conversion into its opposite—the categories of the political.

This is obviously different from saying that nothing can be said of the impolitical itself. If that were true, it would not really be a category (or rather a categorical horizon), but only an example of that philosophical *mana* that is sometimes taken as a crutch in those none too rare moments of conceptual desperation. But anything that can be said about the impolitical has to start with what it does *not* represent. Or, more accurately, it must begin with the impolitical's inherent opposition to all modes of "representation," understanding representation as *the* category of the political at the moment of its emergent crisis. This is how we must read Schmitt's essay, whose fundamental object is the nature of institutional depoliticization in modernity, and more precisely the thesis that this depoliticization is brought about by the rejection of "representation" as the mechanism which binds political decision to the "idea." Schmitt, in other words, considers representation as what allows the passage between the Good and power (a "communication" between the two, to use the terms of Dostoyevsky's anti-Roman stance).

We must make two clarifications on this point (albeit with the brevity necessary to a set of introductory remarks). The first concerns modernity. Without entering into a debate that would implicate practically all recent philosophical literature, what should be emphasized is that any account of the modern must be understood within the register of *conflict*. The modern is constitutively contradictory, in the sense that its extremes remain permanently opposed rather than being resolved dialectically. That is certainly true, and it is perhaps most true, where the modern problem of the political is concerned. Where there is talk of modern depoliticization, or rather of modernity *as* depoliticization or neutralization, these processes takes the form of an *excess* of politics (see for example the works of the young Schmitt, but also a whole host of his interpreters, even those quite distant from him, from Arendt to Polanyi and from Touraine to Dumont). To put this differently, the ever-increasing neutralization of the political is the result of the acquisition by politics of every ambit of life; a process that formalizes life, emancipates it from nature, and effects its loss of "substance." It is referred to as a neutralization because its aim is the exclusion of conflict from the "civil" order. Hobbes's *Leviathan* makes this particularly clear, since Hobbes succeeds in "eliminating" conflict only at the cost of a strategic depoliticization of society in favor of the sovereign. In this sense and on this understanding of the political, it is Hobbes and not Machiavelli who is the true founder of modern politics.

The second clarification also has a genealogical connection to Hobbes's paradigm. It concerns the concept of "representation" [*rappresentazione*] in the modern political and juridical sense of the term [*rappresentanza*]. When

Schmitt sees the death of the former in modernity, he does not mean to deny—on the contrary, he explicitly affirms—that it is precisely modernity, beginning with Hobbes, that opens the history of representation [*rappresentanza*], which is therefore precisely a modern history (a thesis shared by Michel Foucault, though differently inflected). But this is at the same time the history of a modern kind of representation that has been made entirely immanent (emptied, that is, of any substantive content), so it also constitutes the most radical negation of representation understood as a representation of the "idea." All that remains of the idea, which is absorbed—we could say "flattened"—into the *pure image* of a now-absent foundation, is the mere *reference* to something transcendent beyond it that was once both the formative *virtus* and ultimate *telos* of the political. This is the vertical connection that the modern severs with its notion of decision, thus excluding any relation with what lies outside of it (except by analogy or through a metaphorical transposition). It is not that the modern is a simple proliferation of opposing interests with no desire to be united. Rather, it is understood as a self-contained functional whole. It is understood, that is, as a "system" capable of self-governance without any kind of external telos (the Good), nor any logic of an internal bond with its contents (the "subjects" who populate it). Its division into subsystems is organized in precisely such a way as not to require any agreement as to "ideals." And the political is just one of these subsystems, which explains the autonomy it has achieved from the modern at large. At the same time, it also accounts for the entropic hollowing-out we have already mentioned. It is true that not all modern political philosophies produce this same self-destructive result, and in fact several could be seen as points of resistance and contrast. Machiavelli presented an original (but ultimately vanquished) alternative; or we could just as easily say the same of Spinoza, Vico, and in some ways Hegel and Marx. But the fact remains that the "Hobbesian paradigm of order" remains the victorious lineage still widely hegemonic today, from Parsons's functionalism to Luhmann's "system."

The Catholic *repraesentatio* "reacts" to this state of affairs by mending the broken nexus between Good and power, and it does so in two ways: it contemplates that the Good can be *represented* by power, and that power can *produce* the Good (or transform evil into good dialectically). In the course of this volume, this dual possibility will be designated with the expression "political theology." It will be useful to expand on my sense of this term, since my usage departs radically from Schmitt's. It is well known that at least in his mature works, and leaving aside a few complications, by "political theology" Schmitt means the modern process of reevaluation through which certain theological concepts are transformed into equivalent juridico-political categories. Expressing more than a simple parallel, however, this is in fact a process of secularization (despite never amounting to a complete profanation without remainder). My work proposes to alter the potentially polytheistic understanding of this term (that is, a sense that would accord with Weber's "de-souling" [*Entseelung*]). In some ways this shift is also a restoration, since it involves the term's more originary sense—going back to Ambrose and Augustine—which Erik Peterson (but also Eric Voegelin) was to adopt in argument with none other than Schmitt. For Peterson, the concept of political theology is essentially bound to monotheism. In fact, Peterson begins by establishing that monotheism as a political problem has its roots in Aristotle, and specifically in the contestation of Platonic dualism, which culminates in Aristotle's citation of Homer at the end of Book XII of the *Metaphysics*. He writes: "The world must not be governed badly. 'The rule of many is not good, let there be one ruler'" (1076a1). Peterson is thus led to conclude that Aristotle's doctrine "is grounded in a 'strict monarchism' . . . in the divine monarchy, the single rule [μία ἀρχή] of the ultimate single *principle* coincides with the actual hegemony of the single ultimate possessor of this rule [ἄρχων]."[1]

Although it is not possible to retrace the historical and philological genealogy of Peterson's argument here, we can nonetheless identify its critical point: Political theology is a sort of logical-historical short circuit that introduces political terminology (monotheism) into the religious lexicon, thus functioning as a theological justification of the existing order—or functioning, more simply, as the theological representation of power. This is exactly how political Catholicism opposes Modernity's depoliticizing tendency. But this opposition is not necessarily antimodern; on the contrary, if we take the (admittedly atypical) example of Romano Guardini as a model for the kind of position it might encompass, if anything it suggests an "ultramodern" outcome for the "End of the Modern World." Schmitt himself was aware, for that matter, that the Catholic *complexio* is neither antithetical to the sphere of technology, nor concordant with Romanticism's irrational myth and nostalgia. Instead, according to Schmitt, its Catholic theology expresses a strictly juridical logic. Where it differs from the modern paradigm is, as we have said, that its logic is not fully described by a complex of technical procedures, since it also comprehends the "unwritten" [*alogo*] moment of decision. This decision, moreover, has an *essentially* representative quality: it is representative of the *essence*. It is only this grounding in the "heavens of the Idea" that saves it from the ungroundedness of a modern decision. To be a decision as such, Guardini's decision must hold together the two poles—the immanent and the transcendent—from which all of reality is woven: history *and* idea, life *and* authority, force *and* truth. And, once again, power *and* the Good.

If there is a single point where Guardini restores the full significance of political Catholicism (albeit by expanding its limits almost to the point of self-contradiction), it can be found precisely in his *affirmative* conception of power. Because it is also a potential [*potenza*], power [*potere*] is a determination of being. It must therefore not only respect the two poles that belong to being's order, but also act as the very midpoint where those poles encounter each other—and this is what gives rise to a *duty* of power. Man must exercise power in order to obey God, in the sense that it is God who imposes on man to exercise power, in order that he be sanctified. This is why *power is good*: It is the Good's translation into politics. The political *as such* is constituted by this very relation; without it, without the transcendental reference to God's omnipotent will that it implies, there is no real politics but only bare technology. This is why in breaking this relation (or in imposing its different understanding of these terms), the modern is condemned to depoliticization, ceding to secularization and consigning itself to secularized time (the time of the "century" [*secolo*]). Mastering modernity calls for the kind of politics over which, by now, the Roman Catholic Church has a complete monopoly.

This monopoly is both the Church's task and its tragedy. Its task is to defend politics against deracinating attacks from the opposing but complementary forces of capitalism and socialism. Yet this is also a tragedy, because this task is now unrealizable and by definition *utopian*. Thus, the very ground of politics itself is now utopian; the last remaining island in the grand ocean of modern depoliticization (Christian Europe, for Guardini, therefore has an irremediably central and utopian role). The tragic destiny of Guardini's political Catholicism—which is reconstructed in the first chapter of this book alongside the Schmittian failure of *nomos*—seems by now to leave the political with an inescapable dilemma: either the *insula* of the Roman *repraesentatio*, or the ocean of modern depoliticization. Theology or secularization, utopia or entropy, myth or nihilism.

In fact, this apparent deadlock between two seemingly opposed hypotheses opens another historical path, which is one the contemporary state-form, in being *both* "theologized" and depoliticized, has in fact taken. This is the "arcane" aspect of modern politics that Schmitt's opposition seems not to grasp. What he perceives as an antithesis between political representation and depoliticizing neutralization is actually their copresence, displayed in the historical and semantic shift whereby Catholic representation comes to take a modern governmental-parliamentary form. This modern kind of political representation can only represent the various (opposing) interests unleashed by the deformation of the ancient *res publica christiana*; interests that cannot be reconciled or brought into harmony, but at most merely "regulated" by the terms of an "armed peace."

The political resolution to the war of religion can be understood in these terms. Modern politics empties religious conflict of ideological substance, reducing it from a conflict of fundamental principles to a mere play of interests. In this sense, the modern appears as the organization of a void, ridding itself of substance more so than "remedying" it, and doing away with the pretence of any totality. Politics in the sense of the ancient *polis* thus loses all legitimacy. It can survive only through the abandonment (and memory) of itself, and its transformation into *civitas*—the city of plural interests. The state that corresponds to this *civitas* not only ceases to reproduce the order of the *polis*, it can be formed only through its "withdrawal." What is withdrawn, exactly, is any kind of symbolic relation between the political and the social. This break, the abandonment of any need for an "a priori synthesis" of the whole, is what guarantees that there can be an equilibrium of interests. Any such synthesis is then only a *simple* mediation, a pure negotiation between parties wholly governed by economic interests. In fact, the agnostic, neutral state of the liberal-democratic tradition is the state in which the economic can be given "autonomy." This is what liberates the individual from the personal ties and hierarchies of the premodern order, and entrusts them to the "absolute" dominion of the market—just as it is the absolute exchangeability of merchandise that founds the equality of a law oriented to ensuring the equality of opportunity to attain material and symbolic goods.

It is precisely the specific autonomy of the economic, in interplay with the juridical equality that is both its cause and effect, that ensures the central contradiction of depoliticization: its *hyperpolitical* nature. We can put the paradox thus: Depoliticization is the political form within which the autonomy of the economic is established. This autonomy cannot develop "naturally"; it requires a (political) force capable of instituting and preserving the general conditions necessary for it to function, as well as a certain awareness of how it functions in fact. On a different but related level, this same problem affects the continuity of the juridical apparatus. The juridical is "de facto" withdrawn from the obligation to "truth," because that would inevitably lead it back into the same irreducible clash of ultimate values that is tamed by modern polytheism. It therefore becomes by nature arbitrary, unjustified, and changeable—but nevertheless remains bound to a law [*legge*] that must present itself as universal, immutable, and transcendent in order to effectively maintain its authority.

This same dialectic also applies to the state. The state—as we have seen—is born through the process of detheologization that marks modern secularization, and it is therefore formed by the emptying out of any political substance: the fragmentation of political unity into multiple powers, and their neutralization in various contract-structures. Yet this neutralization, in order to function effectively in mediating between differing parties (however artificially), needs a political form—since the negotiation of these parties' power is organized politically. As such it is the breakdown of the old representational arrangement that produces new representational questions. Even if the various interests involved cannot be represented within the same "whole," this whole situation is itself, again, represented. It is precisely ungroundedness—deracination—that offers itself as a new ground; just as it is precisely technology that "provokes" the definition of a new political form, even as it expresses the limitless nature of the will to power.

Naturally, this new form is a mere myth, because it is derived from the very thing that fractured the unity of community and transformed it into a mere *societas*. It is theological to the second degree, so to speak, because it is born from the modern detheologization that is really the theology of secularization, a specifically Hobbesian-Schmittian political theology.

A *political* theology, but its politics is a politics of *depoliticization*. This unsolvable contradiction, or paradox, "theologizes" depoliticization into a new political form. Within it, opposing terms are made copresent, so that each is transformed into the counterfeit shadow of its opposite: technology into "Ethics," law into "Justice," power into "the Good."

The impolitical attempts to rebel against this combination of depoliticization and theology, technology and value, and nihilism and justification. The impolitical, we have said, is something "other" than representation. Or better, it is *the* other of representation and remains obstinately outside of it. But its specific unrepresentability is very different from that imagined by modern depoliticization, because it in no way opposes the political. In this sense, the impolitical is far removed from Mann's term "nonpolitical." It is not an alternative *good* to be posed in opposition to the political. Quite the opposite: It is the *making good* of the existing failure of the political and the "theological" revalorization that attends it. The impolitical is a critique of enchantment, even if this does not mean that it can be reduced to a simple disenchantment, or the carefree polytheism of being "post." It disavows any connection with the great modern deracination, but without any utopian attempt at securing a new ground—which on the contrary it condemns.

Similarly, the impolitical shares nothing at all with an apolitical or antipolitical stance, as is shown by the importance it assumes within the work of Hannah Arendt. It might seem surprising to attribute an impolitical semantics to an author like Arendt, considering her "heroic" commitment to defending the categories of the political in the hour of their grave peril (hers is a different commitment from Schmitt's, but no less ardent). Indeed, if I ascribe Arendt an impolitical stance—only problematically and partially, on the basis of her final writings—it is not because she adopts an external point of view from which to observe the political. Arendt always remains rigorously internal to politics, with the possible exception of the line of flight that her final work opens to the "in-between" time of thought. If Arendt is an impolitical thinker, it is because she gradually constricts the available space in which the political can be positively identified: the result is that any understanding of the political as something plural is fundamentally unrepresentable (as a plurality *or* as natality, considering that the origin, for Arendt, is always plural). Any logical-historical attempt to *represent* the political's plural nature in fact clearly amounts to its negation, since representation's fundamental operation is the *reductio ad unum*. For Arendt it is contemporary totalitarianism that brings this destiny, set into motion by the transcendence-effect of Platonic idealism, to its definitive completion. But it is not that the totalitarian state does something so different from the "bourgeois" state. Rather, the two are if not exactly the same then at least objectively complementary, as suggested by the fact that totalitarianism shares its categories with the depoliticizing processes not only of late liberal society (from which it originates), but of modernity as a whole.

It is thus unsurprising that modernity, with its complex of technology and decision, will and representation, neutralization and theology, would be the main object of Arendt's critique in *The Human Condition*, where she addresses it in tones that are neither restorative nor apocalyptic. It is also given special attention in the essay on revolution, which is the central pivot around which Arendt's writing will take on an ever more emphatically impolitical character. Although the modern is usually blithely understood as the true home of the political-as-plurality (often, unfortunately, in Arendt's name), it is, on the contrary, where plurality is most strictly negated, since modernity always brings about a forced unification. Arendt in fact inscribes this as an originary (not contingent) feature of each of the two poles of modern political constitution: representation and revolution. Ever since its genesis in Hobbes, modern representation has been tied to an autonormative mechanism in which the representative is transcendent over the represented (not in a metaphysical sense, but merely a functional one). This has two effects. First is a "divinification" of sovereignty: Already in Hobbes the sovereign is endowed with divine capacities such as the interpretation of the law and the "creation" of political subjectivity. Second is the depoliticization of society. Indeed, in any modern political constitution the sovereign is sovereign only if it *represents*. But it is just as true that this representation can appear only in a sovereign form, meaning that it is "theological" in a vertical direction, and depoliticizing in a horizontal one. It must take the form, that is, of the *reductio ad unum* of the represented entities—the people, the nation, the state.

This is why the multitude as such cannot be represented: because a political representation can only rivet the multiplicity to the unity of its "imagist" form, which is not concrete but transcendental. The situation is the same for revolution (which is what makes Arendt's discussion of it increasingly marked by an aphasia). At first it is protected from any tendency to unification by its essentially plural and anti-representative nature. But eventually revolution is *necessarily* betrayed by its need for self-legitimation, returning to its premodern etymology (*revolutio*) and to the paradigm of restoration. This fatally binds revolution to its "theatrical" representation: even the American Revolution, which Arendt thought most resistant to this political-theological short circuit, but which inexorably fell prey to it like all the rest. This situation, addressed in a historical register in *On Revolution*, is presented in a more strictly theoretical key in Arendt's incomplete final trilogy through the paradox of the will. Taking freedom as its metaphysical foundation, and being conceived as unpredictable and contingent, the will is eternally divided between willing and not-willing, and it is this binary nature that prevents it from being translated into political action. This could be achieved only by violently suppressing the inner conflict that defines it, in a unification that is even more forced than that of representation: compelling the will to leave itself behind and become suppression, imposition, dominion. This unresolvable situation, whose clearest result is the impolitical landslide of Arendt's final work, seems to be perfectly expressed by the symmetry between representation and decision. In its own way, each denies the multitude, and any political form without the multitude's plurality is pushed to the point of overturning into its opposite, becoming either politically formless (technology), or politically deformed (totalitarianism).

It is this same unresolvable condition that haunts Hermann Broch's "political novel" to the point of "forbidding" its conclusion. That an author of fiction like Broch would be discussed in a political philosophical context will surprise only those who are completely unfamiliar with his work, considering the thousands of pages he devoted to theoretical political problems and to the philosophy of history, above all his brief and extreme political *Kondensat*, introduced and brought to print by none other than Hannah Arendt. This tract begins exactly where Arendt's work halts (not chronologically, obviously), and it has a clarity of perspective that we can attribute to Broch's shift from a fundamentally pre-Hobbesian analytic (like Arendt's) to a decisively post-Hobbesian anthropology. The central feature of this shift is that Broch assumes an idea of the origin that regards it not only as a plurality, but also and above all as conflict: the irreducible conflict of power.

It is not only Hobbes who lies behind this shift, naturally, but also that "strong" triangle of thought comprised by the three most fearsome texts of contemporary political philosophy: Benjamin's "Critique of Violence," Freud's *Totem and Taboo*, and everything written by Friedrich Nietzsche. (We will have the chance to return to Nietzsche and his specific contribution to the "tradition" of the impolitical in due course.) Broch's discussion reflects not only the radical split between Law and Justice shared by all three (which is the central focus and semantic ground for his critique of political theology), but also their common inheritance of the failure of an epoch (and of History as a whole). This failure makes any kind of historical (or eschatological) reintegration of politics and ethics impossible. Politics, as a result, is internally split into two levels (or "poles," as Broch prefers), one negative and one affirmative. On one hand there is the practical efficacy of politics, which is necessarily negative because its conditions are such that freedom (of the self) and servitude (of others) are structurally identical. On the other hand, there is the ineffectually positive pole that the political takes as its unrepresentable presupposition. Broch's "impolitical" perspective lies in his recognition of an absolute difference between a purely negative reality and its purely positive Idea. In Broch there is no sense of any attempt to escape from the political. Since the political is unified with what is *real*, it is declared "ineluctable"—indeed, for Broch the entire lineage of the impolitical lies within, and takes for granted, Koselleck's "politics as destiny." Rather, what is at stake for Broch is the withdrawal of the political from any attempt to valorize it ethically.

It is true that Broch sought to mobilize a neo-Kantian philosophy of history, which was the uninterrupted object of his philosophical research, toward the rediscovery of an ethical foundation for politics. But not only does this project fail due to its own internal contradiction, but it was that same contradiction that would produce the most compelling achievements of the author's fiction, from *The Sleepwalkers* to the *Death of Virgil*. When we read the latter's central conflict between Augustus and Virgil directly against the grain of its dominant interpretation, it offers us the definitive and resolutely contradictory "systemization" of Broch's sense of the impolitical. This impolitical is not only manifested in a *consciously* contradictory way, in a textual-formal sense, as an attempt to reach the Word through the very language that expresses that Word's discursive negation (just as every political praxis is a degradation of the idea it presupposes). Rather, it involves an inherently contradictory *object*. Broch's impolitical stance is itself a contradiction—an inherently antinomian "composition" of contradictions—so its logic must therefore *withdraw* from the inherently non-contradictory language of *Nomos*. It is this contradictory logic that explains both the challenge that Virgil mounts, and its defeat in the final restitution of the *Aeneid* to Augustus. The *Aeneid*, poem of the political, can *belong* only to Augustus, since the idea that Virgil entrusts to it is not something that can be appropriated. Virgil's idea cannot be produced in an image: It is the *just* distance of the *proprium* from the world—*all* the world—and only something that can be reduced to its properties can be captured in an image. Virgil's justice cannot be dialectically mediated with the law [*diritto*]. This is why his dialogue with Augustus can find no point of compromise, no ethico-political synthesis. Ethics is the unrepresentable element of the political: politics listens to the ethical demand only through the "wall of resounding silence" that closes the universe of the *Sleepwalkers*.

Elias Canetti's language is addressed to this very wall, and with an even greater awareness of its internal limit than we can attribute to Broch. The positive "pole" of the political—which Broch understood as an alterity that, while it cannot be expressed, can still somehow be identified as the political's external presupposition (its Idea)—is, in Canetti, radically reabsorbed back into the negative and representable pole *without remainder*. In Canetti's world, there is no other dimension than that of power, which encompasses the entirety of represented reality. It is only this very fullness that allows the nonpower of that which *is not* to show through: not from outside of reality, but from behind it, as its reverse side, or the shadow of a limitless presence. For Canetti, it is in this absence—the unexpressed, the unthought, the forgotten—that the impolitical gathers. It is the silence that enshrouds power, the sliver of light that leaks from the dark fabric of the history of power—or power *as* history, since it is history that sanctions the subordination of the possible to power. History is the translation of the possible into reality—that is, into power. No possible history can break the stride of the *only* reality there is. In this sense, too, the One remains a "theological" characterization of power: something that is coextensive with reality because it excludes every other, unrealized, possibility. This is the decisive aspect of Canetti's thought that utopian-liberatory readings lack the courage to identify: every alternative to power is engulfed by this "unicity" of the real. In Canetti's work, terms such as multiplicity, metamorphosis, or the crowd, though they appear as oppositions to the political-theological syntax of the One, are on the contrary internal to that syntax and subsumed by it. This is the most disquieting "secret" of Canetti's writing: not simply, as is often said, the victory of the One over the many, of the executioner over the victim, of death over life, but their tendency to unification. Not death against life, but a life that produces death.

What has been said up to this point allows us to make a further observation about the nature of the impolitical. We have already seen that the impolitical is a critique of political theology, whether understood in the sense of Roman-Catholic representation [*rappresentazione*] or modern-Hobbesian representation [*rappresentanza*]. As regards the latter, the impolitical is in direct opposition to its every form of depoliticization, and the impolitical is therefore anything but a simple negation of the political. But it is not enough merely to say that an impolitical stance is not disposed to rejecting the political. It is necessary to go further and say that from a certain point of view the impolitical *coincides with the political* (as we saw in Canetti, it could be said that this point of view is located immediately *behind* it). This can be put even more strongly: The impolitical *is* the political, as seen from its outermost limit. It is the *determination* of the political, in the literal sense that it makes visible its *terms* [*termini*][2]—which coincide with the entire reality of relations between people.

When we understand it in this way, it could be said that all great political realism from Machiavelli onward, as the *nontheological* thought of politics, has been impolitical. The grand interpretive tradition, from Croce to Meinecke, has in fact read Machiavelli as an impolitical thinker (albeit unwittingly): If only man were good, that would be one thing, but since he is not, there remain nothing *but* the categories of the political, besieged by their inability to be anything *but* political terms. They are surrounded, that is, by the *other* they cannot be. And even before Machiavelli there was Thucydides, who in the dialogue between the Athenians and the Melians foreshadows the relation between law [*diritto*] (the "all" of the political) and Justice (the "nothing" of the political). It is no accident that Canetti favors those grand negative thinkers (Hobbes, De Maistre, and Nietzsche) who reveal in the simplest terms what La Boétie considered the enigma of "voluntary servitude," or the unsolvable problem of power relations. There exists no real alternative to power, no *subject* of antipower, for the simple reason that the subject is *already* constituted by power. In other words, power inheres naturally in the dimension of the subject, in the sense that its only language is that of power. This is why the conclusion Canetti draws—together with every other impolitical thinker, from Broch to Kafka to Simone Weil (Weil with incredible clarity)—is that the only way to restrain power is to diminish the subject.

Here it is necessary to make two further clarifications. First, what is meant by "subject" here is not the individual, who has already been made impossible as a subject by the reign of technology (defined precisely as a "process without subject"), but rather that abstract subjectivity that remains after the end of the subject-individual. Canetti (but also Broch) expresses this transition clearly when he identifies the characteristics of the powerful subject with those of the crowd, meaning that the crowd multiplies and intensifies the appropriative urges of individuals who are condemned to infinite consumption. The second clarification concerns the specific manner of self-reduction that each of these authors proposes for the subject. This is not simply a matter of disempowerment (a "weakening," if you like) or a "draining" of power, but of understanding power differently. The notion of power that is at stake here—which, although it is clarified in the pages that follow, awaits even further elaboration—is no longer "active," or immediately realized in the "act." Rather, it is internal or sympathetic to the sphere of passion, suffering, and patience (not to use the more conceptually demanding term "passivity").

Simone Weil's concept of "decreation" seems to me to belong within this frame. It refers to the divine, but even more so to the human in that it refers to the subject's own self-effacement. Weil's notion is in fact a perfect fit for the extreme, radical political realism expressed by the idea that in all the world "there is no force but force" (the above references to Machiavelli and Thucydides are in fact Weil's). This formula is another way of articulating the impolitical. It is not a question of rejecting or negating the political categories, as its critics have too often supposed, but of fulfilling them. It is thus unsurprising that Weil's driest political realism *coincides with* her so-called mystical dimension (rather than preceding or alternating with it). Weil's mysticism is essentially none other than that same realism: it is the existence of the political shrouded by what it is not, and *must not* be for fear of relapsing into political-theological idolatry. Weil gestures to this *nonbeing* with the metaphor of the "sovereignty of sovereignty," by which she means that necessity is force's internal limit. Force may be everything, but its necessary limit is that it is everything *and nothing more*. In this antimony lies the contradictory evidence for a Weilian impolitical. What is contradicted, obviously, are not the political categories that fit it like a glove that has been turned inside out, but rather itself: in remaining external to its opposite but without ever being anything other than it, in transcend*ing* [*trascendimento*] the thing whose opposition defines its nature (in Weil this relation occasionally risks slipping into transcend*ence* [*trascendenza*]). It is contradictory, in short, with its own being a category—that is, having an identity, albeit one that is negatively defined.

This is essentially the critique that Georges Bataille directs at Weil, in what will constitute both the final station on our voyage and the final stage in the analysis of the impolitical as a category: its self-negation as a differentiated *identity*. It is as though in order to thoroughly resolve its "negative charge," the impolitical must withdraw even from the extreme point of contrast with the political that defines its border. It is not by chance that Bataille's critique of Weil begins precisely with her notion of the presupposed *limit*—or the presupposed as such. The limit, by Bataille's implicit reasoning, understood as that which *identifies in separating*, is a necessarily dualistic notion, and it is therefore ultimately inclined toward transcendence. For this reason it must be overcome, or more precisely converted and made to move around its semantic axis to its own apparent opposite point: *partage* (sharing, [con-*divisione*[3]])—that which *puts into relation* by *differentiating*. This operation has two effects. First, the rupture of subjectivity, which in Weil had been paradoxically "protected" by its own mystical "self-effacement" because of the *project* of salvation "presupposed" by that practice. Second, difference is made into something "in common," though the figure that more than any other mends the breakdown of relations that so preoccupied Bataille—relations between political and impolitical, life and death, immanence and transcendence. That figure is the "community" of the impossible.

It is not unexpected that this "community" is born in direct "communion" with Bataille's reading of Nietzsche, which is the thread around which his sense of the impolitical is woven—and, at the same time overturned (by the withdrawal from every "term"). It is this reading of Nietzsche (under the influence of Jaspers) that frees the impolitical from the symmetrical logic of binary opposition, and recognizes its originary cobelonging with its apparent opposite. But because of this possibility, what was a negation now comes to be understood as a pure *affirmation* capable of rejecting both transcendence (which, according to Bataille, necessarily ends up involving something "Presupposed"), and the absolute immanence of a theological foundation. Concerning the latter, through Nietzsche Bataille will settle his score with (Kojeve's) Hegelianism in parallel with a critique of Weil the "mystic." The result, for Bataille, is a sharp reversal in the meaning of the expression the "end of history," a theme that, beginning with Kojève's great *Introduction*, was addressed by significant portions of the European culture of the time (albeit in ways that often bore little resemblance to each other). Rather than concluding time in the full Hegelian sense of the expression (at least on Kojève's interpretation, which Bataille accepts), the "end of history" *opens* time to the ecstatic eternity of the sovereign instant and its inherent opposition to the nihilistic will to power.

In this regard, Bataille's anti-Hegelianism matches with the distance that he took from the other great thinker of the *finis historiae*—Ernst Jünger—with whom he is associated by more than their shared sources of inspiration. For Bataille, as for Heidegger, not only Jünger's notion of "mobilization" but even that of "overcoming" remain in the thrall of the "power of the void"—which Bataille's "tragic" on the other hand escapes. But it is not only a conception of sacrifice as the "will to loss" that distinguishes Bataille from Jünger (and from his own group at the *Collège* for that matter, above all Michel Leiris, making his position on the question of nihilism somewhat eccentric). It is also his entire reading of the modern, which poses him—again, asymmetrically—in the position of rejecting transcendence but in no way surrendering to the secular or to an "indifferent" understanding of secularization. In Bataille, the loss of the sacred is understood as the cause of both the "end of the social" and of all political-theological attempts to forcibly reconstruct it, above all fascism.

In response to the theatre of representation that such attempts offer, Bataille counters with something "unrepresentable": the extreme and literally impossible experience of "community." Unlike the community that was theorized by the other director of the *Collège* (besides Bataille and Leiris), Roger Caillois, Bataille's community is "impossible" because it withdraws from its own work [*opera*] (community is thus thought as the very "absence of work," in line with the brilliant readings of Jean-Luc Nancy and Maurice Blanchot). But it is also impossible in the sense that it is constituted not by what binds its various subjects, but by what differentiates them from each other—and above all, from *themselves*: death. Community, for Bataille, cannot be dissociated from death. Not, as the utopian *Gemeinschaft* and Kantian "kingdom of ends" promise, because the collective hypostasis of community can overcome the death of its individual members in an immortal whole. Rather, because community is itself oriented to death. The community is the presentation to its own members of their mortal truth, their finitude, even though they will never be able to identify with it: the death of another contains nothing with which we might identify. But neither does even one's *own* death, as we know from the "expropriated" look in the eyes of one who dies (recalling the impossibility of living with an awareness of one's own death). But the further reason they will not recognize themselves in this truth is because the dialectic of "recognition" belongs to the (communicative) sphere of inter-subjectivity, and not to the "shared" existence of which community is the impossible experience. The fact that the experience of community is impossible is proven by its thoroughly impolitical fate, in the withdrawal from both the grandiose rubble of old communisms and the painful miseries of the new individualism. The fact that this impolitical community has come to the point of a pure and absolute negation is attested by the word *politics*—community—that continues, sovereignly, to *affirm* it.

1

AT THE LIMITS OF THE POLITICAL

HISTORY AND DECISION

In the third section of *The Lord*, entitled "The Decision," Romano Guardini reads Christ's relation to his own death in terms of decision. When death approaches the "moment of decision" draws near—but confronted with numerous warning signs, Jesus is "already in acceptance of his coming fate."[1] Guardini's thesis stands radically distant from that of Bultmann, who not only denies the possibility of "knowing how Jesus would have understood his own end" (in order to protect the absolute character of the *kérygma* from any historical *contaminatio*) but also hypothesizes a possible "collapse of morale." "We cannot veil our eyes," insists Bultmann, "to the possibility that he suffered a breakdown."[2] Guardini's decisionist account, in which He who is "sacrificed" (Romans 8:32) coincides with He who "sacrifices" (Galatians 1:4), is presented precisely in opposition to this one. One notion emerges from the entirety of Guardini's Christology with incisive clarity: Christ is not limited to being the bearer of decision; he *is* decision—the pure principle of decision itself.

In Christ, what it is that decides, that which gives rise to decision, is not so much his teachings or his works but his person [*persona*]. For this reason, Christ's thought is pretheoretical, in the sense of being prior to any theorization. It is his thought that renders theory possible and institutes it. He *is* "beginning," and this is why Christ cannot be "deduced" from a historical situation by the estimations of human psychology. He determines his own history, and he does so essentially through his will: "His will was of great power. It was perfectly at one with itself, without fear, prepared for anything that might happen, conscious that the stake was the one thing of supreme importance—the decisive moment for the whole of existence. It knew also that, in the absolute sense, the "time" had come."[3]

Christ *is* decision, therefore, in the dual sense that he makes it possible and that he himself constitutes it. But this should not be understood as a sort of simple unification of Christ's reality—nothing could be further from Guardini's thesis. The fact that Christ's decision is absolute in no sense resolves the perfect *opposition* entailed by his dual and contradictory nature. On the contrary, this conflict itself is what gives rise to an absolute decision. But although Guardini's position is unrelated to the hypothesis of Christ's integral humanity (a hypothesis that is typical to liberal theology), he is equally far from the opposite yet complementary idea of Christ's absolute divinity. As Karl Adam explained in the same period (the German Catholic theologian perhaps closest to Guardini), the Mystery of the Incarnation stands or falls together with the human reality of God.[4] It is only because Christ is aware of the infinite distance that separates him from God that in that moment he can pray to him, and do so in the language of absolute abandonment ("My God, my God, why have you forsaken me?").

Decision is born within that distance, within that *duality*. It is thus born not despite but *because of* the conflict that constitutes Christ's nature, as that opposition's most proper expression. Without conflict, without opposition, without *bipolarity*—to use the expression that best characterizes Guardini's philosophy—decision would not be decision as such. It would be dulled by a singular, predetermined destiny, lacking the constitutive tension that it must have by virtue of its freedom. It would thus lose the possibility of producing other, infinitely distant decisions, which although distant are nonetheless made possible by this same bipolar relation. And, in fact, in Guardini's universe, Christ's cross, *his* decision, occupies a midpoint between God's decision and man's. This is an asymmetrical relation. God's decision is originary and absolute; man's is derivative and defective. Both, however, are absolutely free. And each is free by reason of the freedom of the other.

One aspect of Guardini's theology was regarded as more scandalous than any other, so much so that it was downplayed with thinly veiled embarrassment (if not explicitly contested) even by "his" Balthasar.[5] It is the idea, expressed in the same chapter of *The Lord*, that man's decision against Jesus, and therefore the redemption offered by Jesus' death, was not a matter of necessity. That "no," suggests Guardini, could have been a "yes," with everything that would have meant for Christ and for man. This hypothesis is anything but a mere detail that could be overlooked or eliminated without consequences for the "system" surrounding it, as Balthasar suggests, for the precise reason that it expresses that system's intrinsically unsystematic nature. This is the aperture, the vanishing point, which both coheres that "system" and gives it its unmistakable place at the extreme limit of Catholic theology. Decision *and* conflict. Decision *deriving from* conflict. Not only is each of the poles and the decision that belongs to it not diminished by the fullness of its opposite, but it is also intensified by it. The freedom of God's decision is *increased* by that of man's, "because human existence was designed to rest not only upon divine creation and bountiful all-inclusive activity, but also upon human decision—precisely *because* God's omnipotence is crowned in the freedom of the individual to accept or reject him. . . . Fearful possibility, yet the gravity and dignity of human existence depends on it. God could not spare us the burden of this freedom. In order that he might exist, his own power had to be curtailed, for had he come to earth as the Omnipotent One, it would have been impossible to reject him."[6]

This is how Guardini will arrive at the conception of history expressed in the final section of his book, entitled "Time and Eternity." It is precisely the "no" directed at Christ—that which should *not* have happened, that which happened *instead*—that destines history to be the potential site of humanity's salvation. Note that if what could have happened did in fact happen (if a "yes" had prevailed over the "no"), history would not necessarily be impossible, but such a history would have been naturalized, galvanized, and eternalized, so to speak, by the certainty of a fulfillment that had in fact *already* taken place. It would have been opened, but then immediately closed by the plenitude of the *right* decision, and thereby sheltered from the risk entailed in new decisions. It would not then be dependent, *in each instant*, on their emergence. It is the "no" to Christ that inflects history in terms of continual decisions, transforming history into a history *of* decisions: "The first unlimited possibility has been lost. Salvation now becomes identified with sacrifice. Thus God's kingdom does not come as it was meant to, in open history-revolutionizing fulfillment; it is to remain to the end of time suspended in the process of coming—its acceptance or rejection, progress or retrogression depending on the response of the individual or group in every period of world-history."[7]

This crucial decision-history nexus not only has implications for the traditional Catholic conception of history, but it also extends to the other of the two terms in question: decision itself. What is it, what *force*, that the historical dimension lends to a decision? Whereas earlier, in his conceptual elaboration of history, Guardini had distanced himself from the idea of a theological *continuum* (theology as the linear historicization of Redemption), here he differs from the antihistoricity of Barth or Bultmann. Not only does their notion of decision not derive from a historical progression, it has meaning only if considered as the rupture of that progression. Their decision refers not to power, to responsibility, or to government, but to deracination, dissolution, and withdrawal. It is, in a word, radically impolitical. It is for this reason that decision can—or rather must—shatter Guardini's bipolarization and *absolutely* separate man from God, nature from Grace, time from eternity. It must dissolve the *complexio oppositorum* of their relation into the terms of a pure alterity.

The intrinsically political *intentio* of Guardini's Catholicism works against this point of view, proposing that the absolute theism of Barth's decision is nothing but the mirror image of modern atheism. In each case the bipolarity is severed, and each achieves the same result: the separation of man and God—albeit for opposite reasons. In absolute theism we have the liberation of God from man, and in atheism the liberation of man from God.[8] At their intersection lies Dostoevsky's legend of the Grand Inquisitor, which in Guardini's distinctive interpretation expresses the exact point where modern atheism encounters Kierkegaardian-Barthian theism and finds its double. In this way, the deformation of the Grand Inquisitor mirrors the deformation of the figure of Christ, who is no longer the Christ of decision (in fact, Dostoevsky describes him as completely indecisive). He is no longer the Christ of decision because he is no longer the Christ of contradiction, of God *and* man. By choosing God, Christ abandoned the world. But in abandoning the world, he loses God at the same time. This is a Christ closed to what is outside of him (but is nevertheless part of him), "a Christ who exists wholly for himself. He does not come to the world from the Father, and he does not go from the world to the Father," hence he does not know—and he rejects—that "middle sphere where man dwells, and where his daily existence unfolds."[9] This zone is not the elevated locus of an absolute, but for precisely that reason it is "the sphere of practical actuation," "the workshop of existence," "the carrier of all essential values." In other words, it is the place where decision finds efficacy and power, where it encounters the world and governs it. It is the point where the Christian decision encounters politics: "Here ideas are converted into forces, impulses into institutions, intentions into ordinances and law. Here one acts responsibly, consequences are accepted, and reality is confronted."[10]

Naturally we should not imagine that Guardini's strongly decisionist language, bolstered by the essentialist and vitalist culture of the time, betrays a relativist-subjectivist or intuitionist-irrational stance unconstrained by the question of "form" (whether understood as "Idea" or as "institution"). The entire Catholic movement that developed in Germany from the end of the First World War was concerned with reconstituting the relation between institution and idea, subjectivity and truth, decision and authority. I speak here of the so-called Catholic *renouveau* (the "return from exile," in Peter Wust's celebrated expression) organized around the journal *Hochland* (directed by Karl Muth and replete with eminent names like Schell, Scheler, Adam, and Guardini himself), whose goal was to break a longstanding Protestant cultural hegemony.[11] To interrogate Guardini's work without reference to the rich network of influences formed by the thinkers and theologians of the time would be to lose not only a sense of its context, but a large part of its meaning (beginning with the teachings of Max Scheler, and encompassing J. Hessen, B. Rosenmöller, R. Schneider, F. Tillmann, and K. Eschweiler, and especially Theodor Haecker and Peter Wust).

It is no accident that these authors share a recurring theme, albeit inflected in different ways: the nexus between *Love and Law*, to borrow the title of Peter Lippert's book, or *Truth and Life*, to cite Haecker's.[12] Here life is liberated from the abstract formalism of neo-Kantian schemes, only to be put through Truth's process of assimilation by different means. But what is absent in these authors is any rationalist presupposition that life is something immaterial [*inoggettività*]—as well as any radical separation between objectivity and existence, form and experience, truth and decision: a separation that, seen from another point of view, is also intuitionist and indeed irrationalist. Decision arrives at a truth—it *must* arrive at its truth—by beginning from life's multipolarity, just as that multipolarity can and must be unified in the truth of decision. Any linear or purely oppositional dialectic between unity and difference, form and decision, or "authority and freedom," to recall the title of a book that was to become exemplary,[13] is therefore interrupted. Authority—the authority of the *veritas*, of the Idea, of the institution—is not the opposite of the autonomy of the spirit, but its *guarantee*, the deeper meaning of freedom.

In 1921, Guardini was already engaged in the front lines of the youth and liturgical movements (*The Spirit of the Liturgy* is from 1917), and it was he who responded to the essay by Max Bondy that appeared that year in *Die Schildgenossen*.[14] Bondy had maintained that the youth movement needed to emancipate itself from false objective truths and must instead assume truth as a function of the historically conditioned self. Thus, authority would be understood as the capacity to adhere to any predetermined aim, and therefore as a purely hypothetical value. Guardini's response was immediate: "Authority has a value independent of any specific goal." It "subsists in and of itself, and not only in the recognition of its purpose."[15] Authority rests on its own truth, by which it lives or dies. To comprehend the significance of this affirmation it is necessary to turn to a text published many years later in *Sorge um den Menschen*, which reprises and develops the thread of reasoning implicit in Guardini's response to Bondy. Its title, *Atheism and the Possibility of Authority*, immediately reveals that its foundation lies in the thesis that atheism excludes authority's very possibility. This exclusion is due to authority's "essence," which Guardini devotes the first part of the work to defining. In the most general sense, it concerns the "necessary participation of the inner initiative of the person at whom the binding act is directed,"[16] while at the same time respecting its intimate freedom, which is possible only if the ends of that attempt to bind are inherently morally good.

But these elements alone (a bond, freedom, and good intentions) are not enough to define authority, since they lack a further essential element: concreteness or empirical reality. For there to be authority, therefore, there must be a concrete person to represent it. This is the most crucial point of Guardini's analysis, whereby the concept of authority is tightly bound to that of representation. It is representation that harbors authority's "essence." Authority is authority if and only if it is represented by such a person: "when the occasion that calls for it is concrete human reality; when it is visible within history, as an individual or as an institution."[17] Now Guardini's attention is wholly concentrated on the three interwoven terms "history," "visibility," and "person." To synthesize the three: Authority requires a visible person, who represents it historically. Here we have almost arrived at a definition of authority, and yet it still lacks the element that will fully illuminate it and allow us to grasp its conceptual "essence." In order to comprehend this point we must introduce the two *exempla* that supply Guardini's terminology with its authentic and unmistakable political resonance: the parent and the State. What does the authority that is exercised, or rather *represented*, by these two juridical persons have in common? It is the fact—and this is what encloses Guardini's entire argument within a Unitarian perspective—that each refers to something that transcends both subject and object as the two parties to authority's operation. More precisely, it remains "above" them: both parent and State "represent an instance that rests 'above' [the subject of authority], bestowing God with a presence as the creator of every life, as the absolute *auctor vitae*."[18]

This is true of the *pater*, but also of the state, directly deriving as it does from the idea of the *rex*, which Guardini interprets in explicitly political theological terms not just as the "head of State (as it is understood today in the functional sense of the word), but the child of a divinity, and particularly informed and protected by that divinity—he is the connecting element between the terrestrial and the divine and his symbols: the crown, the sceptre, the regal mantle, express this."[19] So in modern secularization, not only does the state not lose the theological element that originally characterized the concept of the king, but it also remains inseparably bound to the personal-divine recognition that confers it with true authority: "The State too represents divine sovereignty. In the ultimate instance it is because of this representation that man concedes the State's authority to order the life of its citizenry. Equally, it is in the final analysis this religious valency which renders laws effective on the conscience, beyond personal advantage or punishment."[20] This is the piece that completes the puzzle of authority. The "essence" of Guardinian authority can finally be grasped in two parts: the historical concreteness of the representative, and the vertical transcendence of the "Idea" that functions as the basis of its representation. Their combination, or better, their semantic-conceptual intersection, expresses the essence of authority, and its intimate *political* heart. It is thus unsurprising that these same elements were presented in an extraordinary combination by one writer in particular who reflected, in that same period, on the essence of the political.

ANTIRÖMISCHER AFFEKT

Before identifying this author—whose name is by now obvious (even if, for understandable ideological reasons, it is not found in Guardini's writing)—we will return for a moment to the lively period enjoyed by German Catholicism at the time. Its leading exponents enjoyed the sense of a sudden lifting of barriers, and an escape from the cultural ghetto that had, until then, resounded with the old echoes of the "*los von Rom.*" It is enough to cast one's eyes over the impassioned pages of Hefele's *Katholizismus in Deutschland*, Hermann Platz's *Geistige Kämpfe im modernen Frankreich*, *Kirche und Seele* by the Benedictine abbot Ildefons Herwegen, or the first annuals of the journal *Abendland*, to see the traces of an old wound and the signs of a coming change.[21] Nothing reveals this more clearly than this passage written by Georg Moenius (editor of the *Allgemeine Rundschau*, which was discontinued in 1933, and author of *Italienische Reise*),[22] drawn from the introduction to his German translation of Massis's *Defence of the West*:

> The history of this anti-Roman rebellion has not yet been written. It emerges from the subconscious with a clear will; passing from a repressed instinct to a fully felt emotion. It makes itself felt through the course of German history in all its many variations. In the intellectual sphere this attitude means sacrificing firm principles and precise terms; in the ethical sphere, liberation from the law and from heteronomy; in the religious, an escape from autonomy and from the institution.[23]

As we have said, what is at stake in this reproposition of order, objectivity, and discipline—of all that is symbolized by the name of Rome, with the force of a myth reborn—is not simply a *rejection* of life's quality as a field of flows and becoming, but its placement into an inescapable dialectic with the certainties of form and institution. "The vital forces have need of constraint, and not of freedom," concluded Moenius, resonating with Johann Peter Steffes's affirmations of the same period.[24] "Otherwise life kills itself; every exaggeration of vitality becomes a suicide. Life must be submitted to the guide of an ordering reason; otherwise it produces nothing but disorder and confusion."[25] It is not insignificant that that this imperative to *form* life, to draw a single order of representation from its conflicting impulses, would be made under the rubric of the *antirömischen Affektes*. Although this expression came to Moenius through Hefele's "Die römische Wirklichkeit" (as a specific reference in Moenius attests), both authors had in fact obtained it from elsewhere: Carl Schmitt's *Roman Catholicism and Political Form*, the subject of my earlier allusions.[26]

What Schmitt meant by the expression "anti-Roman temper" is best seen in the context of a broader intellectual inquiry that belongs fundamentally to the theme we have been tracing up to this point, and whose detail bears a striking resemblance to Guardini's own. Consider Schmitt's polemic reference to Dostoevsky's legend of the Grand Inquisitor (which Guardini would take up years later, in exactly the same terms, in his book on Dostoevsky), which invites a withdrawal from the antithesis between the Good and power ("rejecting every earthly power"); from "the incomprehensible political power of Roman Catholicism" that it enables, and from the radical aversion it has generated in its detractors.[27] Here Schmitt introduces the well-known theme of the *complexio oppositorum*: "There appears to be no antithesis it [the Roman Church] does not embrace."[28] For this reason, those who regard the *complexio* as something unilateral and those who tame it by way of a synthesis are both equally far from comprehending it. On close inspection, these two errors are symmetrical, since each is grounded in the *absolute* version of dualism that prevails in the modern epoch—or its absolute immanentism, which is the same thing.

The Catholic *complexio* arises against exactly this conversion of an antithesis into a synthesis, this union of opposed indecisions that voices the spirit of the age. "To [the *complexio*] belong neither the despair of antitheses nor the illusory optimism of their synthesis."[29] This is why it would be wholly misleading to reduce the *complexio* to the spiritual antithesis of technology, or, equally, to a simple defense of romantic and irrationalist mythology posed against the rationality of the modern. Each of these reductions ignores the fact that Catholic theology incorporates an eminently juridical logic. As Weber had in fact already noted, Roman juridical rationalism lives on within this theology—this is precisely how the sacerdotal function can be universalized, which is to say, freed from a purely individual charisma. This does not mean, though—and this is a point that must be forcefully underlined because it gives rise to the central nucleus of Schmitt's argument—that when the sacerdotal function is universalized, the *personal* element of whoever exercises it is lost. If that were the case, if Catholicism were to adhere precisely to classical juridical logic and its *law* [*legge*], the *political* power of the *complexio* would be diminished. But the reason this is not so is that

Catholicism's juridical logic is an eminently *representative* logic: "in its capacity to assume juridical form . . . lies one of its sociological secrets. But it has the power to assume this or any other form only because it has the power of representation."[30]

This emphasis on representation, recalling its place in Guardini's concept of authority, implies two features. It is first of all *personal*: the Church is authoritative because its juridical structure is represented by the concrete persona of the sacerdote who, in turn, through a chain of infinite mediations, represents the person of Christ. This is what confers a specific power and authority on the Church, which in practice means the capacity to create *new* law [*diritto*]. While secular jurisprudence must limit itself to confirming or merely adjusting the law in force, the Roman Church can generate it anew. This is the crux of Schmitt's analysis: The power of the Roman *complexio* resides in the fact that its representational juridical structure contemplates the unwritten [*alogo*] moment of *decision*, incarnated in the personal authority of the pope, and passed down through the person of the individual sacerdotes.[31]

This is only the first dimension of representation: its descending direction, which moves from on high down to the lowest rungs, communicating the power of Christ's decision to even the lowliest ministers. But this aspect must always be understood in its complementary relation with representation's other, ascending direction, referring from the lowly upward: from the sacerdote to Christ, from power to authority, from the decision to the *idea*. It is this complexity that fully expresses the bipolar essence of Catholic representation, diametrically opposing it to the monolinear structure of nonrepresentative thought. It contemplates not only the decision, but also that the decision is grounded in the *reality* of the idea: "No political system can survive even a generation with only naked techniques of holding power. To the political belongs the idea, because there is no politics without authority and no authority without an ethos of belief."[32] As long as the idea survives and the ardent bipolarity of power and authority, person and institution, decision and truth holds firm, the power of the Roman Church remains alive. And, harbored within it, the essence of the political.

Guardini approaches this question from the same point of view. The fact that his work is organized in different ways, offering different emphases that in the end lead him to divergent outcomes, merely conceals the fact—that has until now been overlooked—that Guardini's *Vom Wesen Katholischer Weltanschauung* converges semantically, categorically, and shall we say "topologically" with Schmitt's *Roman Catholicism and Political Form*, which was published in the same year.[33] The affinity goes far beyond an explicit appreciation for Schmitt's writing, stated not long after its publication in one of Guardini's letters from Lake Como (an appreciation made even more significant in light of the reticence Guardini usually showed to contemporary authors and works).[34] Recall the particular "geometric" progression that Schmitt attributed to the representative *ordo* of the Roman Church: a voracious, protean, horizontal extension, attentive to or *governed by* the absolute of a vertically oriented decision, oriented to a "care" for the whole of reality, yet at the same time vigilant against the loss of its singular, particular aspects. This same arrangement also surfaces in the definition of *Weltanschauung*, in Guardini's paradigm. *Weltanschauung* is "an awareness movement that is oriented in a very specific way to the totality of things," but that, in order to realize itself concretely and efficaciously, must substitute the mechanics of a simple knowledge with the impression of an authentic gaze: "*Weltanschauung* is the meeting between world and human, a face to face confrontation, but one that always takes place precisely in the eye."[35]

The role Guardini attributed to the semantics of vision (this too in full sympathy with Schmitt's representational Christology in "The Visibility of the Church") must not be forgotten: it is both decisive and productive of decisions. "Seeing," he wrote in the section of *The Lord* with which we began, "is more than indifferently reflecting (as a mirror reflects all that passes within range). It is a vital process that directly affects our lives. To see, *perceive*, means to receive into oneself, to submit to the influence of things, to place oneself within their grasp."[36] To penetrate the world, and at the same time to be penetrated by it. To know, and at the same time take a position, to decide upon the object of knowledge. But because this is possible, because the gaze of the *Weltanschauung* penetrates the world, it also assumes a *distance* from it. Things are penetrated, but from a distance that liberates us from their immediate power to condition us. It is instead the *Weltanschauung* that makes this power its own, dominating *from above*. For this purpose a position merely *outside* the world is not enough; a place that is *above* the world is required. Only such a vantage could constitute a secure viewpoint for the gaze and enable a decisive knowledge. This position is incarnated in Christ's gesture. "He is 'different' from the world; he is 'from on high.' As such, he places the world into question and obliges it to reveal itself. He is the great unveiling through which the world shows its true face."[37] It is Christ who grasps the world by its essential center, and simultaneously from each of its infinite angles. He sees the whole as each of its parts, and the sum of those parts. He knows and decides. The gaze of the *Weltanschauung* is his gaze. Only those who look with the gaze of Christ "have the power to confront concrete reality, concrete destiny."[38]

This "power" is the power of Rome. Its Church "is the historical bearer of Christ's holistic gaze on the world."[39] For this reason, echoing Schmitt's figure of the *complexio*, "there is no [specifically] Catholic type . . . Catholicism signifies a thoroughgoing adhesion to supernatural Revelation in *all* of its contents, in *all* areas and all involvements in concrete life. It embraces all typological possibilities, just as it embraces life itself."[40] This is a common theme in post-Newman Catholic apologetics,[41] but in Guardini it is brought to the limits of its *vital* significance. It is this relation with life that keeps the power of the Roman Church alive—a power that lives, and continues to live, because it encounters life. And it does so not by indifferently absorbing something that is simply passive and available, but in terms of *direction*.[42] It encounters life *in* and *from* the direction of its truth: "formally put, the Catholic stance consists in the fact that the various types of viewpoint—psychological, ethnological and cultural—are gathered together by an ultimate, general stance."[43] This is the highest *Weltanschauung* of all, because "from on high" it watches, understands, and decides on the infinite variety of the world in its multipolar restlessness. In Guardini's church, finally, that figure of perpendicular intersection inscribed in the metallic pages of Schmitt's *Roman Catholicism*—the figure of the cross—finds its clearest enunciation:

> This universality has two sides: one extensive and the other intensive. By force of the first, the Church maintains its broad gaze, embracing the times, and the coexistence of human forms and differences. This ensures that the Church extends ever wider and inheres within itself ever-new values: it is the evangelical parable of the mustard seed. By force of the second, the Church is able to throw itself into whatever work, conduct, or decision that God, through the situation of the day, desires of it; but it remains elastic, preserving its total being, and it can from there move to ever-new decisions.[44]

This is how the scant, intense fragment "Vom Wesen" concludes, containing within it an interpretive key for Guardini's work as a whole. We have until now labored to clarify the difficult *topos* occupied by the Roman Church, and its inimitable work of preserving Decision within the problem of polar opposition, thus giving rise to the "Grand decision" arising from the tension of its opposites. It is from this "impossible" combination—opposition *and* decision—that its unspeakable political power derives.

As we have seen, this is not the product of an absolutely heterogeneous relation to life, but rather an explicit adhesion to life as something fully concrete. This restless opposition between coexisting elements is the very structure of life itself in its essentially (not contingently) political dimension. This is how Guardini can attempt to express life's "system" in the work that constitutes the true philosophical ceiling over his entire oeuvre: "Der Gegensatz."[45] Much has been said about this system and its consequences, and particularly about the sources from which it was derived (from Plato to Bonaventura, to Nicholas of Cusa and to his contemporaries Mournier,[46] Przywara,[47] Adam,[48] and Roubiczek,[49] and on the Protestant side also Brunner[50] and Tillich[51]). Some have taken issue with its explicitly antimetaphysical and preontological stance, while others have defended its systematic or even neoscholastic character. In reality, the work contains both of these aspects, and not in a neutralized combination but rather as an irreducible contradiction. The fact that this contradiction—which is a good emblem for Guardini's Catholicism as a whole—would end up compromising the coherence of the entire system (or, as we will see, inflecting it in a utopian key) does not alter the fact that this is precisely what lends the text its creative force and makes it a document of extraordinary originality in contemporary Catholic theology.

Guardini's entire oeuvre is animated by an internal conflict that surfaces in numerous logically unsayable thresholds. He systematizes what is by definition unsystematic (the "concrete living being") and categorizes that which escapes every category; he defines, enumerates, and classifies what can only barely, or only sometimes, be named. *Being is united*—reads the initial proposition of the "system"—*by exactly what divides it.* The entirety of Guardini's discursive pattern radiates out from this point, firmly galvanized to the logic of two fundamental laws. First, that reality is dominated by the principle of a bipolar opposition (*Gegensatz*, *Polarität*, *Pol-Gegenpol*); and second, that this opposition is never a simple contradiction (*Widerspruch*), an absolute alterity, or a radical unrelation. For Guardini, all errors—and above all modernity's error—can ultimately be traced back to the contravention of one or the other of these principles, or worse, *both* of them, as in the case of the Romantic sensibility. What in fact condemns the Romantic position to ineffectuality is therefore the same thing that defines its apolitical nature (I underline this fact because it is reproposed point-for-point in Schmitt's *Political Romanticism*): a *confusio* so indecisive that it loses its grasp on the nature of these distinctions at the very moment that it absolutizes them into pure contradictions.[52] This, as Schmitt would not fail to point out, is what ensures its essentially antirepresentative character, meaning that it loses Catholicism's representative *intentio* without being able to substitute for it some other equally powerful form of control over the century—thus ensuring that it passively capitulates to modern secularization.

Guardini poses the tragic seriousness [*der Ernst*] of the "leap" against exactly this *confusio,* introducing a "discontinuity" between elements so that henceforth they cannot be confused with or derived from each other. Guardini's whole system, its categories and its laws, its movement, measure and rhythm, emerges from this originary law [*legge*]. But the same law unmistakably gives rise to his system's internal contradiction: an irreducible tendency to rupture, and therefore to self-negation. The process of rupture can be described in two moments. The first, an internal one and the logical result of the law of opposition itself, consists in the centrifugal push of each of the opposites with their tendency to self-absolutize. It is as if the binary pair unleashes a force of difference that strives to realize each of the opposing terms and everything it contains in its purest form. In fact, this system's productivity increases in line with the relative clarity, distinction, decisiveness and degree of opposition enjoyed by its terms. But it is precisely this differential force, and the maximal productivity that it gives the system, that simultaneously pushes it into crisis. If this force were to prevail—canceling out the opposite tendency to equilibrium—the system would explode. The intensity of its life would be transformed into the ineluctability of its death. As such, the system can be wrenched from this centripetal force only at the cost of its ruin. It is the system that placates, heals, and saves, restoring balance and relation. But it does not eliminate risk: On the contrary, it multiplies it, displacing it onto another front, from the extremes to the center. The risk that belongs to its center (with all that might imply: blockage, stasis, standardization) is no less a risk than that of its extremes, and in no sense does it withhold the system from its fate of breakdown, rupture [*apertura*], *shipwreck*:

> In this way the living relation of polar opposition betrays its idiosyncratic dangers. There are therefore three dangerous points. First of all, each of the two 'external' limit values resulting from the 'pure' realisation of their opposite: this is a shipwreck of the purest kind. Then also the 'internal' limit value of equilibrium between the opposites: the shipwreck zone of perfect harmony. By 'values' I mean final goals, or perfect forms. And by 'limits' we must understand manners of demise. The experience of the opposites as a form of life is besieged at its extremes and assailed from its centre by the vital impossibility of death. In any case, these impossibilities are at the same time the perfect forms of the same life. Bound into perfect fulfilment there is destruction.[53]

With the idea that the system draws closer to perfection to the same degree that it approaches its own "shipwreck," an initial, powerful, quality of beginning [*apertura*] manifests; and at the same time, the inherently (not contingently) tragic character of Guardini's *Anschauung*. But this beginning is still within the system and its self-contradictory logic. There is an opening [*apertura*], but it still resonates within the internal walls of the temple. All along, however, a second and more "catastrophic" rupture [*apertura*] responds to this internal one. The system knocks against the edges of this rupture, grazing itself on its surface. Or equally, we could say that the very outside itself of this rupture is configured into a system: the system of its own alterity. It is at this point that the dialectic of opposites spikes into a conciliatory decision on its contradictory elements or absolute values, finally resulting in a break toward the decisive [*Durchbruch ins Entscheidende*], toward the authentic [*ins Eigentliche*]. Such a break is postsystem [*dopo il sistema*]. Or better, it is presystem, because it is, in fact, what the system presupposes: To remain within conflict and survive is possible only after having made a decision in the face of incompatible values. This is not a matter of something that is temporally or simply logically prior, but something *existential*: a choice that has as its object the *truth of life*. This decision, therefore—in its action, in making a choice and in the risk that entails—does not follow consciousness, but rather precedes it. More precisely, it determines consciousness: The entire cognitive potential of Guardini's system is dependent on this practical decision. Overturned at the threshold of its opening [*apertura*], it remains reliant on the efficacy of an active decision and a language that is necessarily *political* because it is oriented toward the *community* of life. It is no accident that this political inflection, which had covertly governed the entire discussion will, in the end, resound with the tenor of a "mission": "What seems inevitable to us also, in this context, is the mission of 'politics' in our time."[54]

The "political" reference to a decision understood as a break [*rottura*] toward the authentic seems to decisively unite Schmitt and Guardini, thus fully vindicating their 1923 symmetry (which had already been reinforced by their common critique of Romanticism). But at precisely this point, such a stark and unbridgeable distance emerges between the two that their symmetry and their difference appear equally pronounced. In reality, leaving aside the historical-biographical question of Schmitt's profession of faith, whenever we are tempted to speak of Schmitt's writing on Catholicism as analogous with or even as *being* a Catholic position (especially one like Guardini's), we should not forget that a hidden divergence lies within precisely the concept that most justifies the comparison in the first place: representation.[55] This difference is in a certain sense operative in the very text where Schmitt gestures to two opposing ways of understanding the concept in question. On one hand, representation is defined precisely in a Catholic sense, which means, as we have seen, that it possesses both the *complexio* (horizontal difference) and the transcendence of the idea (vertical difference). But representation is further defined in the democratic-parliamentarian (or even monarchical) sense—which elides any transcendent aspect and is in fact possible only in the absence of any transcendence.[56]

We can leave aside for now the problem of whether and to what extent Schmitt himself shifts his prevalent point of view from one of these conceptions of representation to the other. It is true that beginning with his 1923 essay, he considers the Catholic idea of representation, and therefore Catholicism's entire categorical orientation, in terms of a remnant: something that *resists* the converging advance of two opposing and complementary forces, capitalism and socialism. In this sense, the reason Catholicism could attain a monopoly over the political is that it remained alone in its defense.[57] This is also why Catholicism's monopoly is "monstrous": not because of any identifiable *political* objection to it, but more accurately, precisely because of the complete absence of anything of the sort. These factors provide Catholicism with its terribly *utopian* destiny, in the literal sense that its historical and semantic space is ever more withdrawn, so that it inexorably becomes ever more "insular" in the face of grand modern deracination. Deracination, in this way, brings about a sudden reversal of roles: what was the continent (Catholicism) is now an island, and what was an island—modernity, insofar as it is the dissolution or abandonment of the land of tradition—is now the continent.

The radical difference between Schmitt's position and Guardini's is that in Schmitt this inversion of roles—expressed historically by the fact that when the State became a Leviathan it disappeared from the world of representations—is understood as inevitable.[58] The same difference also applies, in fact, to their otherwise common rejection of Romantic thought. Schmitt's reproach of Romanic subjectivism had less to do with the fact that it breaks the bipolar balance between subject and object, or the monistic *confusio* of the transcendental opposition (that is, its inscription within modern secularization), and much more to do with his objection to the weak, inefficacious, and romantically *indecisive* way that break comes about.[59] Though we cannot dwell on this discussion to the extent it might warrant, we should keep it firmly in mind, because it is this same difference that most clearly reveals the distinction between Schmitt's categorical frame and those of both traditional Catholic approaches, and the great "bourgeois" critics of modernization. It is also largely what provoked the staunch Catholic attacks and objections against Schmitt's "political theology." Although this political theology (understood as a "method" and not as a "system," obviously) identifies secularization's zones of crisis and countertendential moments, and even suggests that it is practically impossible to mend its original dualism, for precisely this reason it takes secularization's irreversibility as a general process for granted.

This can be put differently. The fact that secularization is irreversible for Schmitt is confirmed by the fact that in his account of Hobbes's conceptual apparatus, the reference to the personal authority of Christ functions to legitimate the split between inside and outside, therefore amounting to a nullification of the transcendental *Veritas*. The *Veritas* has no force at all beyond that of the sovereign decision, which effectuates the full identification of power and knowledge. Precisely this devaluation of the transcendent *Veritas* (or its incorporation within decision, which amounts to the same thing) marks the truly unbridgeable distance between Schmitt's political theology and grand Catholic representation. Decision and representation remain fundamental references all throughout Schmitt's work, but they are subordinated to a secularizing movement that tends to infinitely separate the levels on which they operate. Each of the terms in question—unity and opposition—is made absolute, to the point where it loses or even *reverses* the meaning it had as part of a principle of bipolarity. So in Schmitt, unity's metaphysical character tends to be saturated to the point of becoming a fully realized monism, while conflict, located on the level of immanence, tends to transform mere contradiction into the equally absolute friend/enemy distinction.

The consequence of all of this is the rejection of any kind of philosophy of history, which becomes something objectively impossible whether in a progressive or regressive sense. For Schmitt, the modern is not just an epoch (the final epoch in a linear development made up of successive stages) but also the point of view, the *only* point of view, from which to observe the past and future alike. The clearest demonstration of this idea is found in the essay on the "Age of Neutralizations and Depoliticizations," with its theory of successive stages with changing central domains.[60] Nowhere more clearly than here is the path blocked against any hope of restoration or any plan of escape. Schmitt's depiction of Europe's "wandering" from a "conflictual domain" to a "neutral" one that itself immediately becomes a new "arena of struggle," gives us a sense of the strict analytical limits he maintains so as not to lose the versatile syntax of modernity's various domains and their unprecedented intertwining, seen above all in the case of politics and technology. Technology introduces a powerful qualitative difference into the procession of centers of neutralization that had, until that point, been simply sequential. Whereas all past centers were able to historically inform their epoch and give it its meaning and destiny (albeit while reproducing and displacing neutralized conflicts to the next level in the sequence), technology, as something purely neutral, remains fully at the mercy of the forces that manage it. The fact that technology is absolutely available is what makes it not only entirely apolitical, but the very principle of depoliticization. Despite this depoliticizing essence, however, it would still be a mistake to imagine that the age of technology could be politically untroubled. It is precisely technology's neutrality that makes it the possible prey of *any* politics that is capable of mastering it. This means that its hyperneutrality ends up overturning into its opposite, so that it becomes the object of maximum politicization—even functioning to inhibit further depoliticization:

> The process of continuous neutralization of various domains of cultural life has reached its end because technology is at hand. Technology is no longer neutral ground in the sense of the process of neutralization; every strong politics will make use of it. For this reason, the present century can only be understood provisionally as the century of technology. How ultimately it should be understood will be revealed only when it is known which type of politics is strong enough to master the new technology and which type of genuine friend-enemy groupings can develop on this new ground.[61]

This is what gives rise to both Schmitt's rejection of every nostalgic, restorative stance (and therefore his acceptance of technology's horizons as the only ones that are effectively available), and his insistence on an idea of the political that can be equal to the situation because it takes the political "void" within technology itself as its starting point. That is: Schmitt recuperates a notion of the political that is capable of accepting the challenge imposed by the time of technology, and "deciding" it existentially. Only a decision that is free of historicist presuppositions and providential schemes can fulfill the "political void" of technology, directing it to its own ends.

THE DUTY OF POWER

Schmitt's position here allows his relation to Guardini to return to center stage. But now the relation appears to be inverted: Whereas in the two authors' otherwise similar writings on Catholicism we could see the signs of an incalculable distance, here those signs reappear to trace out an insistent symmetry. The decisive site of this symmetry is Guardini's analysis of modernity, from *Letters from Lake Como* through *Welt und Person* to *The End of the Modern World*.[62] Certainly, as we have said, like Schmitt, Guardini changes the point of view from which the historical process is judged (for him, this point must always remain the dual perspective of the immanence-transcendence bipolarity). But the two authors converge even more significantly at the categorical and semantic level. Guardini characterizes modernity as rigorously discontinuous—or even exceptional—with regard to its medieval and ancient antecedents; believing that modernity severs the nexus between concept and life, reflection and experience, but also soul and body, man and thing, and so on. More important, however, for Guardini modernity is also discontinuous with the coming epoch "being born out of the womb of history," which history has not yet named,[63] and which is visible from its outermost borders.

What is known about this epoch is its distinctively technological character. It is true that the roots of technology, as the mode of relation with the natural world, are sunk into the course of past centuries. But for Guardini, what was for a long time a question of a quantitative shift in technology has now become a qualitative one. This leap concerns on the one hand the relation between subjectivity and function, and on the other the relation between consciousness, action and experience. Whereas before, in modernity, technology still referred to a subject-human (so-called *Homo faber*) who was considered the unshakeable foundation of its own practical and cognitive activity, now a new kind of technology is born precisely from this subject's irreversible breakdown. This is what gives rise to technology's specific epochal relation with a multitude that is understood not as a simple sum of single individuals, but as the "social structure" of a different "law of standardization."[64] All of this results in a radical transformation in the constitution of subjectivity, which is marked by a growing disjuncture between the ambit of knowledge and action and that of experience. And because of this disjuncture, it is marked also by a particular kind of man, conceived as "nonhuman" insofar as it can no longer be defined by the foundational category of the subject.[65]

However, this fact must not bring the individual, expropriated of its natural character, to an attitude of resistance or rejection (in some ways specifying that this unnamed epoch is "posthuman" recalls some moments in Jünger even more so than Schmitt). Rather, the individual "must make a decisive effort to overcome his prejudices, to expose himself freely to an order which may menace his very essence, stamped as it is with the forces of history,"[66] and thus *favorably* take on all the innovative potential of this incipient "genetic" mutation. Guardini's position not only leaves well behind the antimodernism of the Catholic right (from Maritain to Del Noce), but it strikes decisively at all explicit and implicit critiques of civilization (albeit from a perspective, it must be said, that is far from modernist or generically liberal). Technological secularization is not only considered inevitable but is also augmented and brought to its full "maturity" and extreme consequences.[67]

But what does it mean exactly, to bring technology to its extreme consequences? The answer to this question is contained in those of Guardini's works that are dedicated to the theme of power, culminating with *Die Macht*, which finally make explicit the profoundly political soul of his entire message.[68] To bring technology to its extreme consequences means to reckon with its specific function, and what it installs at the center of existence: *power*. "Science, as the rational comprehension of reality, and technology as the sum of scientific possibility, together stamp existence with a new character: power, or dominion, in what we might call the acute sense of the word."[69] In making technology and power synonymous, Guardini's discussion finds an initial connection with Schmitt's analytical frame. Technology is essentially domination, and all those who account for it weak or pacifist terms will inevitably come up against the harsh fact that technology is power.[70] But the analogy with Schmitt also concerns the specific quality that this identity assumes: an absolute availability. "Power awaits direction,"[71] and thus it may be used to ends that are entirely conflictual. So much so that precisely because of its intrinsically apolitical nature, technology (recalling that this is also Schmitt's thesis) calls man to the most intense politicization: the great decision. Not only is this assumption of technology as power (and the existential decision on that power) not incompatible with the theological task of ultramodern man: It is the direct consequence of that task.

Here Guardini opens a bold political-theological chapter, *The Theological Concept of Power*, which attributes the necessity of human authority, the *duty* of power, to a particular command from God.[72] In order to resemble God, and therefore true man, the human must exercise power: "Man cannot be human and, as a kind of addition to this humanity, exercise or fail to exercise power; the exercise of power is essential to his humanity. To this end the Author of his existence determined him."[73] This has a further consequence: not only the exercise of power, but simply power itself. But this is a power increased to the nth degree: a power—to arrive at the definition most true to Guardini's thought—that is *capable of mastering its own power*. It was the failure to attain this kind of power that "shipwrecked" the modern, in severing the human-God bipolarity in favor of the former: not an excess of human power, then, but a lack of it. Modern man's rejection of God meant the refusal to govern its own power, a renunciation of that supreme power that only a power over power can offer. As Guardini elaborates, it is "ascesis" that could supply such a power, in that ascesis is understood as an extreme mastery of one's own power.[74] This is not a Weberian "ascesis," naturally—which, as a renunciation *for* economic profit, can objectively be seen as a kind of depoliticization—but an ascesis *from* the economic, toward the fulfillment of the political. It is a power over power, which is to say, the power of the *Idea* (according to the *powerful* representative logic of the Roman Church).

Guardini devotes his argument precisely to the misunderstanding of the concept of "ascesis" in the "liberal" or "bourgeois" mentality. Instead of "openly taking the defense of power," these accounts prefer to "hide it behind aspects of 'utility,' 'welfare,' 'progress' and so forth,"[75] thus erroneously giving it an apolitical inflection and losing sight of its decisionist potential (this, too, is strongly Schmittian). Against this "weak" economic reading of power, Guardini believes it is necessary to return to its essence, which is that it has the decisive option over the great questions of existence: "At the center of the endeavors of the coming culture will loom this problem of power. . . . Every decision faced by the future age—those determining the welfare or misery of humanity and those determining the life or death of mankind itself—will be decisions centered on the problem of power."[76] This is why one must "know and agree that the import of the coming culture is not welfare but dominion."[77] Never before has the world required power, direction, command as it does today; never before has the world "shrunk to a single political field with no gaps or empty spaces"; never as today has "governing—in the true sense of observing, judging, comprehending, directing, evaluating the given part in view of the whole" become so "particularly urgent."[78] At this point the coming epoch, the epoch still without name, begins to take shape. It is the time of the fulfillment of technology, but at the same time, *precisely for this reason*, the time of the maximum politicization of life:

> The fact that the earth confronts us as a definitively limited field of a specific size gives rise to a distinctive pressure from *outside*, a frontier pressure, whether national, economic, cultural, or indeed intellectual and spiritual. This pressure gives distinctive importance to all intrinsic points of integration and forms of relationship. And it especially gives political importance to, for example, humanity, the cultural circle, the nation, and personality.[79]

This is why to have "an elemental relationship to technology"[80] can only mean to reconquer "an originary relationship with power,"[81] to confront the risk it bears and rediscover its positive potential: The danger "does not belong exclusively to the negative symptoms of the coming culture.[82] If it did, we could only conclude: then away with it! But danger is an integral part of the coming world view, and when rightly understood, it lends that view a new earnestness. To the end of time there will be no human existence that does not live with peril."[83] To fully live the coming time can only mean "to live with danger, or at least know that . . . [one] can and must learn to;" to realize the "greatness" of the power that this offers us and to *decide* on it.[84] In this time, the clash between the forces triggered and "provoked" by technology becomes decisive in every sense. It is more than ever the time of absolute decisions, a sentiment that can countenance absolute imperatives:

> The coming man is decidedly un-liberal, which does not mean that he has no respect for freedom. The "liberal" attitude is that which declines to incorporate absolutes into existence because their *either-or* engenders conflict. It is far easier to be able to see things in any light, "the only important thing" being "life" and "getting along with others." Values and ideas are but a matter of personal opinion . . . . [But] the man under discussion knows that unless freed from such attitudes man can never cope with the existential situation we face today. What will count will not be details or elaborations, but fundamentals: dignity or slavery, growth or decline, truth or lie; the mind or the passions.[85]

But if the time of decision is coming, what will be its specific *space*? Where does decision fall? What is its historico-epochal *topos*? The answer to this question gives us an opportunity to offer some final considerations on Guardini's thought, and at the same time to situate it once more in relation to Schmitt's. No great contemporary political theorist more than Schmitt made the problem of historico-political space the center of their research, as *The Nomos of the Earth*[86] attests. On this book's grand canvas, where his reflection on the space-politics-decision nexus is at its most concentrated and clear, Schmitt displays the self-negating procedure that characterizes his great works, wherein the object of his analysis shifts and migrates beyond the very lines that seem to define it. Here, decision falls in a space in flight and so becomes a decision not *of* but *from* that space. This internal upheaval grips Schmitt's text, withholding it from its own topic of inquiry and any "definition" of its object, thus precluding any systematic or constructive outcome.

In this way it draws a line of pure negativity between its point of departure and point of arrival, crossing out what can no longer be because it is the process of an irreversible dissolution.

The object involved in this case is naturally the *jus publicum* and its European space. Torn from its borders, multiplied, but also shattered into segments that disperse its original centrality, the *jus publicum* was once central but is now reduced to a remnant, a residue, the trace of a definitively broken order. The order in which it now finds itself—it would be better to say disorder—is the result of the continual rupture and upheaval of its ancient roots. But in Schmitt's analysis we can also hear something like the familiar echo of a terrible scourge. Was this now-wrecked European center not itself the product of a more ancient but no less traumatic deracination? Was it not also wrenched from something that existed before it, something that is now borne within it in a dismantled form? Was that *jus* not erected on the rubble of the *respublica christiana*, decreeing its end? The Europe of states, and its new law, are born from the breaking of the union between Roman law and Roman Church and therefore between *auctoritas* and *Veritas*—even if residues and fragments of that union remain within the new order in the form of "political theology." These same fragments are the agents of its future dissolution, beginning with the First World War when the criminalization of the enemy and the resulting transformation of war into an international policing operation evoked the theological phantasms of the *bellum justum* in an attempt at a new organization of the world.

This organization, however, stands no chance of completion—if by completion we mean the construction of an international peace. That peace was made dependent on the identity between power [*potere*] and faith, and staked into the center of Europe by the Catholic *repraesentatio.* But this identity is not only exactly what the *modern* Europe of States was born and raised against, it is now even further removed from the internationalization of the economy and the formation of the world market, which have relegated Europe and its law to the periphery of the earth's new empires. In a sense, this destiny was already implicit in the first great European decentering, brought about by its appropriation of the new world—a process through which, paradoxically, statal Europe had celebrated its centrality to the modern age. Europe is now "appropriated" on the very ground it had made its own precisely by a process of appropriation. And it is now paying for that first betrayal, that first abandonment of the Christian center, without which, or outside of which, Europe witnesses the space of its decisions being carted away. It can thus no longer decide on even its *own* space. Schmitt's *Nomos* embraces this space's impossibility, standing opposed to any attempt to refound it. The fractures, the battle lines, the wars that fragment the space of the new order from within and without, give the sense that it is utterly ungovernable. If the Europe of states can no longer be the ancient *res publica christiana*, then the new poststatal space can no longer order the history of the world: and this double, intertwined movement expresses the entire meaning of Schmitt's *Nomos*.

Guardini's conclusion is completely in line with this one. What he shifts and overturns is the premise, not the consequence, of Schmitt's reasoning. For Guardini too, outside of its relation with Christianity Europe cannot but disappear as the subject of world history; and outside of Europe's gaze, the history of the world inevitably loses its meaning. But—here Guardini's tendency to utopian resolution flares—it is not entirely certain that this will occur. It is not a forgone conclusion that the world loses Europe, because it is not yet given that Europe loses the word of Christ:

> Without doubt, the Europe of the mandate for which we have spoken does not yet exist. We spoke of a law according to which the existing marginal pressure around a certain sociological field acts such that the particular territories situated in this field are joined together. Besides which, however, we must not forget that the word 'law' can be used only in an improper sense when it comes to historical events. It is not an expression of necessity, but a form of becoming endowed with significance. It is a fatal error to see within history a process that necessarily proceeds by way of determinate forms. History is not a natural process, but a human becoming, which is not completed of its own accord, but must be willed.[87]

The fact that natural "law" [*legge*] misfires, such that the reality of Europe fails to be captured by the order it necessitates, results directly from the fact that Europe's task and reality is precisely the liberation of the world from the law of necessity [*legge*]: it is an expression of history as the very principle of being unconditioned by natural law. Europe—to respond, at last, to the question that opened this section—is the *space of decision*. And it is the space of decision because it is the space of Christ. The *topos* of the Christianity-Europe nexus recurs with impressive frequency within the Catholic thought of the time, assuming various tones and meanings according to the politico-cultural position of its interpreters. What is shared, however, among such diverse sensibilities as Maritain[88] and the frankly reactionary Massis or Belloc,[89] is the idea that it was not the Occident that vitalized Christianity but the reverse. In fact, to outline this position, whose classic expression comes from Karl Adam's *Christus und der Geist des Abendlandes*:[90] Christianity, born of the Orient, was developed in the Occident—until the Occident betrayed it. This betrayal sealed its fate and brought about its undoing. This is what leads to the final prognosis: Only the reconquest of its Christian roots can save the Occident and mend its ancient fracture with the Orient. This is the great task that falls to Catholicism because it alone, in its capacity for synthesis—the Schmittian *complexio*—can bring this task to completion. From Herwegen[91] to Moenius[92] to Wust,[93] this theme unites the entire front of German Catholicism.

But none of these authors' arguments has a force to match the "politico-theological reflection"—as the author himself defines it—that is Guardini's remarkable "The Saviour in Myth, Revelation and Politics."[94] This reflection—with its *powerful* utopia—seems to give the rest of Guardini's work a clearer and more intense significance. Again Christ is at the center of the frame, and once more he embodies the principle of history. Precisely for this reason Christ stands in contrast to the world of myth, to which certain traditions (the Gnostic tradition, for example) had sought to assign him. Christ stands opposed to all mythical temporalities like "once upon a time," or "ever since that day;" or the functionally identical always-future of the "to come." On the contrary, "Christ is purely and precisely historical."[95] This is why, evidently, he does not make up one of the rank and file of "saviors." He shares nothing with their meaning and destiny, and nor does he come bearing their inheritance: an uninterrupted chain of references and correspondences that follows the order of the natural cycle. Birth, death, then another life and another death: this rhythm accurately describes the work of the saviors, and its cadence assumes *their* particular brand of salvation. They are indeed saviors, and they do in fact redeem, but only within the cycles internal to this event. Their role is not to "test" nature or to break down its walls, but to confirm it, to exorcize its traumas and prepare a salve. The saviors do not disrupt nature's circle, but rather galvanize and reproduce it.

Their action is purely horizontal. They do not know history's leaps (or they know them only to erase them).

But Christ is different. He escapes their power and saves from their brand of salvation: "Who therefore is Christ? He is the one who redeems precisely from what the saviors mean. He liberates man from the ineluctability of life and death, of light and darkness, of ascension and fallenness. He shatters the enchanting monotony of nature, which although it seems to be saturated with every sense of existence, in reality dissolves all personal dignity."[96] What he saves from, precisely, is the continuous whole that involves an *indecision* between opposing principles. For the saviors "there is no good and evil in the true sense, that is separate from the either/or of moral decisions."[97] Christ, on the other hand, decides. He separates and chooses: "He founds absolute differences. He makes clear the meaning of personal decisions that are valid for eternity."[98] This is why Christ has determined and continues to determine the *political* role of Europe as history *and* decision, decision *within* history: "What we call Europe, that context of countries and peoples that lies between Africa and the Arctic, Asia Minor and the Atlantic Ocean, and whose history begins in the third millennium before Christ with Greece's primitive age and extends through to our time, is decisively defined as a whole by the figure of Christ."[99] The reason Christ defines Europe—note that this is what distinguishes Guardini from the reactionary strands of political Catholicism—is not because he protects it from the ultramodern, technological outcome of its history, but rather because he entrusts it to precisely that outcome: "Nothing is more mistaken than the opinion that modern dominion over the world in terms of consciousness and technology must have been attained in a struggle against a Christianity that desired to keep man in an inactive subjection. The opposite is true: The enormous risk of science and of modern technology, whose capacities we witness with a profound disquiet after recent discoveries, became possible only on the foundation of the very personal independence that Christ gave to man."[100] Romano Guardini's entire political utopia, and the vital contradiction that it contains, is concentrated into these propositions (which echo Novalis's old prophecy of *Christenheit oder Europa*). It is utopian and contradictory for a twofold reason: not only because Guardini thought Europe would remain central forever, but above all because he entrusted its centrality to its Christian origin, which is itself the paradigm and theological form of the most extreme historico-epochal deracination: the Cross that casts its rays far from its center. And yet it is within this utopia that his voice most clearly responds, like an unfaithful echo, to Carl Schmitt's—and vice versa. One adhering strictly to the reality of the modern and the apparent eternity of its season, the other striving to overcome it but being bound, at the same time, to its ancient theological roots. One clinging to its desperate realism, the other suspended by its utopian hope. And at their intersection lies a change of epoch that has not yet concluded.

2

THE UNREPRESENTABLE POLIS

THE REPRESENTATION OF DIFFERENCE

If we were to express in one phrase the "oppositional symmetry" between Schmitt and Guardini established in the previous chapter, we could say that it concerns the meaning each gives to the term "political theology." Although in the 1920s their similarities were emphasized by a shared semantic frame of reference, at the end of their intellectual lives, the radical differences between the two were to come fully to light. At one extreme lay Guardini's attempt to overcome the modern division between power and faith through the "ideal" management of technology, and at the other, Schmitt's taking that same division as the truth of the political-theological analogy between church and state (in an expression of a pure functionalism). Yet, as we have seen, the fact that such different projects continued to share a common conceptual vocabulary, so that their differences remained encased within a political-theological protocol, is materially significant. Indeed, it is within this broader consonance that the Catholic *complexio* reemerges—as the message (in Guardini), or as "memory" (in Schmitt). The appropriately named *complexio* is able to accommodate the most diverse political theologies (just think of the postconciliar political theology of Metz and Moltmann). The *complexio*, however, is also the categorical seed from which the political-theological paradigm will be first hollowed out from the inside, then thoroughly negated—giving us our first view of the operation that is the unifying theme of this volume.

This is seen clearly in the work of another German Catholic thinker, Eric Voegelin. Unlike Guardini, Voegelin does not limit himself to a position within the borders of political Catholicism, but decisively exceeds those borders with conclusions that disrupt any form of political theology.

Thus, it is no accident that Voegelin would mount a substantial critique of Schmitt, appearing in his long review of Schmitt's 1931 *Constitutional Theory*[1] (albeit one with numerous concessions). Voegelin's opposition is not easy to grasp, partly because of the inherent complexity of some of the categories involved—not least that of "representation," which we have already discussed. But the difficulty is compounded by the constant slippage of meaning that these categories undergo within Schmitt's theoretical framework, a fact we have already seen. For example, Schmitt's 1923 essay seems to outline a position in some ways not dissimilar to the one Voegelin held in his 1931 attack. The similarity goes beyond the fact that each attributes an "incomprehensible political power"[2] to Roman Catholicism (a position that was anything but rare at the time), or that each regards the *complexio* as the source of that power, from either a socio-institutional or theological point of view. That explanation, too, was widely accepted in the apologia of the period. Rather, it concerns the fact that each considered the *complexio* logically bound to the hinge-concept of "representation," as we saw in the previous chapter, with the result that their common position was in contrast with the nonrepresentational thought by which it was increasingly surrounded:

> From the standpoint of the political idea of Catholicism, the essence of the Roman-Catholic *complexio oppositorum* lies in a specific, formal superiority over the matter of human life such as no other imperium has ever known. It has succeeded in constituting a sustaining configuration of historical and social reality that, despite its formal character, retains its concrete existence at once vital and yet rational to the *n*th degree. This formal character of Roman Catholicism is based on a strict realisation of the principle of representation, whose particularity is most evident in its antithesis to the economic-technical thinking dominant today.[3]

The basis for this antithesis with nonrepresentational thought emerges clearly from the very essence of the principle of representation as formulated in this passage and enlarged in the discussion that follows. It consists in "a specific, formal superiority" over the matter of life, every *single* element of which it nonetheless conserves. This superiority is thus not an erasure or a simple domination. It is rather what renders the *complexio* possible and politically productive, since no vital opposition, no aspect of life, is sacrificed to the representative form that unifies it. Representation is representation only if it protects the *plurality* of the elements that are represented. Yet for this to be possible, a third element must stand alongside the representative and the thing that represented—or rather, *beyond* them, *transcending them both* and specifying their manner of relation. Schmitt defines this third element as the "idea." As we suggested in the previous chapter, "no political system can survive even a generation with only naked techniques of holding power. To the political belongs the idea, because there is no politics without authority and no authority without an ethos of belief."[4]

This is precisely the point of difference from nonrepresentational thought. Whereas in Weber's well-known equation nonrepresentationalism reduces the concept of authority to that of power, thus condensing all of reality within a single technical and mechanistic order, representative Catholicism conserves and exalts *difference* according to two distinct but intertwined levels. A "horizontal" plurality-difference between represented elements is conserved within the representational structure only if we assume an even more marked "vertical" transcendence-difference between the representative and the "idea" in whose name it represents. Without this double bipolarity—or a bipolarity that can be seen from two points of view—the entire system of representation collapses, and so too, therefore, the political system. If this bipolarity is destroyed as the transcendent pole is forgotten, and all of the real is thus enclosed within a single monistic principle, then grand political representation can only abdicate the political field to its *modern* adversary: "Economic thinking knows only one type of form, namely technical precision, and nothing could be further from the idea of representation."[5] The loss of this bipolarity signals the end of representation, and with that the end of the political. Notwithstanding the otherwise rich thematic frame presented by Schmitt's book on Catholicism, it is this specific passage that must be brought to bear on the present discussion.

Voegelin's critique will address this exact point. He, too, confronts a wide and tightly connected range of questions that cannot be reproduced here even in part—spanning the problem of the Weimar constitution, his relation with Jellinek and Kelsen, and the critique of the norm. What remains central, however, is his argument against Schmitt's new monistic point of view and the fall of bipolarity that accompanies it. It is as if here Schmitt had drastically reduced the capacity for differentiation of his 1923 understanding of representation. Elements that had in 1923 been carefully separated and distinguished were now violently concentrated as a result of an "obsession" with unity that leaves no space for anything outside of itself. And, according to Voegelin, it is precisely this obsession that draws Schmitt's account—considering Schmitt is usually so ready for concrete existential reality to rupture the false coherence of theory—toward a relatively commonplace kind of abstraction.

But of what is Schmitt's concept of state unity an abstraction? Not the state's historical existence as the *will* to power (the will being a theme we will revisit shortly), so much as the properly political existence that such a will would express. Politics should be understood here as Voegelin intends it: a unity that only functions, or that only has meaning (Voegelin would never use the former expression), if it manages to safeguard difference. This is really a question of two differences, as we have said: first, a difference between represented subjects (Voegelin, in the Catholic tradition, prefers to speak of "persons"), and second, a difference between the practical sphere in which persons "live together" (the Aristotelian *philia*) and the transcendental foundation that gives that living its specific value. According to Voegelin, these two differences—the "horizontal" difference internal to the sphere of immanence and the "vertical" distinction between immanence and transcendence—are directly related. The former presupposes the latter, in the sense that it is only a conscious acceptance of the latter (Voegelin's "noetic comprehension")[6] that allows the ontological possibility of affirming the former.

Voegelin will go on to formalize this thesis as a necessary connection between three kinds of representation: elementary, existential, and transcendental.[7] But already the text of his 1931 critique makes the central issue clear: "And here we face a problem the principles of which Schmitt has unfortunately not worked through: a State is fundamentally not a datum, but is present always solely in the actions of persons. . . . Each person in the state has his political status, even if this status should be characterised by the absence of all political rights, and to this extent each person 'represents' the political unit, even if neither the individual nor the sum of individuals are the political unit."[8] This means it is not the politico-juridical form that creates persons, but rather it is the concrete person that produces the politico-juridical form. The representative function relies on a solid anthropological structure,[9] and any mechanism designed to reduce the concrete, metaphysically founded subject-person to its formal features—which is Voegelin's accusation against Schmitt—will render representation meaningless. Representation rests on two dimensions: one "lower" (the plurality of persons) and one "higher" (the transcendence of its foundation). The fact that this foundation is not something that can be known, that for Voegelin it is grounded in an experience of mystery, does nothing to change the fact that the very possibility of the notion of representation depends on it. As he will say later in *The New Science of Politics*, the anthropological principle—the Platonic *metaxú* and the Aristotelian *philia*—requires the theological principle as the source of its meaning: "The truth of man and the truth of God are inseparably one. Man will be in the truth of his existence when he has opened his psyche to the truth of God. . . . If now the Platonic terminology be adopted, one may say, therefore, that the anthropological principle in a theoretical interpretation of society requires the theological principle as its correlate. The validity of the standards developed by Plato and Aristotle depends on the conception of a man who can be the measure of society because God is the measure of his soul."[10]

Without this metaphysical bipolarity, the political is maimed: deprived of its true, vital substance, and reduced to a pure surface. Even if that surface covers all the conservative inclinations of the will to existence and all the aggressive tendencies of the will to power, it will always lack any ontologically constitutive relation with its underlying reality. This is what rivets Schmitt's political will to the conceptual language of scholars like Jellinek and Kelsen (if not their substantive content): "The political will found in a political existence is the ultimate unity, one behind which Schmitt does not penetrate in his discussion of principles, which means he breaks off further advancement in the construction of political realities by way of his own system."[11] Such a will remains entirely unfounded, and for that reason it is in turn unable to offer a foundation for authentic political action. Equally, the concept of decision that is this will's logical consequence is destined to lose its affirmative power and fold circularly in on itself (despite Schmitt's placing it in convenient opposition to the abstract pure norm): "The new contents that this perspective brings into focus issue in some conceptual formulations peculiar to Schmitt, such as existence and decision, in which the will, which is necessary to grasp the element of the people constructing the state, remains central. Yet these concepts too are still captivated by the image of unity, and they are not fully detached from the realm of juridical thought with its complex syntheses of persons."[12]

This point requires further consideration, because it will also arise in Arendt's thought, albeit inverted, so that its logic appears to be reversed. What does it mean to say that in Schmitt the will is inextricably connected to the "representation of the whole"? How could a faculty like the will, traditionally associated with the capacity for choice, discrimination and decision, be associated with the representation of a whole? The question invites comment on the theme of unity in Schmitt's thought. In short: if his unity is a product of the will, this means that it is the result of a *separation* or exclusion, and it is therefore a *negative* unity. Note that this separation has nothing at all to do with Voegelin's bipolarity—it is rather its exact opposite. While the latter permits and produces a true, substantial, positive and affirmative unity (the Aristotelian *philia* between subject-persons who are different but in reciprocal communion), the Schmittian separation produces a unity that is only *functionally* a unity, because it is based on the distinction between friend and enemy. That is, it is capable of defining friendship only on the basis of enmity (through negation).

There is thus a reciprocal relation between unity and decision. *This* unity is the result of the will-decision, just as the will-decision is the result of *this* unity; and neither can do without the other. Just as this unity, in order to be a unity in the sense just indicated, needs the will to distinguish it from (or *against*) everything outside of it; so too the will, to be able to act and in order to will *decisively*, must be unitary. Something intrinsic to this conceptual arrangement seems to exceed the distinction between the categories of representation and identity, considering that the classic philosopher of representation (Hobbes) and that of identity (Rousseau) both arrive at a unification of the will (the former in sovereignty, the latter in the *volonté générale*). Indeed, remembering that in Schmitt, representation loses the balancing and differentiating principle of bipolarity and thus tends toward identity, the problem Voegelin poses is not actually the choice between identity and representation,[13] but rather between representation's classical and modern conceptions (or, more strongly, between "classical (Greek *and* Christian)" and "modern" representation). As his critical stance on Hobbes's notion of the will suggests, this is the real question for Voegelin, and he will in fact attack Hobbes and Schmitt for the same reason.[14] The difference between the two, which is certainly marked if not decisive of Voegelin's argument, is that while the former opens modernity, the latter closes it. But each works, in any case, *from within it*. Whereas the will is still vitally dual in Saint Augustine, the modern current drags the will into the vortex of unity, diminishing one of the poles (the transcendent) and thereby making the other absolute: "Saint Augustine distinguished between the *amor sui* and the *amor Dei* as the organising volitional centres of the soul. Hobbes threw out the *amor Dei* and relied for his psychology exclusively on the *amor sui*, in his language the self-conceit or pride of the individual, alone."[15] Before Schmitt, and with Schmitt, Hobbes opens the history of radical immanence, and the radical immanentization of history.

We can now bring together the discussion up to this point. We will leave to one side, for now, the question of Voegelin's accuracy in his interpretation of Schmitt. This means we leave open the following questions: (1) Whether Schmitt can be read as the political philosopher of radical immanentization or if, on the contrary, this immanentization leaves beyond itself (or even within itself) irreducible fragments of transcendence. (2) Whether the category of "representation" in *Constitutional Theory* is so radically different from that in *Roman Catholicism and Political Form* (that is, whether it is so entirely "horizontalized").[16] (3) Whether Schmitt's 1923 essay already contains the concept of will-decision (in the papal person) that becomes absolute in his later works. What matters is that this is Voegelin's reading of Schmitt, and that this reading is enough to situate it on the other side of the battle line that, according to Voegelin, divides the political philosophical debate into two conflicting camps: "The true dividing line in the contemporary crisis does not run between liberals and totalitarians, but between religious and philosophical transcendentalists on the one side, and the liberal and totalitarian immanentist sectarians on the other side."[17]

ORIGIN AND FOUNDATION

The phrase just quoted was not in fact directed at Carl Schmitt, but at another protagonist in that debate, Hannah Arendt, who by then was already the celebrated author of *The Origins of Totalitarianism*. The brief but intense 1953 debate that followed Voegelin's critical review of that work, and the radical positions it uncovered, would illuminate the subsequent output of both authors. It was almost as if their thought diverged only within a shared set of questions that aligned their positions to a far greater degree than either of them realized. So much so that the basic theoretical disagreement that concludes the debate between Voegelin and Arendt in 1953 now gives the impression of a mutual misunderstanding—or at least suggests that neither saw how their differences, however pertinent and material, were possible only within a common frame of inquiry. I refer not so much to those topics through which the canon of critique somewhat habitually associates the two authors (together with Leo Strauss): practical philosophy, the return to the Greeks, and the critique of modernity. These points are, in fact, where their difference is clearest and most profound.[18] Rather, their similarity concerns a conceptual or more precisely semantic current within which even the most glaring distinctions appear to move in a similar direction.

We turn now to the substance of the 1953 exchange, arising, as we said, from Arendt's great work on totalitarianism. After an introduction of the book's interests that was by no means merely formal, Voegelin proceeds to level two accusations against it. The first of the two charges is inconsequential: despite being aware of the extent of the problem in question, "Dr. Arendt . . . does not draw the theoretical conclusions from her own insights."[19] But the second and more serious complaint is decisive for Voegelin. He suggests a conceptual connivance, or mental complicity, on Arendt's part, with the object under analysis: totalitarianism. "This book on the troubles of the age . . . is also marked by these troubles, for it bears the scars of the unsatisfactory state of theory to which we have alluded. It abounds with brilliant formulations and profound insights—as one would expect only from an author who has mastered her problems as a philosopher—but surprisingly, when the author pursues these insights into their consequences, the elaboration veers toward regrettable flatness. Such derailments, while embarrassing, are nevertheless instructive—sometimes more instructive than the insights themselves—because they reveal the intellectual confusion of the age, and show more convincingly than any argument why totalitarian ideas find mass acceptance and will find it for a long time to come."[20]

According to Voegelin, the truth is that Arendt does not have a true philosophical method, and this is why she succeeds in understanding certain fundamental characteristics of the totalitarian phenomenon, but not its "essence." If she had been able to identify this "essence," and not fallen short at recognizing a certain "phenomenal difference" that obscures its "essential sameness,"[21] then Arendt would have understood the factor common to historical events that connects them beyond the centuries and even millennia. More specifically, she would have realized that the origin and essence of totalitarianism lies in its immanentism, which, according to Voegelin's well-known theses, joins recent European history to the Joachitic heresies of the late Middle Ages with the red thread of Gnosticism. According to the final blow leveled by Voegelin, this same immanentism burrows a visible path through Arendt's book where she seems to allude to the possibility of a change in human nature. This allusion appears to Voegelin as a "symptom of the intellectual breakdown of Western civilization,"[22] the breach through which the enemy first gains a foothold and then thrives. As we said earlier: in the battle between philosophers of transcendence and philosophers of immanence, Arendt is situated on the other side of the barricade. This suffices, for Voegelin, to discredit her position.

Though Arendt's response may have been constrained in form by the protocols of respect, the same is not true of its substance. After explaining that the difficulty of the book is that it "does not belong to any school and hardly uses any of the officially recognized or officially controversial instruments"[23] (which accounts for the originality of her style, a combination of knowledge and imagination), Arendt directly returns the accusations of her distinguished interlocutor. First, on the concept of history, which according to Arendt Voegelin locks within a theory of secularization so that factual distinctions are sacrificed to a presupposed conceptual identity: "The reason why Professor Voegelin can speak of the 'putrefaction of Western civilisation' and of the 'earthwide expansion of Western foulness' is that he treats 'phenomenal differences'—which to me as differences of factuality are all-important—as minor outgrowths of some 'essential sameness' of a doctrinal nature."[24] Arendt continues by addressing the relation between theology and politics. Voegelin characterizes her position in terms of immanentism, she maintains, because of his undue introduction of "semi-theological arguments in the discussion of totalitarianism."[25] Deepening her attack, Arendt affirms that this essentially instrumentalizes theology, and that in many respects this approach borders on "the last and perhaps the most dangerous stage of atheism":[26] its use in a legitimating function. "Those who conclude from the frightening events of our times that we have got to go back to religion and faith for political reasons seem to me to show just as much lack of faith in God as their opponents."[27] To summarize the exchange: although for Voegelin Arendt lacks a real hermeneutic key capable of philosophically driving out totalitarian immanentism (and, more importantly, unwittingly falls prey to it); for Arendt, Voegelin cages the totalitarian event within a traditional philosophy of history and slides, in the end, into a true and proper political theology.

As I suggested at the outset of this discussion, my impression is that each of these thinkers is mistaken; and that each pushes a defense of their own opinion to the point of misunderstanding the nature of the other's. First, take Voegelin. Arendt saw his perspective, as we have said, as a "philosophy of history" and as a "political theology." Not only is neither of these two descriptions adequate to Voegelin's actual position, but I would even go so far as to say they are its opposite: Voegelin's is an "anti–philosophy of history" and an "anti–political theology." We can consider this point one term at a time, beginning with the anti–philosophy of history. It is by now commonly understood that Voegelin's philosophy is not a philosophy of history in the usual sense, which would assume a linear paradigm in which outcomes are predetermined according to a succession of events, and successions of events are reconstructed according to a given outcome. On this point we need only recall that he interrupted and revised his *Order and History* project, which was originally conceived as a succession of phases arranged along a single line of development. On more than one occasion, furthermore, Voegelin will declare that no *eidos* of history can be reconstructed or predicated: "All these interpretations, which pretend to tell you what the meaning of history is, presume that one can know history as a complete thing. To put the matter in technical language, history is considered '*modo futuri exacta*,' in the mode of a perfected future, as if one knew what the end would be. In fact *one does not know what the end will be, and therefore any pronouncement on the meaning of history is impossible*."[28]

This quotation is from the essay "Configurations of History," perhaps the place where Voegelin most fully interrogates his own concept of history. Not only does he reprise his argument against any simplistic chronological notion of time[29] and restate his overcoming of Jaspers's "Axial" or fundamentally horizontal paradigm, but Voegelin also emphasizes and intensifies his understanding of historical time as discontinuous and unpredictable through the category of "exodus" that appears in the final part of the essay. Here he defines history in terms of "epochal leaps" (Voegelin uses the concept-term "irruption" [*Einbruch*], of which Schmitt was also fond[30]) that continually lacerate historical time's unitary fabric with a series of catastrophic events, thus producing new and unforeseen morphological configurations.

All this leads us to critically reassess Arendt's characterization of Voegelin as a traditional philosopher of history. It also suggests common ground between the two authors, precisely in that each subjects traditional philosophies of history to a kind of deconstruction. However, remaining wary of the opposite error of overassimilation, there is in fact one thing that fully justifies Arendt's claim to difference: their respective concepts of the "origin." We will note the semantic transliteration of this concept in Arendt's theoretical apparatus later, remaining for now with Voegelin. We have said that Voegelin discounts the category *telos* as a possible site through which to unify historical time. But that cannot mean that any and all unitary considerations of historical time are ruled out—if that were so, we could not even speak of history. Voegelin might deny the "goal" [*il fine*] (or the "end" [*la fine*]) as a vantage point from which to reread the entire sequence of historical events, but there is a different point that can give a meaning to historical enquiry (destined, though it is, to remain partially unsatisfied): that point is the *origin*.

It is the origin that makes history legible. But here additional caution is required. This origin is not *itself* legible. On the contrary, it could be said that for Voegelin history is made legible by the illegibility of its origin, by the fact that the origin cannot be known precisely in historical terms.[31] This reflects Voegelin's idea that history is not a human process but a "divine-human" one: "In time but outside of it," or "with a view to 'eternity,'" as he further specifies in the essay "Eternal Being in Time."[32] If this were not so, and Voegelin understood the origin as a fully knowable event, then it would acquire the metaphysical characteristics of a "foundation"—chief among which would be the ability to determine subsequent events. In that case, it would retrospectively assume the predetermining role that he denied to the *telos*, thus amounting to the simple, symmetrical reverse of a traditional philosophy of history. Again, this is not how Voegelin's notion of origin ought to be understood. While he does speak explicitly of "foundation" (there is even a chapter of *Anamnesis* entitled "The Consciousness of the Ground"[33]), he does so in a wholly negative way, denying any possibility that it might be positively affirmed. Not only this, but it is only an awareness of the "tension toward" the foundation that charges the historical experience with meaning, which requires that such a foundation can never be attained:

> The tension toward the ground is the structure [*Sachstruktur*] of consciousness, but it is not an object for propositions: Rather it is a process of consciousness that operates with its own levels of transparency. In the noetic experience consciousness attains its maximal luminosity, in which it becomes able to express the tension toward the ground of its own logos; in the full presence of the luminous exegesis of its own logos, consciousness can go on to constitute the field of past historical phenomena as a field of less transparent phases of the same endeavour to grasp the truth of the ground. Without the dimension of the luminosity of consciousness, there is no aetiological dimension available to consciousness, and without both of these there is no historical-critical dimension of participatory knowledge.[34]

This fact has two closely related consequences. First, what Voegelin calls the "foundation" functions *as* a foundation only to the extent that it continually withdraws from its own definition. Second, history cannot be unified except by an ever-keener awareness of the necessity of that withdrawal. In this sense, we could even say that what unifies history is an awareness of its own unrepresentability; its disjuncture with any project of immanent self-interpretation. As we know, for Voegelin it is philosophy that introduces this disjuncture. Philosophy is not born with history, but *falls into* it at a certain stage of its development, bringing with it its truth. But again, this is a truth that cannot crystalize into a response to the question that called it into being, and that in the end coincides with an awareness of its own limit in confronting that obscure "foundation" which gave rise to it and which it can yet never fully reveal. This is how we should understand Voegelin's suggestion that the most important part of knowledge is the distinction between the knowable and the unknowable (though not in a Wittgensteinian sense). When philosophy erases this distinction, when it surpasses this limit (or worse, makes it immanent in a *telos*) it crosses over into gnosis.

The theme of gnosis, and its role as the key concept in Voegelin's interpretation of modernity, is well known as the most suggestive aspect of his work—and the most self-contradictory. Just think of the conceptual discordance involved in adopting "secularization" as a hermeneutic device, and at the same time obscuring the evident connections between Augustine Christianity and modernity.[35] This is not the place to fully take up this question,[36] and I do so only insofar as it allows us to address Arendt's second allegation, that Voegelin's perspective amounts to a form of political theology, where that term describes a short circuit between the political and theological lexicons that has a legitimating effect.

Voegelin's *New Science of Politics* can easily be read as essentially offering a critique of this form of political theology. In his 1938 essay on political religions, Voegelin had already posed the concept of "differentiation" as fundamental to any assessment of the epochal relation between politics and religion, through the distinction between *überweltlichen Religionen* and *innerweltlichen Religionen*. *The New Science of Politics* brings this thesis to maturity, with the proposition that the level of development of a given society—like that of the philosophy that interprets it—is proportional to the level of its internal differentiation. The very idea of representation, which is the specific object of Voegelin's analysis, is directly informed by this internal differentiation in the sense that "articulation . . . is the condition of representation."[37] "Articulation," here, refers to the relation that exists on one hand between a society and its representation, and on the other between these two elements and the transcendental idea that gives the representation-function its significance. As we have already seen in detail, it was precisely this bipolarity that Voegelin wanted to defend when he attacked Schmittian representation for being too unbalanced in favor of "identity," in his review of *Constitutional Theory*. Now, regarding the question of political theology, the critical point is that for Voegelin the reason Christianity's soteriological form of representation should be considered representation's epochal high point (as opposed to its modern *degradatio*) is not actually because it reunifies the order of experience that had been differentiated since the very birth of philosophy, condensing it into a single existential level. On the contrary, it is because Christianity amplifies and intensifies this differentiation, separating it even more radically.

The chapter in Voegelin's *New Science* devoted to the "struggle for representation in the Roman Empire" insistently addresses this very point (this chapter, not coincidentally, follows Erik Peterson's anti–political-theological argument, as I mentioned in the introduction).[38] The struggle for representation places two sides into opposition. First, Roman political theology—from Varro to Cicero to Celsus—which strives to bridge the soteriological difference and thus renew the ancient alliance between the political city and its gods. Second, that of Christianity—from Saint Ambrose to Saint Augustine—intent on reasserting and emphasizing that same difference. The latter aims to safeguard the absolute nature of the city of God, but, we should be careful to note, it does so partly in order to preserve the terrestrial city's autonomy. This aspect of Voegelin's thought, which completely reverses Arendt's image of him as a political-theological thinker, deserves particular emphasis. When Voegelin underlines Ambrose's conviction that "the legions make Victoria" and "not Victoria the Empire,"[39] or when he notes that "what St. Augustine could not understand was the compactness of Roman experience, the inseparable community of gods and men in the historically concrete *civitas*, the simultaneousness of human and divine institution of a social order,"[40] he interprets Christianity as the movement of thought that in defending the autonomy of the transcendent sphere, also guarantees the sphere of the historico-political by default (a sphere that Augustine believed was condemned to be *saeculum senescens*, but not for this reason any less *absoluta* than the other).

It thus comes as no surprise that Voegelin situates Christianity within the category of de-divinization: "The clash between the various types of truth in the Roman Empire ended with the victory of Christianity. The fateful result of this victory was the de-divinization of the temporal sphere of power."[41] This is why Voegelin is at odds with any form of political theology, be it the premodern Gnostic variety (the attempt to redivinize the world by making the transcendent *veritas* immanent), or the modern Hobbesian one (the elimination of *veritas* altogether). Each of these forces an integration of elements that were once rigorously distinguished—first in Greek philosophy, then in Christianity. The resulting simplification radically alters the notion of representation [*rappresentanza*] that modernity inherited from the preceding order, which now loses the essential differentiating function—articulation—that had characterized it up until that point. This unifying transformation is effectively completed with Hobbes: "The covenanters do not create a government that would represent them as single individuals; in the contracting act they cease to be self-governing persons and merge their power drives into a new person, the commonwealth, and the carrier of this new person, its representative, is the sovereign."[42]

CONSTITUTION OF THE NEW

Naturally, this might raise our interest in Voegelin's interpretations of Christianity, modernity, and the relation between the two. But to return to the initial question of the relation between Voegelin and Arendt, it seems to me that this point reveals another similarity between the two thinkers that concerns their critiques of political theology. It is true that Arendt and Voegelin handle the category of "political theology"—and therefore also its critique—through different and in some ways opposing questions, and perhaps this explains why each misunderstood the other. Whereas Voegelin's sense of the term is geared toward an integration of the two lexicons (political and theological) that elides and "makes horizontal" the transcendental break; in Arendt, on the contrary, political theology is the outcome of a process of scission that gives rise to transcendence-effects within the political world. From the latter point of view, all of Western politics from Plato onward is "contaminated" by a theological "disease": It is precisely to Plato that Arendt traces the logical and semantic split that breaks the originally undivided figure of the *arché* into a double of "beginning" (*archein*) and "achieving" (*prattein*), such that it falls to the *archein* to rule [*dirigere*] without acting, and to the *prattein* to act without ruling (that is, to execute).[43]

From this point on it can be said that no form of politics, whether theoretical or practical, has escaped this theological destiny: not even modern revolutions, which are the only events Arendt does not present as entropic.[44] (This claim is perhaps the clearest evidence of the exclusively critical rather than constructive character of Arendt's analysis.) In modern revolutions, it is as if two tendencies, two forces, clash and are held enthralled by their own conflict. On one hand, there is the potent force of the *new*: Revolution is "a new experience which revealed man's capacity for novelty."[45] For Arendt, the fact that this *pathos* of novelty is something completely new that had never been realized before the two great modern revolutions spectacularly refutes Voegelin's understanding of the principle of secularization. "The theory that Christian teachings are revolutionary in themselves," writes Arendt with explicit reference to Voegelin, "stands no less refuted by fact than the theory of the non-existence of an American revolution. For the fact is that no revolution was ever made in the name of Christianity prior to the modern age, so that the best one can say in favor of this theory is that it needed modernity to liberate the revolutionary germs of the Christian faith, which obviously is begging the question."[46] From this point of view, revolution is the exact opposite of secularization. If secularization means continuity, revolution means—or *is*—difference: precisely historical difference. Or, we could say, history *as* difference.

Yet, this is only one side of the problem. History, or a historical event, must not be confused with the knowledge of that event. We must not lose sight, most importantly, of the shifts and displacements that give this knowledge its character. It has been said that the *pathos* of novelty exalts the protagonists of the modern revolutions.[47] But Arendt's point is that this *pathos* "came to the fore only after they had come, much against their will, to a point of no return."[48] This is no small distinction, because it expresses the absolutely decisive feature of the "revolutionary spirit": the simultaneous presence of two directly opposing tendencies. One innovative, induced and provoked by the force of facts, and another, more originary and conservative but no less forceful, that vindicates the original etymology of the term *revolutio* with its connection to restoration and reintegration. Throughout history this combination has resulted in a kind of "analytical strabismus": to look on the future with the eyes of the past, to interpret the novelty of a revolution as the repetition of a past event; beginning with the foundation of Rome, celebrated by its interpreters as the refounding of Troy.

It is precisely the question of the "foundation" that permits a fuller analysis of this tension. Although it is expressed subjectively by revolutionaries themselves, revolution's essential contradiction cannot be reduced to a simple psychological difficulty; rather, it pervades the very structural semantics of the revolutionary event. We have seen how such an event implies a radical break from the preceding situation—a true and proper decision. Yet, from the very beginning Arendt clarified that the concept of revolution was not fully expressed by the idea of the destruction and upheaval of the old: that it requires revolution's other, equally essential aspect, the foundation and constitution of the new. It is this aspect of revolution, its constructive projection, that distinguishes it from the simple notion of rebellion. As such, to achieve a true revolution it is not enough to overcome the old tyranny; it is also necessary to construct a new freedom: "to constitute," according to Montesquieu's pregnant expression, "a political freedom."[49] Only when we are able to reconnect those terms that are generally understood as mutually opposed—such terms as revolution and constitution, deracination and foundation, freedom and power [*potere*]—will the revolutionary dialectic be understood in all its complexity.

However, and this is where the contradiction in point emerges, if revolution is not only a liberation from the past but also a constitution of the future, this means that it cannot be inflected in terms of pure decision. Or it is perhaps better to say: To avoid being limited to "deciding" on the old, and to be able to influence the new, that decision must be taken on the basis of a particular principle. This is why all the great theorists of revolution, from Machiavelli to Robespierre, regarded themselves as bound to evoke the legislators' divine inspiration, thus articulating their break with tradition in a language that remained political-theological. Yet, it is also the reason for the failure of the revolutions they theorized. Revolution requires a new foundation, a transcendent principle (law, authority, legitimacy) to which it can appeal, an Absolute—albeit a new one—into which it can sink its roots. But was revolution not defined as *modern* precisely because it was part of a plan for liberation from the Absolute in all its forms? This is the vicious circle that closes in on every revolution.

On every revolution? At least one, the American Revolution, seems at first glance to escape this cycle. It is well known that Arendt regarded the circumstances of the American Revolution as historically exceptional because of the absence, if not of a "social question" as such (which America in fact had in racial discrimination), then surely of any mass poverty comparable to Europe's. That there had been an experience of self-government prior to the revolution was also unique, owing to the existence of plural governing bodies with separate powers. But this pair of objective factors would not, on its own, have been enough to prevent the American Revolution from taking the usual degenerative spiral, had it not also been paired with a *subjective* factor that suddenly arose for its protagonists: the plan to break with the past and proclaim themselves originators—Founding Fathers—of a wholly new experience. This does not mean, Arendt continues, that they escaped the natural impulse to refer to an earlier exemplar, but in choosing the Roman republic for this role and emphasizing certain of its qualities, they were able to convert a self-legitimating and therefore fundamentally conservative need into a potentially innovative force.

We shall see how. The problem of every revolution, we have said, and more generally the problem of every political organism, is that it requires a source of authority that is structurally superior to political action as such, but that this normative principle is as contradictory as it is necessary. At the moment of its constitution, not even the Roman republic could do without such a principle—at least, not without falling prey to the unavoidable arbitrariness that is inherent in every beginning. This arbitrariness, Arendt suggests, consists in the confusion of power and authority, or more specifically, the elimination of authority in favor of power [*potere*]. But the American Revolution has a decisive difference from all those previous: the use of the Senate to conduct authority back to the act of state-foundation itself. The constitutive relation between authority and foundation, created by attributing authority to the very act of foundation, was the vital element that the people of the American Revolution borrowed from the Roman *exemplum*. And in doing so, they managed the priceless feat of keeping the font of authority intact, without also making it transcendental to political action:

> The very fact that the men of the American Revolution thought of themselves as "founders" indicates the extent to which they must have known that it would be the act of foundation itself, rather than an Immortal Legislator or self-evident truth or any other transcendent, transmundane source, which eventually would became the fountain of authority in the new body politic. From this it follows that it is futile to search for an absolute to break the vicious circle in which all beginning is inevitably caught, because this 'absolute' lies in the very act of beginning itself.[50]

The unique result of the American Revolution thus owes everything to the solidity of this miraculous equilibrium: "that beginning and principle, *principium* and principle, are not only related to each other, but are coeval."[51] The dawning moment of its *incipit* thus entirely contains and defines its particular achievement. On close inspection, Arendt credits its success to the very exclusivity of its experience of the beginning, radically underlining that it was something entirely new—even considering the Roman precedent whose decisive element it reproduced at the moment it determined its own authority. Although in both the Roman and American institutional models authority is incorporated into the act of foundation instead of being a product of power, in fact it is on the question of authority that the clearest difference between the two emerges. Not simply because the American revolutionaries transferred authority from its seat in a political institution (the Roman

Senate) and into a judicial one (the Supreme Court), but because this transfer breaks the bond with tradition that *political* authority had preserved. In Rome, it was the Senate that bound together [*religava*] permanence and flux, and *permanently* augmented the political beginning, preserving its duration in time: "The uninterrupted continuity of this augmentation and its inherent authority could come about only through tradition, that is, through the handing down, through an unbroken line of successors, of the principle established in the beginning."[52] This line is exactly what is broken by the American Revolution, and this is what makes that revolution a completely new experience—a *novus ordo saeclorum* that opposes, rather than reproduces, the Roman *magnus ordo saeclorum*. But it is also this break that will, *in time*, determine its dissolution.

Here Arendt's discussion seems to double back on itself, pushing the contradiction expressed by revolution to the very limit. Though situated in a temporal "void," in the interval "between a 'no longer' and a 'not yet'" that seems to suspend time in a pure present, revolution irresistibly, again, falls prey to time. Indeed, it is revolution's extreme alterity—its defiance of time, its temporal unrepresentability—that condemns it to the disastrous repetition of past experiences. Something in this account exceeds the question of any specific historical event and expresses a constitutive aporia of modern politics as Arendt conceives it. Not even the American Revolution could make it possible to found freedom stably *as* a plurality, to constitute freedom in an enduring *space*—which is not only a historical impossibility, but also a logical and semantic one. Freedom as plurality, the freedom of the plural beginning, is literally unimaginable. It is beyond every possibility offered by representation, whether on a temporal or spatial plane. From this point of view, Arendt's radical incompatibility with Voegelin comes to light as something far greater than a simple political or categorical divergence, and appears as a genuine semantic difference. The representational semantics of Voegelin's political Catholicism conflicts with Arendt's Jewish rejection, and even "proscription," of representation.[53]

Great care certainly ought to be taken where Arendt's relation to Jewish culture is concerned (and not just because of the practical difficulty of defining "Jewish culture"). Nonetheless, it is possible to read the entire final section of her book on revolution through this question, devoted as it is to a critique of the principle of representation. First, there is her federalist polemic against representation's centralizing effect. Here Arendt's passionate defense of all experiences of self-governance comes to the fore (the French Commune, American townships, the Russian soviets, the Hungarian *Rätesystem*), experiences that are born in every revolutionary explosion and that are regularly swallowed by them as well. Alongside this defense is her corresponding attack on party politics, which Arendt holds responsible for the degradation of participation into consensus, action into execution, politics into administration. But because of something it does *not* say—or rather, because of something that cannot be expressed—this text seems to concern *every* political form. This something is the unrepresentable center of revolution, its originary fire: the coincidence of origin and principle [*principio*] that releases the political's plurality, the political *as* plurality. It is this plural essence that is utterly unpronounceable in the language of representation. This is because of a dual principle: the language of representation unifies what is plural, *and* divides what is unitary. Or better, it unifies represented subjects precisely by separating them from their representative.

It makes no difference whether we understand political representation as a simple suppression of direct action by the people, or a government of the people controlled by the people themselves. In either case, it is a question of "the age-old distinction between ruler and ruled which the Revolution had set out to abolish through the establishment of a republic."[54] From this perspective, none of the variations attempted by representative governments between the eighteenth and nineteenth centuries does anything to modify the essence of the representative principle: a unity—always and forever a "political-theological" unity—constructed by the representative's transcendence over what it represents. The will of subjects, and with it their decision, is subordinated to the transcendence of representation. The will therefore *cannot decide freely*, because representation severs the immediate relation between freedom and will, interposing the filter of an absolute *mediation*. This, in the end, is what impedes political action, translating it [*tradurre*] into administrative technique and thus betraying it [*tradire*]. Here Arendt's criticism of the principle of representation reaches its height and *seems* to overbalance into its mirror image: immanence instead of transcendence, identity instead of its representative, the will against its representation. The backward thrust of her forceful argument seems to push her onto the path of an unconditional praise of decision: dissolving the will of the bonds of representation, reopening it to freedom, liberating it to decision.

This is merely an impression. Arendt's path is not toward an immanent, self-legitimating decision, and her critique of representation cannot retreat into an apologia for the will since that path is blocked by the outcome of the French Revolution. If the American Revolution is the revolution of representation, the otherwise similar French Revolution is, by contrast, the revolution of the will. This will is presented as the very negation of representation—as something that cannot be represented: "a people that is represented is not free, for the will can not be represented."[55] Rousseau is at the origin of this thesis,[56] which *appears* to radically overturn the Hobbesian perspective.[57] If representation severs the relation between will and freedom, then the will can regain its freedom only by expelling representation.[58] This would require the fall of all the categories of representative thought, beginning with "consensus" (which is bound to the old concept of *volonté de tous*, and is therefore unfit for the task of the *grande* decision).

The general will [*volontà generale*], by contrast, is the will of a *unity*: "It was of greater relevance that the very word 'consent,' with its overtones of deliberate choice and considered opinion, was replaced by the word 'will,' which essentially excludes all processes of the exchange of opinions and an eventual agreement between them. The will, if it is to function at all, must indeed be one and indivisible, 'a divided will would be inconceivable'; there is no possible mediation between wills as there is between opinions."[59] Those who wish to bury the originary link between plurality and revolution under the flag of unity (nation, state, party) will appeal to exactly this notion of the will as a *union sacrée*,[60] thus conceiving the nation as a single body, an individual. As such, here the fundamental contradiction and *inconsistency* of the political—the impossibility of there being a political plurality—is once again clear. Nothing less than Rousseau's will, which "bound the many into one"[61] could safeguard it. But what struck Arendt was not only this nexus between will and unity, but also the specific site through which it forms: namely, the friend/enemy distinction.

> For his construction of such a many-headed one, Rousseau relied on a deceptively simple and plausible example. He took his cue from the common experience that two conflicting interests will bind themselves together when they are confronted by a third that equally opposes them both. Politically speaking, he presupposed the existence and relied upon

> the unifying power of the common national enemy. Only in the presence of the enemy can such a thing as *la nation une et indivisible*, the ideal of French and of all other nationalism, come to pass.[62]

Here our discussion of Arendt, which began with Voegelin's critique, seems to address a different adversary. The object of her critique is no longer Voegelin's *Repräsentation*, but Schmitt's *Identität*. Schmitt's conceptual scheme depends on the presence of the enemy, real or imagined, since it is only the enemy's *absolute* difference that unifies the will. If the risk of representative democracy is depoliticization (arising from the subjugation of the political to administration and bureaucracy), then the risk of direct democracy is a hyperpoliticality organized around the dominion of the one through the *exclusion* of the other. The unity dominates the plurality, but it is dominated in turn by the principle of exclusion. Importantly, this can be an exclusion of the external enemy, but also—and here is Rousseau's philosophical "one step further"—an internal one: "Rousseau himself, however, went one step further. He wished to discover a unifying principle within the nation itself that would be valid for domestic politics as well. Thus, his problem was where to detect a common enemy outside the range of foreign affairs, and his solution was that such an enemy existed within the breast of each citizen, namely, in his particular will and interest."[63] Only if the individual internalizes the principle of exclusion can the conditions exist for the will to be permanently unified, in taking a *philosophical foundation*. From a certain point of view, Rousseau thus goes even further than Schmitt. Here friendship is not just a function of enmity, but of an enmity that is enhanced and multiplied by the number of individuals that comprise it:

> The oneness of the nation is guaranteed in so far as each citizen carries within himself the common enemy as well as the general interest which the common enemy brings into existence; for the common enemy is the particular interest or particular will of each man. If only each particular man rises against himself in his particularity, he will be able to arouse in himself his own antagonist, the general will, and thus he will become a true citizen of the national body politic. For 'if one takes away from [all particular] wills the plusses and minuses that cancel one another, the general will remains the sum of the differences.' To partake in the body politic of the nation, each national must rise and remain in constant rebellion against himself.[64]

Here culminates the contradiction of a *political* will, the unsustainable nature of any one to one relation between the will and the political. The individual will can be, and is, united with others (thereby becoming capable of decision) only if it is divided from itself, or indeed if one of its parts is subjugated to and annulled by the other. This is perhaps the strongest attack against the subject-person ever registered in political philosophy. At the same time, it amounts to further and perhaps definitive disproof of the political as the space of common deliberation, since any "decision in common" would necessarily entail the struggle of each individual against themselves. Rousseau's reasoning closes its own circle: The will coincides with one's interests to the extent that those interests coincide with conflict. This means that the political can take up the will's point of view (and reach *the* decision) only when the will-decision is directly subsumed under the dimension of conflict. With this immediate relation between politics and conflict—essentially a translation of politics into war—the will's "political dream" dies. This unworkable situation may well be at its clearest in the connection between Rousseau's philosophy and the result of the French revolution. But as we have seen many times, its fundamental contradiction applies so generally that it can no longer be said to belong to any particular historical juncture, and demands the reconstruction of its very conceptual origin. The failure of revolutionary will that closes *On Revolution* thus refers Arendt on to a more complex task, framed by a complete genealogy of the category of the will.

This genealogy is the object of *Willing*. We are familiar with the basic problem: the relation between freedom and the will. Can the will *found* freedom, in the sense of constituting its enduring political space? In an essay from 1960, Arendt offers a very neat response—perhaps altogether too neat: "Freedom as related to politics is not a phenomenon of the will."[65] This essay is from a time when Arendt's argument about *vita contemplativa* was more direct, and the reason for her negative answer is that the will is "inactive." Since freedom is identified with action, the will—like all inactive faculties—necessarily suffers *unfreedom*, or freedom's impossibility. But the initial binary position that opens the second part of the essay is tempered by a steadily more complex discussion. In short, what prevents the will from being free is not the fact that "the faculty of will and will-power in and by itself, unconnected with any other faculties, is an essentially nonpolitical and even antipolitical capacity,"[66] neither that the will is fundamentally a command that feigns obedience. Rather, it is that the command of the will is contradictory in itself: "In other words, the two-in-one of solitude which sets the thought process into motion has the exactly opposite effect on the will: it paralyzes and locks it within itself; willing in solitude is always *velle* and *nolle*, to will and not to will at the same time."[67] The unfreedom of the will comes from the fact that in expressing an intrinsically contradictory form of command, it is ultimately *impotent*:

> Historically, men first discovered the will when the experienced its impotence and not its power, when they said with Paul: 'For to will is present with me; but how to perform that which is good I find not.' It is the same will of which Augustine complained that it seemed 'no monstrousness [for it] partly to will, partly to nill'; and although he points out that this is a 'disease of the mind,' he also admits that this disease is, as it were, natural for a mind possessed of a will: 'For the will commands that there be a will, it commands not something else but itself . . . Were the will entire, it would not even command itself to be, because it would already be.' In other words, if man has a will at all, it must always appear as though there were two wills present in the same man, fighting with each other for power over his mind. Hence, the will is both powerful and impotent, free and unfree.[68]

Arendt's *Willing* follows the line traced by the end of this passage, but resituates it within the slightly different context of her gradual reevaluation of mental activity. Though remaining separate from practical and political activities, here mental activities are not subordinate—on the contrary, Arendt seems to suggest that it is precisely because of their distance from political action that the mental faculties conserve their particular positive quality.

For Arendt, this is certainly true for thought. It is true for volitional acts too, but with a decisive difference: whereas thought always refers to something that *is* in that moment or *was* in the past (despite being dislocated from its immediate "reality"), the will always refers to something that *might be*—or better, *could* be, in the future. Now, it is this intentional quality, its orientation to the future, that gives the will those features that thought as such lacks: it is contingent, circumstantial, unpredictable. It is these qualities that highlight the will's utmost freedom: "the notion of an unfree will is a contradiction in terms."[69] Here we find ourselves a long way, or so it seems, from the radical antithesis between freedom and the will in Arendt's 1960 essay. Her position seems to have been reversed so that the two terms become synonymous. Yet, a closer view of the problem will recognize that this is not a matter of a mere reversal, but a new articulation of the planes of Arendt's discourse. We shall see how. The first reason the will should be considered "free"—as theorized by Duns Scotus, the foremost medieval philosopher of the will—is its ability to differ from and resist both the exigencies of desire and the dictates of the intellect. Each of these is *determined* (in its own particular way) by irresistible forces (one by the force of impulse, and the other by the principle of noncontradiction). The second reason for the will's freedom is already implicit in Scotus's position and relates to the distinction between the will, as the *free* capacity to begin something completely new, as against mere free choice, which is *constrained* to choose between two or more given possibilities. The will remains *pure* will, and is *not* transformed into action. "In other words, the human will is indetermined, open to contraries, and hence broken only so long as its sole activity consists in forming volitions; the moment it stops willing and starts to act on one of the will's propositions, it loses its freedom."[70] The conclusion Arendt reaches here is, in fact, not different from the one found in the preceding essay. The fact that the will is now considered free in itself in no way contradicts her earlier conviction that it could not found a political freedom, because the will's freedom—with its mental form—remains free only if it does not seek the translation into *political* freedom that means its negation.

A brief conceptual genealogy of the will should help us understand the reason for this paradox, and so enable us to consider the reason for its poor philosophical fortune—but also its necessarily *theological* paradigm, which is perhaps the same thing. It concerns first, the Christian linear (rather than circular) conception of history, and second, the Judaic concept of creation *ex nihilo*, as against the eastern theory of the world's emanation from preexistent forces. The Judaic conception contemplated experiences that "were not political and did not relate to the world, either to the world of appearances and man's position within it or to the realm of human affairs, whose existence depends upon deeds and actions, but were exclusively located within man himself."[71] This is what produces the fundamental contradiction that plagues the idea of the will for the length of its tormented conceptual history: it cannot be pronounced politically, or even *practically*, at least since Paul, for whom the will shares thought's dichotomous structure—the "two-in-one"—but transforms it into a conflict. This conflict is not simply between an "I-will" and an "I-cannot" but between an "I-will" and an "I-will-not"; that is, between one will that commands and a second, internal to the first, that *dis*obeys. Such an irresolvable conflict necessarily paralyzes the will, and its only means of escape would be to recompose itself into a *unity, deciding itself* as "one," and acting unitarily—but in doing so, losing itself as a "will" and negating itself in decision-action, a decision formed *in* action.

If this means Paul's Christian will can never be pronounced politically, Epictetus's Stoic version fares no better. In fact, here the will's failure is redoubled, especially considering that Epictetus considers it omnipotent (at least within its sphere of activity, restricted to those things that depend upon man). The reason the will's failure is twofold is that, in deciding not to will what cannot be realized and preferring to will the inevitable, it both transforms into a doctrine of fate (*heimarmenē*) and fails to overcome its existential impotence over the factual world. It is only with Augustine that the will's inherent conflict is assuaged—at least in a certain sense: Not because Augustine gives no place to the unavoidable dichotomy between willing and not willing, which on the contrary he strongly formalizes, or because he accepts the extreme possibility of stoic self-repression—after all, he declares "not willing" to be absolutely impossible. The will's conflict is settled, rather, through a theologico-semantic shift that converts the will into love, making love into the only *power* [*potenza*] of the will ("*Volo ut sis*,"[72] in the terms of a will to divine sacrifice). But here, too, above all in *On the Trinity*, the will can attain power—thus overcoming its contradiction and repairing itself—only by leaving itself behind and transforming into something else. Achieving action suspends the conflict that saw *velle* and *nolle* face off each against other: but only through a coup d'état (as Bergson put it)[73] that suppresses freedom.

And so we are right back where we began. The will's conflict is *politically* insuperable: it cannot be overcome within the horizon of the political. The will entails conflict because it cannot will without the opposition posed by its own not willing. This conflict impedes the translation of the will into action, and true decision: in order to decide something practically, to act decisively, that conflict would have to be overcome, resolved, absorbed. The will is reunified though willing's dominion over not-willing. Only in this way can it regain its power, experience its omnipotence—and annihilate its contradiction, as the early Nietzsche suggested. But as Nietzsche would realize, even before Heidegger, this is an entirely mythical solution. It leaps over the problem instead of resolving it; quite simply, by disregarding its terms. The will can certainly ignore the conflict, or it can dominate it, *but only outside of itself*—by making itself into mercy, pity or love, or command, imposition, or domination. Not the will, in any case.

Against such solutions, Nietzsche's "yes and Amen" and Heidegger's *noluntas* offer the impenetrable *irresolvability* of the impolitical. Each renounces the will's *positivity*. The only positivity to be found in the will lies in its negative quality; that is, in the disjuncture its negativity produces. To make the will into the source of politics by forgetting this disjuncture, simply uniting the will with politics or with power, would be to lose both. It would drag the political into the will's internal contradiction, or unify the will under the political's command. Arendt's entire conclusion in *Willing* is addressed to this unbridgeable distance that separates the freedom of the will (the "two-in-one" of the *velle* and *nolle*) from political freedom (the "many-in-one" of the *polis*): "Philosophic freedom, the freedom of the will, is relevant only to people who live outside political communities, as solitary individuals."[74] This is the reason for her disagreement with all those who maintain, from Jaspers to Buber (with whom Arendt's "philosophy of communication" has too often been compared), "that the intimacy of the dialogue, the 'inner action' in which I 'appeal' to myself or to the 'other self,' Aristotle's friend, Jaspers' beloved, Buber's Thou, can be extended and become paradigmatic for the political sphere."[75] Now, having reached the conclusion that mental activity can never be assimilated to political action, we are returned to the point from which we set out: the impossibility that the will could ground a political freedom.

"This impasse, if such it is"—concludes this passage, and indeed the book—"cannot be opened or solved except by an appeal to another mental faculty, no less mysterious than the faculty of beginning, the faculty of Judgment, an analysis of which at least may tell us what is involved in our pleasures and displeasures."[76] It is well known that Arendt's book on judgment, intended as the last in *The Life of the Mind* trilogy, was never written. Death surprised the author just as she had typed the title of the volume and two opening epigraphs, so any suggestion of the path she might have pursued can only be hypothetical—besides, of course, what can be found in the postscript to *Thinking*, where she sets out a plan based on her writings on judgment prior to the drafting of *The Life of the Mind*.[77] Taken together, these offer less a true and proper resolution of the impasse, and more a sense of Arendt's gradual shift to the outer limits of the political and into the impolitical terrain that is both the final resting place of political thought, and at the same time, its fullest realization.

We are now very familiar with the impasse at issue: it describes the fact that it is impossible to found a political freedom that is capable of resisting representation's centralizing effects. Political freedom, wishing to remain plural, can never be represented as a unity. The will cannot be entrusted with this task of foundation, because in seeking power—in wanting to be political and converting itself into decision—it becomes an even more immediate unity than a representational one, acquiring its identity through the exclusion and elimination of the other. If unity achieved through representation is the unity of the "partocracy," a unity of the will-decision tends toward totalitarianism. So the will remains the faculty of "beginning," the new, the unforeseen. But the will voices precisely the arbitrary and baseless aspect of beginning, the pure immanence to itself that it assumes when it is not animated by a principle [*principio*], when it is a pure upheaval of the old and not yet a constitution of the new. If Arendt were to give credence to *this* beginning—and to the faculty that corresponds to it politically—she would be endorsing Modernity's own interpretation of itself as self-authorizing: Modernity as the forgetting of tradition, the absence of foundation, radical abandonment. Yet, as Arendt well knows, this is nothing but modernity's specific utopia. The political philosophies underlying the two great unifications of Hobbes and Rousseau can be seen as belonging to this utopia in opposing but complementary ways; the former taking the form of representation, the latter, the general will. Each is based on the reduction of the multitude of opinions to civil war, and on the total (if not indeed totalitarian) exclusion of conflict—which is not really excluded at all, but remains as the only possible sense of political plurality, the political *as* plurality.

It is this vanquishing of the will, along with all the other modern political categories, that motivates Arendt's turn to the spheres of judgment and thought—a move that clearly involves a displacement of categories going far beyond a simple switch from one mental faculty to another. In fact, *The Life of the Mind* marks the passage from one phase of Arendt's writing to the next: from the early writings, where attention was focused on the reevaluation of practical activities (*vita activa*) in order to declare them superior to theoretical ones (*vita contemplativa*), to a more mature approach where her task is essentially to mark the distance between them. Or, more specifically, to stress the *need* for that distance. Certainly, the work is concerted in its critique of the fatal separation between thought and action by which Plato raised the former over the latter. But even when this dominance is contested, the underlying separation remains. It is precisely a *fatal* division; thus no amount of minimization, and no ideological short circuit between its terms, can hope to mend it. On the contrary, every modern attempt to overcome the separation by a theoretical coup d'état has had a catastrophic result. Each has led to a political *philosophy* destined to suffer its own failings in practice even before it suffers them in theory. The examples are plain to see, and there is no need to run through them here. It will be sufficient to consider what it has meant, for the history of the world, that it has been considered necessary to govern politics by the infallible *necessity* of a given philosophy. Naturally, for Arendt, a return to the old superiority of contemplative life is not an option, and nor is giving philosophy less responsibility than politics. Something else entirely is required: a more complex relation, and a gradual displacement beyond the necessarily unifying structure of the categories of the political. It is the impolitical that names this shift.

In fact, Arendt turns to judgment for its fidelity to the plural. In its constitutive plurality, judgment produces sense and significance precisely through a multiplicity of opinions. This is not the place to retrace the hermeneutic and theoretical path by which she arrives at this definition, but it is enough to note that Arendt frames her interpretation, in the footsteps of Kant's reflective judgment, in terms of "taste," "imagination," and "common sense." Through these elements, Arendt recognizes in judgment precisely the possibility of judging the particular without mortgaging it to an abstract, normative, transcendent universal, which she achieves by posing judgment from the (eminently plural) point of view of *others*, or more precisely, possible external spectators. Judgment is thus made impartial, but in a way that escapes the reified objectivity of scientific truth and, at the same time, remains outside the groundless subjectivity of purely individual choice. Even more important, judgment can contest—precisely by *judging* it—that conception of history (once again a *philosophical* conception) that is limited to deducing the "after" from the "before," thus subordinating the "after" to the meaning imposed upon it by that "before," and therefore also subordinating the event to the process, the effect to its cause, and contingency to necessity. In a word, such a conception of history subordinates the "fact" [*fatto*][78] to progress, and it is this philosophy that Kantian judgment can oppose: "Since Hegel and Marx, these questions have been treated in the perspective of History and on the assumption that there is such a thing as Progress of the human race. Finally we shall be left with the only alternative there is in these matters—we either can say with Hegel: *Die Weltgeschichte ist das Weltgericht*, leaving the ultimate judgment to Success, or we can maintain with Kant the autonomy of the minds of men and their possible independence of things as they are or as they have come into being."[79] We will leave aside for now the question of whether Arendt's readings of Kant and especially Hegel are acceptable.[80] More important here is the opposition between judgment and the philosophy of progress that Arendt draws from those readings. The very nature of the idea of "progress" excludes any possibility of a point "at which we might stand still and look back with the backward glance of the historian"[81]—as Arendt writes in conclusion to her book on Kant's political philosophy. When history is interpreted as progress, when it is officially endowed with a general meaning, and when that meaning coincides with its ultimate end, judgment is always deferred to a conclusion that never arrives.

This same problem can be described from another point of view. Like the will that is its most privileged faculty, the philosophy of progress is always oriented toward the future—even when this future is considered a result of the past. But the past remains precisely *its* past, a past oriented toward and therefore *annulled* by the future. It is the past *of* the future. No wonder, then, that its result is oblivion. It is modernity that brings this oblivion, or rather the very tradition that modernity presupposes itself to have destroyed, but that on the contrary it secretly produces. In a philosophy of progress, the destruction of tradition means the past becomes an oblivion, erased and forgotten by tradition. Arendt's call for judgment overturns this logic. For her it is rather (self-legitimating) tradition that is destroyed, or whose destruction is acknowledged, so as to regain a clear gaze on the past and return it to light. In the absence of tradition, the past changes. It is judged not according to its victories, but its *factual* truths: *victrix causa deis placuit, sed victa Catoni*[82]—so reads the quotation that both closes the postscript to *Thinking* and opens *Judging*'s title page. The historian's judgment is removed enough in space and time to be able to "recount" the past without being directly involved, and it is this judgment—the judgment of the spectator-narrator, not the actor—that reestablishes the truth and the unpronounced power of the *fact* [*fatto*]. This is the judgment capable of reestablishing the force and the dignity of the past, and this judgment alone can condemn it. Equally, it alone can redeem the past, by giving it a different meaning from the one assigned to it by the violence of tradition: "What guides this thinking"—Arendt is speaking of Benjamin here—

> is the conviction that although the living is subject to the ruin of the time, the process of decay is at the same time a process of crystallization, that in the depth of the sea, into which sinks and is dissolved what once was alive, some things 'suffer a sea-change' and survive in new crystallized forms and shapes that remain immune to the elements, as though they waited only for the pearl diver who one day will come down to them and bring them up into the world of the living—as 'thought fragments,' as something 'rich and strange,' and perhaps even as everlasting *Urphänomene*.[83]

Because it displaces the point of view from the actor to that of the spectator-narrator, Arendt's judgment already makes an initial retreat from the terrain of the political. But with the question of *thought*, this retreat, or "withdrawal," takes on an unmistakably impolitical tone, implicit first of all where Arendt describes thought as "out of order."[84] By this she means that in thought there is an arrest of all those activities "so necessary for the business of living and staying alive," and on the other, the inversion of "all ordinary relationships": "what is near and appears directly to our senses is now far away and what is distant is actually present. While thinking, I am not where I actually am; I am surrounded not by sense-objects, but by images that are invisible to everybody else. It is as though I had withdrawn into some never-never land, the land of invisibles. . . ."[85]

With this reference to the invisible (and the idea that thought escapes the categories of the political because it is withdrawn from the visibility of representation), Arendt enters a more "profoundly" impolitical dimension. The transition results from (or better, is presupposed by) her critical inversion of "ordinary relationships." What are at stake here are the relations involved, not the values: Impolitical thought does not substitute new values for existing ones. "It does not create values; it will not find out, once and for all, what 'the good' is; it does not confirm but rather dissolves accepted rules of conduct. And it has no political relevance unless special emergencies arise. That while I am alive I must be able to live with myself is a consideration that does not come up politically except in 'boundary situations.'"[86] The impolitical sense of this passage lies not in some simple absence of "political relevance," but rather in the political quality that absence assumes in those "particular emergency situations" that Arendt defines, using Jaspers's expression, as "boundary situations." It concerns an absence that is made a presence, or a presence that resounds, silently, in an absence. Or better, a presence that *transcends itself* into absence. In fact, with his use of the term "boundary situations" Jaspers refers precisely to *transcending*, and not a "transcendence" (where the latter is understood as a metaphysical hypostasis of the act of transcending): "This term was coined by Jaspers for the general, unchanging human condition—'that I cannot live without struggling and suffering; that I cannot avoid guilt; that I must die'—to indicate an experience of 'something immanent which already points to transcendence' and which, if we respond to it, will result in our '*becoming the Existenz we potentially are.*'"[87]

This immanence that "already points to transcendence," a transcendent immanence, or a transcendence excavated from immanence, is the mode of the impolitical. It is not a space—and even less a value—situated outside the political and indifferent to it, but rather the transcending that is *within* the political as an affirmative category. It is the void, the absence, that the political opens when it puts into play its own dimension of presence (that is to say, of representation), thus also radically putting it into question. The impolitical consists in the political's exit beyond itself that never amounts to a transcendence. For this reason, it is part of life. It is life withdrawn from its pure immanence to itself and its rush to transcend existence (or the rush to understand existence as transcendence). "Here the point is that whenever I transcend the limit of my own life span and begin to reflect on this past, judging it, and this future, forming projects of the will, thinking ceases to be a politically marginal activity. And such reflections will inevitably arise in political emergencies."[88]

With this, the impolitical critique of the political reveals itself to be anything but apolitical or antipolitical. It is rather a critique of any political-theological valorization of the political, a critique of its assumption of a political *value*. Arendt says as much, referring this time to Socrates, whose "midwifery," "which brings out the implications of unexamined opinions and thereby destroys them—values, doctrines, theories, and even convictions . . . is political by implication."[89] The specific political sense of an absence from the political (or equally, the absence *of* the political) had been explained earlier in Arendt's text through a proposition of Socrates's own, according to which "it is better to be wronged than to do wrong."[90] This proposition is incomprehensible in the language of the political, and indeed political language responds to it, through the mouthpiece of Callicles, by claiming that "to suffer wrong is not the part of a man at all, but that of a slave for whom it is better to be dead than alive, as it is for anyone who is unable to come either to his own assistance when he is wronged or to that of anyone he cares about."[91] The citizen cannot comprehend Socrates's proposition because it stands radically opposed to any political logic—whether understood "realistically" (in the "appropriative" sense of the will to power), or in the "utopian" sense, in terms of a "communicative" relation between equals. But Socrates is precisely "not talking here in the person of the citizen."[92] He "talks instead as the man chiefly devoted to thinking. It is as though he said to Callicles: if you were like me, in love with wisdom and in need of thinking about everything and examining everything, you would know that if the world were as you depict it, divided into the strong and the weak, where 'the strong do what they can and the weak suffer what they must' (Thucydides), so that no alternative exists but to either do or suffer wrong, then it is better to suffer than to do. But the presupposition is of course: *if you are in love with wisdom and philosophizing*; *if* you know what it means to examine."[93] Only by beginning from this "assumption" can the political appear as the world's *only* language. But for that very reason it can be subjected—by a thought that wants to *remain* as thought—to an operation of internal transcendence capable of overturning its "ordinary relations," and "ordering" those relations in light of *that which cannot be seen*: in light of that invisibility, or absent object, that is thought.

But thought does not reside in that absence. Nor does it abandon its responsibility to the *present* life. Quite the contrary. The present is rather *the* place of thought, as Arendt tells us, through the Kafkaesque parable to which she eventually resorts.[94] This is the answer to the question about the space of thought that pervades Arendt's entire book and is confronted in the final chapter, entitled precisely "Where Are We When We Think?" Arendt figures thought at the intersection of two opposed and competing forces, understood as the past and the future, within and against which thought fights a never-ending battle. The place where the "he" of Kafka's title combats those domineering forces is obviously the present—the *instant* of the present, as Arendt immediately qualifies, recalling the allegory of Zarathustra at the gateway—understood as a now that is held in the thrall of a clash between past and future. The present is therefore the place where the instant struggles against a time that flows without interruption, continually transforming being into becoming and so annulling it. Thought can never renounce this struggle. If it were to do so, considering itself above the parties to the contest, an external arbiter or a spectator to the game of life—and thereby averting its gaze from the *reality* of the political—it would only repeat the old dream of Western metaphysics: a land without time and devoid of worries, inhabited precisely by thought.

This not Arendt's solution. Thought cannot betray life, abandon its *true* place, and opt out of the struggle. But why must it be *this* struggle? What is its particular responsibility—and how is it specified philosophically? Arendt's response can be found the metaphorical figure of a diagonal line, which begins from the intersection between past and future (and is therefore rooted in the present), proceeding into infinity without "positively" adhering to either one axis or the other. Her response, it seems to me, is this: to remain faithful to the present and not betray it through utopian escapism or weak disenchantment. But equally, and this is the decisive point, to do so without placing the present into the continuity of time, without adhering "positively" to the flux of history, and without "programatically" filling the lacuna that the present excavates between past and future. Thought rather *preserves* that void, that disjuncture or distance, because that is the only way it can protect itself from the domineering force of the existent, and the unifying violence of *its* history: "Kafka's time parable does not apply to man in his everyday occupations but only to the thinking ego, to the extent that it has withdrawn from the business of everyday life. The gap between past and future opens only in reflection, whose subject matter is what is absent—either what has already disappeared or what has not yet appeared."[95] This absence *in* the present, this decoupling from the present, this disjuncture between that which merely exists and yet is *all* that exists, bears the title "impolitical." And only this impolitical light can illuminate a final quotation from Cato that was dear to Arendt: *Numquam se plus agere quam nihil cum ageret, numquam minus solum esse quamcum solus esset.*[96]

3

POWER AND SILENCE

POLITICAL BIOLOGY

We can now offer some remarks summarizing the preceding discussion. The conclusions we have reached concerning Arendt's reflection on the political seem to present a major difficulty for the prevailing interpretation of her work, which is usually framed in terms of the utopia of the *polis*, or at best in terms of a practical philosophy. In fact, the notion that the political plurality is unrepresentable (an idea that Arendt came to in the final phase of her writing, as we have seen) reflects the breakdown of any direct, symmetrical connection between the political and the conceptual. It is not that Arendt's intense and at times single-minded interest in the political ever falters, nor indeed her impulse to think the political ever more radically. Rather, it is this intensification that prevents her from conceptualizing the political in any direct, traditionally "philosophical" manner. This is clearest in the critical opposition to "political philosophy" that runs throughout the entirety of her oeuvre (her objection, that is, to political philosophy understood as a politics grounded in a specific philosophy, or worse, a philosophy that is established by a given politics). The political can never be conceptualized in a positive form, but only by beginning from what is thrown into relief at its extreme limit, by beginning from that which defines the political negatively by constituting its contextual background, and at the same time its opposite.

The notion of the impolitical concerns precisely this gradual constriction of any positive field for the political. As we have said, this constriction is the result of the very radicalization it undergoes in Arendt's thought. Let us allow our attention to rest on the term "impolitical" for a moment. It is quite clear that the impolitical has nothing whatsoever to do with any form of depoliticization, whether explicit or implicit. Its essence is rather exactly the opposite. It is the extreme outcome, the "ulterior" outcome, in the strong sense of the word, reached by a political critique of depoliticization; and for that reason its relationship to it is one of intrinsic opposition. Arendt elaborates this impolitical conclusion clearly only in her incomplete final trilogy. Whereas her work up to and including *The Human Condition* is marked by a political objection to the intrinsically inactive character of the mental faculties, in her final work this stance is replaced by a reconsideration of those same faculties as the site of a possible distance from the modern world's notion of "praxis," with its servile adhesion to the existent. For this reason, paradoxically, when the political situation becomes critical, when "everybody is swept away unthinkingly by what everybody else does and believes in,"[1] the political's innovative function takes refuge in the impolitical realm of thought, which thus assumes the role of a check on and supplement to the temporarily dulled and degraded active faculties.

In fact, when they are read within the horizon opened by her later books, although they seem to be (and in fact are) marked by a more directly and "fully" political emphasis, Arendt's earlier works can be seen to contain elements that prefigure this analysis. Consider her great work on totalitarianism, where Arendt poses a fundamental dichotomy between totalitarianism and politics, and expands the positive identity of the political to cover the entirety of all the historical, logical, and semantic space that is *not* occupied by totalitarianism. But these positions are tempered by the subtly contradictory thesis that sees totalitarian experience born within—and not outside and against—late liberal society.

We will return to this discussion. For now, it is enough to register Arendt's growing tendency to leave behind the bipolar split between totalitarianism and political society that she herself had established, in the interests of implicating "liberal" modernity in an ever more unstoppable process of depoliticization. Although it was already at work throughout the section of *The Human Condition* that addresses the modern, this tendency is at its strongest in Arendt's book on revolution, where the "area" of political entropy, so to speak, is extended well beyond the problem of totalitarianism, reaching the entire modern horizon of representation, whether liberal or democratic. As we saw in the previous chapter, at the onset of modernity Hobbes and Rousseau had already marked out the modern's depoliticizing path: a forced convergence of technology and decisionism, within which political plurality (the political as plurality), is inexorably crushed under the monolithic boot heel of unity. This is both the most general conclusion reached by Arendt at the end of her research, and the most "scandalous" (its Jewish aspect?): Political plurality can never be represented, whether by the political entity [*rappresentanza*] or the representational image [*rappresentazione*]. Or rather, it can be represented only on the moving screen of revolution.

But even in revolution it can be represented for no longer than a moment. This moment is the moment of origin, or of the beginning, which Arendt isolates and exalts with a Machiavellian emphasis. Only the origin is the place of potential [*potenza*], which is why it is necessary to have recourse to it, to return to "beginnings,"[2] when the revolution threatens to stabilize and so necessarily to lose itself in the inevitable bureaucratic-representative apparatus, thus also losing that very combination of plurality and politics from which it originally emerged. It is at the point of this opposition between the Machiavellian origin and the Hobbesian-Rousseauian social contract where the critique of the modern, and its constitutively (not contingently) depoliticizing charge, forcefully emerges—which leads us back to the problem raised at the outset of the chapter. In the modern—or equally in a stage that comes after it but is touched by its invasive shadow—the political, for those who still resort to it (and nobody does so with a greater passion than Arendt), cannot be named except in the negative: Its exigency is felt, but it can no longer be positively represented.

But it is also said of Arendt's work—both as a whole and in its individual parts—that it does not entirely move in this extreme direction, that it retains discursive segments that shackle and restrain it so that it only goes part of the way in its anti-Hobbesian intentions; that it thus cannot succeed in reaching a stable post-Hobbesian position and so occasionally stalls in a pre-Hobbesian one. This is the case not only in Arendt's first works, where an affirmative space is reserved for a political-plurality, cast in the image of the Greek *polis* and posed in opposition to totalitarian homogenization, but also in her final ones—and particularly the book on revolution insofar as it concerns precisely the question of the origin and its ambivalent relation with *violence*.

From this point of view, *On Revolution* should be read together with Arendt's anti-Sartrean (or, more precisely, anti-Fanonian) pamphlet *On Violence*, so that a certain internal contradiction emerges. On one hand, the moment when a revolution begins is declared necessarily violent, in at least in some respects (as Machiavelli had already forcefully underlined, making him precisely the "ancestor of modern revolutions"[3]). But on the other, because the political is concentrated and sheltered within precisely and *only* that beginning, as we have seen, such a beginning cannot contain moments of violence, since "politically speaking . . . power and violence are opposites; where the one rules absolutely, the other is absent,"[4] at least, not without being broken from within. Arendt's conclusion is that freedom—which she identifies with power only to the extent that the latter can be distinguished from dominion—cannot spring forth from violence. Yet, that is exactly what regularly occurs in revolutions that succeed. So Arendt's contradiction has its roots in an even more glaring incongruity: her interpretation of the logico-historical moment of the origin as a plurality but *not as a conflict*.

It is precisely this impasse that prevents Arendt's anthropology from overcoming Hobbes (and from this point of view, the same could be said for Machiavelli). It is also what lends her idea of politics an ingenuously positive quality, taking the model of the Greek *polis* or the Roman *civitas*, harbored within her otherwise radical critique of the modern. But if the distinction between the governing and the governed (or more acutely, between the dominators and the dominated) has no place in the originary political scene (the Freudian *Urszene*);[5] if, similarly, there is no role there for the vertical break that disjoins power from freedom and makes the two separate and opposite, or for the violent tendency toward unification, or for the friend/enemy distinction—if, in short, all of these things have no part in politics' primal scene but rather intervene at some later moment to disrupt the peaceful plurality of the "beginning," as Arendt seems to believe—then despite her every metacritical caution and the radicality of her interpretation, then her thought of the political will always contain a *positive* representation of the "beginning" [*principio*]. The beginning may thus be degraded, but it is never definitively abandoned. In other words, the beginning is retranslated into that political *philosophy* from which Arendt herself had always quite rightly wanted to withdraw it.

This problem can be viewed from another perspective. It has to do with the relation between politics and law [*diritto*], and the political critique of the law that Arendt began but never definitively completed. It is well known that for Arendt, the function of the law is the protection of freedom-power (which, in the final analysis, is politics) from violence, whether external or internal to the political organism. Political power must be protected from the twin risks of being made absolute (vertically) and becoming fragmented (horizontally), and it is the juridical order that fulfills this need for stability and continuity (from this point of view law is much stronger than custom or tradition). Two consequences arise from this metapolitical inflection of law as something presupposed by politics, something both preceding politics and circumscribing its space of operation. The first is law's *necessity*: Politics cannot exist, or at least cannot endure, outside the legislative order. But the second is the thoroughly *negative* nature of this necessity: the rigid exclusion of the law from the world of action (politics), which is confirmed by the fact that it belongs to the sphere of *poiesis* and not *praxis*. The law is only ever a *limit*: "positive laws in constitutional government are designed to erect boundaries and establish channels of communication between men whose community is continually endangered by the new men born into it,"[6] as Arendt wrote in the conclusion to *Origins of Totalitarianism*. But this means—as she would insist in her 1970 essay on civil disobedience—that the law can "stabilize and legalize change once it has occurred, but the change itself is always the result of extra-legal action."[7]

In this essay, which is also dedicated to the relation between law, politics, and violence, the contradiction within revolution that we have just noted is spectacularly brought back into play. The essay focuses not merely on the distinction between politics and law, between (human) power and (institutional) law, but also, more precisely, on the primacy of the former over the latter that results from the purely negative nature of the law-limit. This primacy of the political is also what gives rise to the *political* legitimacy of civil disobedience, which is seen to break the conservative stasis of the juridical order. Here we are only a short step from a critique of law that rather than regard law as protecting the political from violence, would acknowledge it as violent in itself at least in some circumstances, in the sense that it impedes the innovative and liberatory function that for Arendt characterizes political action. From this point of view, the law is above all what distances us from the origin, blocking its transformative potential. Civil disobedience responds to law in a political language, offering a projection into the future that is at the same time an appeal to the very "beginning" that is constrained by the law in the present. That "beginning" contains, as we have seen, a necessary seed of violence. Yet, this political language, in order to remain political, must necessarily be nonviolent (which is in fact exactly what characterizes civil disobedience). Here we have reached the height of the contradiction. In order to defeat the latent violence of the law, the political must have nonviolent recourse to that origin that is always violence: it must combat the violence of a nonviolent law with the nonviolence of a violent origin. In order to move beyond this summit, and at the same time shed light on the passages that led to it, our discussion must take leave of Arendt's lexicon so as to encounter other authors and other texts, while following the path offered by her themes.

One of these texts in particular was edited and introduced by Arendt herself, with an intellectual engagement so intense that it is, at times, difficult to fully comprehend. The text is Hermann Broch's "Politik: Ein Kondensat,"[8] which is the only piece of writing that Broch fully and systematically devoted to a reflection on the political. More important from our point of view, it is also one of the long and involved works on the philosophy of history and the psychology of the crowd that grounds his frayed image as a political thinker. The essay opens with two related affirmations. The first is the necessity of anthropology as the foundation of political theory (and practice), since "every politics begins with man because it is exercised by man, for man, and often against man."[9] For Broch, anthropology is the first stage of the ongoing process of descending to the roots that marks every truly political reflection, or, better, "metapolitical" reflection.[10] The second concerns the fact that this anthropology, though given a positive inflection by every humanism of our tradition (whether theological or secular), eventually comes to speak the bitter language of the negative.

> In his metapolitics, Saint Augustine sought to extract the essence, aim, and means of political action from the conception of man as the image and likeness of God. Augustine therefore based his analysis on the positive pole, and for this reason he failed in practice, just as Plato's analogous concept had also failed. In the realm of things, nothing can in fact be

> defined in positive terms—and less than never is it possible to excavate a model for moral comportment from an absolute. All ten commandments (except those addressed directly or indirectly to the absolute, which, however, add the quotidian caveat "if you wish to live well,") refer to the "negative pole" and are based upon the formula "thou shalt not."[11]

As was true of both Nietzsche and Freud, but in some ways not of Arendt, here we are rooted in a fully Hobbesian territory.[12] This is confirmed by the reasoning that follows this passage (and coheres the entire discussion), questioning the utility of the notion of natural law and the foundation for human freedom that it offers. Broch's thesis, as original as ever, is that while the claim to freedom on the basis of a natural law might hypothetically be valid for a "parliament of animals," is not so in relation to humans. This is because of the simple fact that freedom as it is universally intended and above all practiced by man is inherently unnatural, since "it is configured solely as a rebellion against the social community."[13] It is not that men do not realize the convenience of institutional relations, which give rise to all kinds of association, from the family to the state. Rather, it is that the "anarchic" tendency, which expresses the most profound and unspeakable sense of human freedom, gives those institutions the same aggressive character that is typical of the individual, so that "every institution (like every individual) aspires to a total freedom of action, an unlimited power in relation to its members, and also, revealing its anarchic character, in relation to all equivalent institutions."[14]

Moreover, if "the struggle of all against all" were fought only on the basis of rationally pursued interests, insists Broch, then we could understand politics as the "mechanism of this equilibrium of interests"—a common enough approach. But this should entail "a rational process that would not concern (as it instead does) a desperately anarchic and chaotic character occasionally revealing some partial objective which, when seen as a whole, reveals nothing but an absurdity."[15] It is true that rational interests are often discernible, but their influence is minimized by the fact that they are indistinguishably jumbled together with the irrational impulses that are man's most authentic "political biology." Politics, "born of struggle, becomes more conditioned by struggle than it can condition it in return."[16] This is in line not only with the crudest political realism, but its most extreme variety. Since it is born from chaos, the *Tohuwabohu* prior to creation, the political has no chance of overcoming that chaos. It can only organize it institutionally and "refine" it into a state. This is thus the state of chaos, the state of the struggle of all against all. Hobbes is assumed here, but also overcome as far as any optimism for a normative contractual solution is concerned. There is no *solutio*, no contract, that is capable of pacifying this conflict, given that it emerges precisely from that contract's *impossibility*. In this sense, continues Broch, Machiavelli's or Clausewitz's analyses have an "incalculable advantage" since they do away with "every form of mystical optimism about the necessity and possibility of definitive political solutions."[17] Such solutions are impossible for politics because one of its constitutive elements—the tendency to freedom—is in direct opposition with the other: the tendency to *subjugation*.

This is the conclusive summit toward which Broch's entire discussion will converge. The identity between freedom and slavery, autonomy and subjection, signals the "zero degree" (*Nullpunkt*), the "negative pole," "that our epoch has reached."[18] Though it marks contemporary politics in particular, the kernel of this identity is present in *every* politics. To continue to adopt a positive anthropology means to fail to grasp "that the desire to enjoy an absolute and untrammelled freedom . . . constantly pushes us to enslave our neighbour. . . . It is a diabolical mechanism that has functioned in every epoch thanks to the infernal interchangeability between masochism and sadism; a mechanism that grips the slave himself,"[19] along with all political regimes—including democracy which, though it is relatively preferable, at best fragments subjection into a series of localized microservitudes. It also penetrates and perverts the dynamics of revolutions[20] (here is Arendt's great impolitical theme again), as we will see more clearly later.

This is truly a limit-point: an absolute negativity, the death of the political, or the political *as* death. It is the border beyond which no further progress can be made, at least not along the path of that "evil" that for Broch marks out the political's "gnostic" course. But because it cannot be crossed at the level of evil, this same point may—and almost must *necessarily*—deliver us onto a different discursive plane, which is exactly what happens in Broch's essay. Narrowing to the point of its negative climax, the funnel of Broch's discussion is suddenly inverted and it begins, in a kind of semantic mirror image, to widen out again toward a "positive pole." This pole will assume many names—freedom, humanity, justice—without being completely defined by any of them. Which of these it might definitively be is left undetermined, as befits the logic of Broch's enterprise, which understands this positive pole as something unrepresentable. As we have seen, the political is represented and representable only negatively, in its aspect as evil. But precisely where this evil is at its most radical and absolute, at its very outer limits, the very exclusivity of the nexus between politics and evil gives rise to something that, although it cannot be positively realized, or rather precisely *because* of this fact, overcomes this evil and in a certain way also redeems it. This something is the impolitical. The term "impolitical" should not be understood here in the usual sense, or in Mann's sense, of the "unpolitical,"[21] something extraneous to the political or in a simple categorical opposition to it. Rather, the impolitical dimension describes a tension between the inside and outside of the political, determining the political's conditions of existence precisely in being situated outside of it, in the form of its implicit but immovable presupposition.

The second half of "Politik: Ein Kondensat," on "human rights," is entirely geared toward the definition of this presupposition, through a reversal of the "negative" procedure found in the first part of the essay (even though Broch is aware that such a definition would be impossible). Whereas the first half began with the idea of freedom in order to end up at the concepts of slavery and death, the second begins with the ideas of slavery and death[22] and strives toward the idea of freedom. In this way, Broch purifies freedom of its humanist valorization as a metaphysical foundation, and realigns it with the purely unrepresentable: "Human freedom, which is a component of this divine affinity, is then no longer dogmatically situated at the beginning but only at the end of the series of definitions, as their ultimate object—an object that can be infinitely approximated, but is in itself unreachable."[23] For Broch, the "ideal" vehicle for this process is the category of the "earthly absolute" (*das Irdisch-Absolute*), which he poses (alongside physics and thermodynamics) as an "insurpassable limit" or "absolute zero" that cannot be crossed. But he also presents it as an "excess of content" that, although it cannot be described in discourse, remains firmly grounded in an antimetaphysical and antitheological signified that is precisely "earthly." This is why it can be inflected only negatively—unlike the old metaphysical Absolute of which it is a necessary secularization.[24]

The earthly absolute can be sharply contrasted with the strictly deductive logic of the "right as such" (*das Recht an sich*). Like mathematics, the latter derives its legitimacy from the transcendental absolute of the *Logos.*

And like mathematics it can be known only *formally*. Precisely because of its indifference to contents, the "right as such" is destined to come into conflict with itself. Its juridical indifference betrays the demonic aspect that always accompanies law[25]—an intuition that certainly links Broch to Benjamin,[26] but also to Freud.[27] And because it remains neutral on phenomena like slavery and the concentration camp, the "right as such" always and inevitably ends up negating the very content that is its precondition and on which it depends: the human end of justice.[28]

As Broch wrote to none other than Hannah Arendt, again in a tone reminiscent of Benjamin,[29] the necessary impossibility of positively identifying justice as such—the fact that it inevitably becomes "punishment"—comes from the fact that "down here one cannot operate except through models," whereas "justice is determined from on high (*von oben*) and it does not permit the construction of models."[30] "The appeal for justice"—he writes at the end of the "Kondensat"—"seems almost to spring from a meta-law that is even more difficult to formulate than divine or natural law, situated beyond both of these and human law alike. Though this meta-juridical edifice is even less visible than the others, now and then it can be glimpsed within them, becoming concrete in a rather crepuscular way (for example with the abolition of slavery). But it is nonetheless as compelling as the 'I' itself."[31] These two qualities, "crepuscularity" and "necessity," the necessity that the positive pole be untranslatable, and the untranslatability of its necessity, are the ultimate terms by which that pole is manifested and concealed. The positive pole is not necessary *despite* being crepuscular, but *because* of that fact. If it could always be fully recognized and identified from all angles, if it could be positively translated into norms and institutions, then the law [*diritto*] (and the politics that would result from it) would be at one with itself. But then it would lose the alterity that redeems it "from on high," thus depriving man of its distant echo and the ineradicable hope this echo brings:

> Certainly this law, too, is exposed to the same positivist objections that were so often directed at divine and natural law. One can in fact deny the value of any attempt to comprehend and define that which is destined to remain invisible (wondering, then, whether this pursued entity is doubly invisible); one can sustain that man cannot access the sphere of the Platonic idea, whilst admitting, by intuition, that this may be the very seat of his being; and one can even define this return of attention toward the orig-

inary homeland as audacious and risky—as dangerous as the freedom that comes from it. But it remains the case that the image of this homeland produces that incessant nostalgia that accompanies us all our life.[32]

DEPOLITICIZATION AND REVOLUTION

If we were to name the most far-reaching theoretical consequences of Broch's "Kondensat," we would have to say that it entails the manifest end of political theology, understood in the Catholic sense of a possible and necessary relation between the Good and power. This is why, in addition to more explicit and avowed sources, I have insisted on the more hidden but certainly more essential link to the Benjamin of "Critique of Violence." In Benjamin's essay, an awareness of historical failure, or more decisively, the failure of history,[33] sharply distinguishes the level of (political) power from that of the (ethical) Good, according to two propositions: the impracticability of a politics conceived in ethical terms, and the unthinkability of an ethics devised from political ones.

Having set out these propositions, however, we must carefully avoid a misunderstanding that might artificially simplify things. The impossibility of any positive reconciliation of power and the Good is not Broch's starting point, but rather, not forgetting that the "Kondensat" is among his final works, the failed destination of his life's work: It can be said without hyperbole that for his entire life Broch sought the systematic affirmation of both a political ethics and an ethical politics. Furthermore, in the expanse that lies between his initial hypothesis and final conclusion, Broch was to establish a complex dialectic of opposing impulses—violent oscillations as well as true and proper oppositions—that would attend and condition his writing for the length of its complex and eventful course.

An initial clarification should therefore be made on this point. When we speak of "oppositions" in Broch's work, we refer not just to some personal limitation (an inability to recompose in his writing certain logico-linguistic impulses that tend in opposite directions), but also to his *object*. Broch assumes as his object the very impossibility of overcoming oppositions by means of discourse—an incapacity to *say* them in discourse, and so to mediate them—because discourse, language, is constitutively inadequate to the task of comprehending the noncontradictory truth that weighs at its depths without ever being able to rise to its surface. This is a limit of the instrument more than of any individual interpreter. In fact, the only kind of interpretation capable of avoiding blindness and aesthetic-romantic repression (which Broch calls *Kitsch*[34]) is one that intentionally problematizes this limit, even as it constantly, desperately, yearns to transgress it. This describes the responsibility of the writer in the contemporary world quite precisely: to understand his work as the home of unresolved contradictions, as a "composition" of antinomies (in both the mathematical and musical senses of that expression), which cannot be mediated by any discursive *nomos*. Because it is based on the principle of noncontradiction, *nomos* is what promises to liberate us from opposition. But this *nomos* is only the ground zero of blindness; situated at the very farthest remove from the light that filters down to us precisely *antinomically*, through contradiction, within and at the same time beyond linguistic convention—even if every expression, every "saying" (along with every number and every musical note) bears its essence. This essence, however, is inexpressible by individual linguistic elements, inappropriable by any signified, and above all, unrepresentable in history.

It is therefore unsurprising that those of Broch's writings that seek to resolve the opposition between ethics and politics (which he found in Weininger and Kraus) through a new and essentially Kantian theory of history will not achieve their aim. (Broch absorbs this Kantianism through Chamberlain,[35] as well as through the dual traditions of Marburg and Heidelberg, to say nothing of Vaihinger's oblique but intense influence.[36]) To take but one example, consider the 1918 essay "Konstruktion der historischen Wirklichkeit,"[37] which addresses precisely the fertile intersection of ethics, politics, and the theory of history. Only a theory of history, says the central thesis of the essay, can foster the political ethically, and correspondingly only an ethical perspective can give the political a concrete historical realization. This is what drives Broch's call to absolutize the category of "reality," thus bringing it to the level of both *Logos* and *Ethos*. But it is precisely this absolutizing procedure that reproduces the original "fracture" (the "antinomic-antagonistic state of affairs" [*antinomisch-oppositioneller Sachverhalt*])[38] that his discussion was originally designed to overcome. This is the central point of the essay, and of Broch's self-critical gesture: An antinomy cannot be resolved within the discursive system that logically produces it. The two questions that result from this state of affairs are whether a new theory of history can be redefined on the ground of ethics, and whether this theory can be translated historically into an effective criterion for a practical politics. Even with all its "methodological" merits, Kantianism does not seem, to Broch, to be well suited to respond to the problem raised by the "disaggregation of values" (*Zerfall der Werte*) and their undue absolutization. So at this point other paths open up for Broch, though without ever fully closing off those that had come before. His *Offener Brief* to Franz Blei goes precisely by the title "Die Straße"—and it is here that his reflection on the nexus between ethics and politics seems to assume another, more disquieting direction than that raised by a Kantian theory of history.[39]

Written directly after the proclamation of the democratic republic, this letter is particularly significant. Besides bringing our discussion to the question of the multitude that circulates within the unfinished *Massentheorie*, it also offers a basic outline of Broch's stance on Catholicism and modernity, and above all the relation between them, which goes far beyond the linear, oppositional relation traditionally suggested by critics. If Broch had arranged the Catholicism-modernity relation with everything positive on one side and everything negative on the other, then his rejection of the "mass aggregate of mouths, noses, beards and stomachs" that is the multitude would have been much less ambivalent than it in fact was.[40] This ambivalence—a disgust for the crowd that is paired with hope and expectation—comes from the connection he saw between the multitude and the category (or rather "spirit") of "community"[41] (with the possible exception of the national multitude). It is the "communal sentiment of metaphysical truth (*das gemeinsame metaphysische Wahrheitsgefühl*)" that "grounds ultimate insight within a faith,"[42] thus implicating the multitude in a true and proper renunciation of the human spirit. The crowd also entertains a connection to that "cheap ecstasy of the communal rhythm . . . that cheap aid without insight, with which for example Christianity, as a cult, is replete."[43] This puts Catholicism into opposition with any experience of God understood as an individual and "personal" affair.

For Broch, the fact that Catholicism is marked by this communitarian dogma means it is bound to a spiritually immature exterior element that does not affect the modern multitude. This is what sparks his disagreement with Blei's Catholic-communitarian, rather than communist, point of view. But the reason that the communitarian dogma does not touch the multitude—and now this is what separates Broch from the apologists for secularization—is not because the multitude resists dogmatization as such, but because, on the contrary, it is itself the bearer of that other, more potent principle of dogmatization: an absence of all principles that allows it to pass indifferently from nationalist delirium to socialist enthusiasm. It is from this vantage point, at a distance from the modern decline [*Zerfall*] but *without* reproposing the Catholic community, that Broch can introduce the brief *excursus* on the "essence" of the political whose semantics were already introduced in his "Kondensat." "So," Broch proposes in the explosive opening to the second part of the letter, "the horror is that it is necessary to dogmatize and degrade the idea! That the essence of the political lies in this degradation; that the political is necessary by virtue of the spirit of this age, and that it would be positioned as its ultimate debasement."[44]

It is the declared *necessity* of the political that separates Broch from those, like Blei, who think nostalgically of restoring a premodern community. But the fact of this necessity must not hide its cost: the degradation that it necessarily entails. Here the central presupposition of Broch's political philosophy surfaces (or better, the presupposition entailed in the *impossibility* of any such philosophy). The political can be considered *purely* political insofar as it is an idea, but it is then thoroughly unrepresentable—except in the evil, the negative, of its practical realization. What Broch's conception excludes is the affirmative symmetry between the Good and power that is still espoused by Catholic political theology. In order to be pure, the political—that is, the *idea* of the political—cannot become power (or law, *Gewalt* in Benjamin's language). It must remain as Justice: "The concept of the Political coincides with that of Justice. Another politics, one that does not aspire to Justice, does not exist. A politics of interests is not politics, but only a more or less concealed version of commerce. The result of Justice is freedom. A pure politics is nothing but an idea and, as such, it has a supreme necessity and has nothing to do with any kind of physical obscurement. Pure politics is born from the autonomy of the spiritual, while the old politics, which was oriented toward a *telos*, was the servant of existent society."[45] This absolutely pure politics that is unrepresentable by interests, or even by preestablished ends, cannot help but become dogmatic, and therefore corrupt, when it comes into contact with that multitude to which it *must* be addressed, since it is democratic in principle:

> It follows that not only is a pure politics democratic, but it must address itself to the crowd as such, as the sole object that informs it, and who at

> the same time functions as its sole motor. This pure politics is therefore destined to be dogmatised within a multitude composed of an aggregate of mouths, noses, beards, stomachs. There exists no other fate for this pure politics than its absolute debasement as an empty slogan destined for the multitude, and the higher and more pure the moral will that is manifested in this political, the more profound is its fall and its prostitution to the cheap ecstasy of the multitude.[46]

Since it knows nothing of political Catholicism's old communitarian spirit, the multitude necessarily arrives at the worst possible degradation: that mix of "pleasure" and "dogmatism" typical not only of the philistine bourgeoisie, but also of its equivalent in the social realm, the socialist worker. This purely negative representation of something purely positive (but unrepresentable) belongs to its time—or rather, it is its very spirit. With this, we are a long way from the neo-Kantian utopia of a new philosophy of history built on the old "alliance" between ethics and politics. History now appears as radically fractured—and engulfed—by the absolutization of relative values to the point of their hypertrophy, making the political an "absolute kingdom," an ideal category, and at the same time degrading it to the rank of a mass ideology. But this does not detract at all from the fateful character of this event. If the political is the evil that represents the good, this evil can only be its destiny: "The political is simply the ineluctable (*das Unabwendbare*). Within it, as is evident in the character of practical politics . . . the most miserable thought possible is brought to the world. This is the final and most severe brutalization of man: radical evil as the necessary consequence of the dogmatization of what is moral *par excellence* (*das Sittliche schlechthin*)."[47]

The extreme words of "Die Straße" certainly do not represent the entirety of Broch's early political reflections (but given the complexity of Broch's dialectical thought and its situation at the limit of logical contradiction this should not surprise us). On the contrary, the first of the two political writings he completed before the drafting of *The Sleepwalkers* even seems to be proposed in a constructive spirit. Taking the oxymoronic title "Konstitutionelle Diktatur als demokratisches Rätesystem," this essay was composed around the time of the discussion of the consular system in the convulsive phase between 1918 and 1920, before the republic assumed its definitive constitution. Besides the suggestions it put forward (significant proposals for a kind of transitional compromise between a consular system and a parliamentary one), the essay also displays what are by now the unmistakable traits that never fail to disrupt Broch's political philosophy from within, along its entire course from "Die Straße" to the late "Kondensat," perhaps even throwing them into sharper relief by virtue of their practical setting.

It is true that this essay contains notable points in common with the Austro-Marxist and Social Democrat thinkers of the time, from Kautsky to Bauer to Adler; and that these similarities significantly distinguish Broch's project from those of conservative Catholics like Othmar Spann.[48] But here it is much more important to note the linguistic-conceptual and thematic dissonances with the social democratic tradition, which Broch encountered but never really made his own. This can be seen from the very beginning of the piece, where the dictatorial principle of the state as such, with its paradigm in the Russian revolution, is contrasted with a principle of justice that coincides with the freedom of the individual and is expressed by democracy. ("Every state is the realization of the power of its idea . . . every healthy State is dictatorial."[49]) The ideal type of the socialist state results precisely from the encounter and the fusion between these two extremes—*total* dictatorship and *total* democracy—in a risky semantic synthesis brokered theoretically mostly in Broch's writings after the Second World War.[50] How can this fusion be realized? How is "individual anarchy" brought together with the "anarchy of the state" without thereby destroying democracy? The practical solution proposed by Broch moves toward a bicameral system that assures a representative to all economic groups, in line with the program set out by his friend Paul Schrecker.[51]

But what is even more important as far as the author's "political philosophy" is concerned is the point of departure that enables this frankly improbable structure: the principle of depoliticization (*Entpolitisierung*) that is actually its most direct negation. What makes depoliticization necessary is the fact that the liberation of the proletariat is only a means to an end (the freedom of man as a whole), and that "only in this socialization of culture's goods can the liberation of man be achieved: it is given only through the depoliticization that converts the State into a society. Just as it is only in this depoliticization of free man that it can become clear why what is serious in the political (*das Ernsthafte in der Politik*), and so what is serious in social-democratic thought (the economic base), must be apolitical. But revolution as such is always political."[52] In light of the categories already introduced in "Die Straße," this passage reveals a clear contradiction between the aim of depoliticization (which becomes most explicit when Broch suggests directly connecting the electorate to its representatives in the House without the bureaucratic mediation of political parties[53]) and the outcome that flows from it. The implicit presupposition of Broch's discussion is that there is no practical politics capable of effectively realizing the "idea" of Politics-Justice. This contradiction is, in fact, the only way to convert the negativity of that fundamental presupposition into something positive (that still has a negative form, however: *de*politicization)—so that unlike revolution, which attempts but fails to effect that *impossible* translation, the only way to respond to the absolute seriousness of the political (or the idea of the political) is to depoliticize reality. Importantly, though, this depoliticization is diametrically opposed to political indifference, as Broch does not fail to underline. It is, on the contrary, maximally political. Confronted with an effectual politics that *must* betray its idea of Justice (nothing is more irrevocably effectual than a successful revolution), the only possible solution is to be sought within the ineffectual incorruptibility of the impolitical:

> The aim of the council system is the complete depoliticization of humanity, and it can endure only until humanity throws off all political shackles. Those who want revolution for revolution's sake insert the political into the consular system, and they will, with their childish impatience and greed, acquire that blood debt whose worst crime is the degradation of man. Only when the political State is fully traversed by the apolitical idea, will it become a society of free men.[54]

Given these premises, it is not surprising that the second of Broch's "political" writings of the period is dedicated to a categorical deepening of the concept of revolution that was assumed as the negative pole in the first; a concept that, like the "multitude," would remain a fixed *topos* in Broch's oeuvre. I refer to the 1922 essay "Die erkenntnistheoretische Bedeutung des Begriffes 'Revolution' und die Wiederbelebung der Hegelschen Dialektik," which took the form of a commentary on two works by the neo-Kantian Arthur Liebert (*Vom Geist der Revolution* and *Wie ist kritische Philosophie überhaupt möglich?*).[55] Here, too, as the title suggests, Broch seems a long way from the semantic excesses of "Die Straße," and more disposed to a conciliatory spirit (by which Liebert's Kantianism is integrated into the Hegelian dialectic), with the additional effect of alleviating the strict anti-revolutionary prejudice of his earlier work.

Yet, neither here will Broch fully do away with the negative tones and antinomous values that were destined to bloom ever more forcefully in the great novels of his maturity. Broch's essay opens precisely with a definition of antinomy (under the influence of Liebert). He had already encountered the antinomy of the New (*das Neue*) and the Old (*das Alte*), in the work entitled *Theorie der Geschichtsschreibung und der Geschichtsphilosophie* (which concerns an *Antinomie*, but also, more sharply, a *Kampf*). There it was resolved through the distinction between "individual systems," in which there is no discontinuity that is not absorbed by its overall unitary context, and "pluri-individual systems" that are accessible by a *novum* (when one manifests itself); through psychological phenomena such as the "wonder," the "discovery" or the "upheaval"; or equally through the emergence of a "genius subject" who is capable of historical intuitions.[56] In the essay on revolution (again, in Liebert's footsteps), this antinomy is dramatized as the clash between "historical becoming" (*das geschichtlich Gewordene*) and the "ahistorical Absolute" (*das ungeschichtlich Absolute*),[57] and it is revolution that expresses the essence of this conflict. Naturally, Broch hastens to specify that when one speaks of an "ahistorical Absolute" in the sense of a human autonomy from all conditioning, it is always a question of something that is borne by the human and acts within history, so in the final analysis it is therefore a historical phenomenon. But precisely within this copresence of the historically conditioned and the ahistorical absolute there lies "*die Tragik aller Revolutionen*." That is, the antinomy that revolution cannot resolve, because it is *constituted* by it:

> But in this . . . also lies the tragedy of every revolution. It is a tragedy in that not only does the continuity of historical life not permit a radical break, but it is precisely the very logic of the revolution that eliminates that break. Every revolution is, in its essence, fundamentally "exigency." In any case the concept of exigency presupposes the concept of something to which the exigency is in a relation of validity and in relation to which it generally makes sense; something, in other words, that submits to that exigency. But this 'something' is again, precisely only historical life—that complex that, through revolution, should be destroyed.[58]

In other words, the antinomy between old and new, continuous and discontinuous, static and dynamic is not external but internal to revolution itself. Or to put it more precisely, the antinomy is between revolution's absolutely unconditioned form, and its absolutely historical content: "here, in the collision between these two absolutes, the deepest root and the particular ground of revolution's antinomous principle shows itself: it is the logical antinomy between form and content."[59] Nothing can undo revolution's logically and historically unresolvable knot: neither Broch's formal appeal to the Hegelian dialectic nor his hybrid of Marxism and Kantianism undertaken in the tracks of Vörlander, Masaryk,[60] Adler (and on the bourgeois front by Liebert himself under the banner of Liebmann's imperative "back to Kant!"[61]). It is this same knot, freed of the methodological trappings of his younger writing, that will appear in all its starkness in the final section of the *Sleepwalkers*.

All the categories in the 1922 essay are also to be found in the recurring logico-historical excursus interspersed throughout the narrative of *The Sleepwalkers*, bearing the title "disintegration of values" [*Zerfall des Wertes*]. But there, these categories are so generalized and radicalized that they resist any conciliation, compromise, or indeed any dialectical amelioration whatsoever. This is true most of all for the concept of revolution itself, whose specific meaning is expanded and made to coincide with the "European spirit" at large—that is, with modernity as change. This is a long way from the dream of a new *Christenheit oder Europa* that was common in the German Catholicism of the time (recalling our discussion of Guardini). Here Europe, or Europe's spirit, is the Europe of the protestant "revolution." Or better, Protestantism *as* revolution. It is this Europe, with its opposition between the "sea" of abstraction and the "land" of Catholicism, that relieves the world of the bonds of its old political theology; making its islands into continents, its streams into great rivers:

> It looks as though the current of the absolute Abstract which for two thousand years has flowed through the ghettos like an almost imperceptible trickle beside the great river of life should now become the main stream; it is as if the radicality of Protestant thought had inflamed to virulence all the dread ruthlessness of abstraction which for two thousand years had been sheltered by insignificance and reduced to its minimum, as if

> it had released that absolute power of indefinite extension which inheres potentially in the pure Abstract alone, released it explosively to shatter our age and transform the hitherto unregarded warden of abstract thought into the paradigmatic incarnation of our disintegrating epoch.[62]

When the Protestant revolution overcomes the antinomy of the late scholastics, thus beginning a process of man's gradual interiorization, it falls into the opposite extreme: pure abstraction. From that point on, the break with tradition becomes a betrayal. The opposing poles that were still dialectically reconciled in Broch's essay on revolution are radicalized here to the extreme point of their nonrelation, which, paradoxically, converts each into the other. In this way, the "relative" (the polytheism of values produced by the European spirit) is itself made absolute. With this absolutization of the relative, each of the now separate spheres of the old Catholic *organon* appears "unfettered in its autonomy, each resolved to push home with radical thoroughness the final conclusions of its logic," to the point where each seeks to "embrace the whole of the world," overwhelming all other values and exterminating them "as a cloud of locusts lays waste a field."[63] This is precisely how the autonomy of a politics reduced to pure technique abandons the world to its most total depoliticization.

There is nothing to surprise us here. It is simply that those two opposing vectors making up man's freedom, while they were harmonically reconciled in the 1922 essay (the irrational impulse of *Leben* on one hand, and the rational one of the *Geist* on the other), now clash in a merciless battle that turns each term into a pale imitation of the other.[64] Every system that is not a total system but only a partial one, which by its "logical genesis or "logical basis" is compelled "to be revolutionary,"[65] expresses a certain rationalizing logic because of its tendency to specialization. But to defend itself against the scission that made it the fragment that it is—to defend itself, that is, from a further fragmentation that would destroy it from within—that system must pluck a handful of "good" irrational forces from the mass of irrationality that it combats, and cling to them, thus giving rise to a struggle between the rationality of the irrational and the irrationality of the old reason.

> For revolutions are insurrections of evil against evil, insurrections of the irrational against the rational, insurrections of the irrational masquerading as extreme logical reasoning against rational institutions complacently defending themselves by appeal to irrational sentiment: revolutions

> are struggles between unreality and reality, between tyranny and tyranny, and they are inevitable once the release of the super-rational has drawn in its train the release of the irrational, once the disintegration of values has advanced to its last integral unit, the individual; for the individual, isolated and autonomous, stripped of all its prejudice, is defenceless before the invasion of the irrational.[66]

In this inevitable perversion of revolution—according to the classic image of the serpent that devours itself—those who are outcasts, those who are destined to be first "stripped of values," "must also be the first to hear the voice of murder."[67] Here opposites converge. Those who were victims become the new executioners and the old executioners become the new victims; and so the political cycle touches its *Nullpunkt*, the zero-degree that is rendered in Broch's "Kondensat" through the bivalent metaphor of the "earthly Absolute." Just as in that essay, here too the limit-point—beyond which there is nothing lower—is necessarily the conflictual impetus for the identification of a new form of politics:

> And it seems almost like an outcrop of the same logical necessity that the transition from any value system to a new one must pass through that zero-point of atomic dissolution, must take its way through a generation destitute of any connection with either the old or the new system, a generation whose very detachment, whose almost insane indifference to the suffering of others, whose stark denudation of values provides an ethical and so an historical justification for the ruthless rejection in times of revolution of all that is humane.[68]

But—and this is always the conclusion—only on the condition that this generation is "silent," since "only such a silent and self-contained generation is able to endure the sign of the Absolute and the rising glare of freedom."[69] This generation should be mute, so as to be incapable of any affirmative utterance of its own power [*potenza*]. But it should also be blind, so as not to represent that power in a scene that would betray its message. This must be a generation prepared to receive the "political" sense of its existence—the "We" of *The Guiltless*[70]—only in a reflection, like an "image in a dark pool," or through "the mute vibrations rolling like an impenetrable wall of deafening silence between man and man, so that no voice can rise beyond it or through it, and man must tremble."[71]

THE STATE OF ETHICS

It is from within this silence that Broch's Virgil speaks at the hour of his death. From outside of it—without the inversion of perspective it brings about for the "voice" that must nevertheless express it—it is very difficult to apprehend the true sense of Virgil's conflict with Augustus, which is both the most relevant part of *The Death of Virgil* and a kind of summary, and symbolic enaction, of Broch's entire reflection on the political and its fate. Critical discussions of this book have dwelled on two main points: the semantically ambivalent figure of Augustus, and relatedly, the fact that Augustus prevails over his antagonist Virgil—in a victory that is not only "historical" (the final triumph through the conquest of the *Aeneid*) but also logical—even as the author fully sides with the latter. Yet neither of these questions can be resolved within the traditional paradigm, which sees Augustus as the exponent and bearer of a politics liberated from ethical reason, and Virgil as the defender of a politics that is founded ethically.

This perspective seems to me to require an almost complete inversion. It is rather Augustus who represents the ethical state (vindicating—only partially, as we will see—the observations of those who have identified Hegelian rather than dictatorial strains in the kind of state he advocates): "You make time responsible for the actions of men;" he retorts to Virgil, "you consider it responsible even for the loss of perception . . . by this you release men, and naturally yourself also, from every responsibility; that is dangerous . . . I prefer to make men responsible for the time they live in."[72] Augustus's defense of human free will, with all of the ethical consequences that follow from it, carries a further connotation. Human action is ethical to the extent that it confers meaning upon the passage of time (recall the relation between ethics and the theory of history established by Broch the neo-Kantian). More precisely, it is ethical action that gives time its form. This is why, when Virgil observes that "in a mysterious way we are captives to time, it flows on mysteriously . . . an empty stream . . . a stream on the surface, and we know neither its course nor its depth,"[73] Augustus counters that man is stronger than time. Far from being "held into time," he "holds time in his hands."[74] In order to be able to affirm his nature as an ethical subject, therefore, man must "shape" time [*formare*]. But in order to do so—proceeds Augustus's reasoning—he must organize himself into a state. The state is time's true form: "And I cannot admit that the course of duty is altered through time . . .

man bears the responsibility for the duties and tasks which he has set as the goal of his actions; at all times he has to adjust these to the community and to the state, and when he fails to do so, then the time is formless. Man, however, has to shape time, and he shapes it within the state; this constitutes his highest duty."[75]

The presupposition underlying Augustus's position is that rather than being its negation or constriction, the state is the highest and most definitive realization of the ethical subject. This is what lends Augustus, his very physical presence, the *auctoritas*—in the sense of both historical representation and logical coherence—that Broch-Virgil seems not to be able to contest, despite his best attempts. Augustus's achievements—the social transformation from an agrarian to a mercantile state and the pacification of the empire (and therefore the world)—are inscribed within an ethico-political logic that Virgil's argument cannot dent (from an ethico-political point of view). Not even by invoking freedom, since the very mission of the state, as the bearer of the historical *telos*, takes the production and expansion of freedom as its object:

> Freedom? Certainly, certainly, I am responsible for the freedom of the Roman people; no one shall disturb it, neither Antonius nor any other. This is the task of the Roman state, and for this it must be made firm. By letting the people participate in the state's momentum, we give them the feeling of freedom for which men strive, since this aspiration is intrinsic to human nature and must be satisfied. The one and only place to shelter this feeling for freedom is in the commonwealth of the state: here it is accessible to everyone, even to the slave, and it is more than the freedom of the soil, of which you speak; it is the freedom of a divine order![76]

Unlike the freedom of popular ideology, continues Augustus, which behind its apparent radicalism inevitably privileges one social class or another (the slaves, or the farmers), the freedom brought about by the state is a true freedom. Not a freedom for the individual or the group, but the freedom of the people as a whole. So, in that it is a state of freedom, Augustus's state is also the *people's* state in the literal sense that it belongs to them. The state, but also whoever (far from being its owner) is its legitimate representative (like Augustus himself): "Ourselves a part of the people, we are the property of the all-commanding state, we are owned by it with all that we are and have, and in belonging to the state we belong to the people; for just as the state personifies the people, so must the people personify the state, and if the state has unrestricted rights of ownership over us and our achievements, the same rights come in turn to the people."[77] This is the ultimate characterization of Augustus's state: The duty that it prescribes is symmetrical with the right it assigns to its citizens (even the duty of sacrificing his *Aeneid*, and its artistic value, to the state). The state of freedom, the state of the people, is also, and above all, the state of *right* [*diritto*]. This is what subordinates the logic of the individual to that of the collective, and precisely by this subordination makes it pleasing to the gods: "The gods have no care for the individual, they are indifferent to him and they take no note of his death; the gods turn toward the people, their own imperishability turns toward the imperishability of the people, which they wish to maintain, perhaps because they realize that their own would vanish with that of the people."[78]

The right of the people is the bond between the state and *its* gods. The very existence of the gods depends on the maintenance of that state, just as the state depends in turn upon the existence of those gods. From their position in the heavens, the gods are deeply rooted in the state's "terrestrial" quality: "The reality of Rome is earthly, its humanity is earthly,"[79] and the state looks to the sky because the sky is grounded in the earth. It is the sky over *that* earth. This is the relation that sanctifies power [*potere*], and permits the unity between power and the Good claimed by Augustus's "political theology," which coincides here, yet again, with that of the Roman church—both the power of the Good, and the good of power. The right and *jurisdictio* of the state belong to this theology, so although they belong to the mortal world they are at the same time "symbols" of immortality: "for only as a symbol may a mortal fit himself into imperishability, into an imperishability which, like the Roman state, stands by virtue of its own reality above any symbol whatsoever."[80] This immortality not only transmits to the people the image of their own power [*potenza*], but also, through the person of the one who represents them, redeems the evil that it inevitably bears:

> The state, in its twofold reality, has not only to symbolize the gods; it is not enough for it to have built the Acropolis for the glorification of the gods, it has also to set up a symbol for the people who constitute the second half of its reality, a strong symbol that the people will see and comprehend, a strong symbol in which they in turn will recognize themselves, the likeness of their own power to which they may and will bow, sensing

> that power within the earthbound always inclines toward the criminal—Antonius was an example of this—and that only a bearer of earthly power who is at the same time a symbol of eternity precludes this kind of danger.[81]

This is the rhetorical high point of Augustus's entreaty; his Hegelian political-theological conclusion. Because of its divine origin, power has the ability to transform evil into good. But this same point also offers a foothold for the entirely distinct logico-linguistic code by which Broch-Virgil will bring about an inversion of its meaning. This new code is not simply independent of Augustus's account. Considered not from the usual point of view, as the problem of the ethical foundation of the political, but rather as a Gnostic strategy for placing all of the political into default, it is also a rereading and overturning of all of Augustus's affirmations by means of an *argumentum e contrario*. This result is achieved not by opposing the content of those affirmations, but by inverting their form. It is not power that transforms evil (into Good), but evil that transfigures, or better, *reveals* power's real essence. Thus, the mechanism for the transposition between power and evil remains constant, but its subject and object positions are reversed. Augustus's discourse is thus transformed, we might say, from a point of view that is situated *behind* it. And it is from this specific inversion of perspective that the "dual semantic foundation" that had always been harbored in the figure of Augustus finally becomes comprehensible: his captivating smile had seemed "something malicious and cruel,"[82] the purple of his toga suddenly seemed to have "turned a black-violet," wrapped around a figure that had become marked "by severity, by obduracy, by sharpness"[83] along with the very landscape he moved against. "Existence was motionless, motionless the one who stood there at the window, no longer Octavian, but a gentle and stern and strangely rigid picture, almost beyond anything human, while on every side the state expanded in far-reaching, spectral lines."[84]

In this new "black" and literally diabolical light, the state that had been presented as the political realization of ethics now assumes its true guise (noting that it *really was* in fact the politicization of ethics, but precisely for this reason, according to the principles Broch set out in "Die Straße" and "Kondensat," it was therefore also the *perversion* of ethics). Its guise is no longer Hegelian, but rather "Augustinian": it is the *civitas homini*, or even more so the *civitas diaboli*. The authentic character of its progressive *telos*, and the "historicism" it represents, is revealed to be a total surrender to becoming, a pure nihilism: "Possibly I was shown just a little too much of death, because, really, my friend, life means as little as death; life leads to death and both amount to nothing."[85] And if Augustus's philosophy is nihilistic, if life and death count for nothing, then so too the subjectivity brought by the state—the *subjects'* state, as Augustus says—will be nothing. Rather than the state of the subject it will be the state of *subjugation*, and a subjugation to the state:[86] "verily, it is a hard humanity which the state has to offer, all the harder as the state, serving the commonwealth and, in so doing, personifying it, demands service in return from the individual, and his full subjugation to the power of the state, aye, going even further, it demands the right to requisition the life which has been protected by the state's power whenever that life is needed for the protection and safety of the community."[87] Here we are well beyond the (already absolute) Hobbesian state. Here, to be precise, there is no notion of "absoluteness"; there is rather the translation *in politicis* of an ethic of totality that, in order to be realized, requires the elimination of the individual as its condition of fulfillment:

> I have, to be sure, been active in ameliorating the lot of the slaves, but the welfare of the Empire demands slaves, and they have to accommodate themselves to this fact, disregarding the rights due to the oppressed for which they might clamor; truly it was most unwillingly and against all my desire for clemency, that I have had to accustom myself to limit by law their widespread emancipation, and should they rebel against this, should another Spartacus arise as their leader, like Crassus I should have to let thousands of them be slain on the cross, as much as a warning to the people as to divert them, and in order make them, who are always ready for cruelty and fear, realize with fear and trembling, how impotent the individual is in comparison to the all-commanding state.[88]

Here the most hidden, profound meaning of the people's state, the state of the masses, is brought to light. Precisely insofar as it is constituted by and for a unification of the multitude ("I have to reckon with established facts and I must not overlook anything that may be relevant to a unification of the masses"[89]), this state reproduces and redoubles the inner ambivalence between "panic" (the contraction of the "I") and "ecstasy" (the expansion of the "I") that elsewhere Broch (and others) describe "scientifically." The result is that the power [*potenza*] of the crowd is derived from the power of its leader, with whom it is bound in a mutual identification that can never be severed. But the *individual* man[90] cannot grasp this fact, because it has to do with the political's inherent *reductio ad unum,* which is expressed through the *exclusion* of the individual. The individual is incapable, precisely for being but one individual, of "participation in the power, the divinity, the expansive freedom, and the eternity of the one who sat over there in the palace."[91]

If this is Augustus's state, if the letter of its law is the suppression of every other law [*diritto*], then Virgil will stand wholly opposed to it. The situation recalls the strict Benjaminian opposition. Faced with a law of this kind—and the gods who secure it to its earthly bounds—it is only the absolute "unboundedness" of Justice that can offer any response: "Even though now you may still have to protect the boundaries of the state, oh, Caesar, the kingdom will be unbounded; even though now you still feel you must separate major rights from minor ones, justice will become indivisible, the community will be vulnerable in the individual, and the right of the individual will be protected by the community."[92] Its freedom will be unlimited, "for the kingdom of freedom into which your state will blossom, the kingdom of true reality, will not be a kingdom of popular crowds, not even a kingdom of the people, but rather a kingdom that is a community supported by men of awareness, supported by the individual human soul, by its dignity and freedom, upheld by its power to reflect the divine likeness."[93] The state of law's [*diritto*] political theology has its echo in the "image and resemblance" of the state of Justice. This is the "positive pole" to which Broch will refer in his "Kondensat." But here, as in that essay, its visage bears no resemblance to any other. Its face, to be precise, is the very absence of a face. Any "image and resemblance" in the state of Justice can only be a resemblance *without* image. This is why Virgil yields to the Emperor, to the superiority of *his* logic and the cogence of *his* law [*diritto*]. The restitution of the *Aeneid* to Augustus—wasn't it his poem, after all?—in no way signals a reconciliation between the two interlocutors, but rather the definitive splitting of their two discourses. Power is returned to the only language that can represent it—a negative language—while the "positive pole" is withdrawn from any kind of representability. If "death on earth is not to be exterminated . . . [and] man is separated from men by the struggle for power wherever people dwell side by side,"[94] then "it was above an earth in repose, not above the states that the star would wander,"[95] because "freedom inheres in us; the state is ludicrous and earthly."[96]

The impossibility of joining ethics and politics is the only message that Broch consigns to *The Death of Virgil.* Far from aiming to achieve the conjunction, Broch assumes its impossibility in the most radical sense, moving well past any kind of constructive approach. Between ethics and politics there lies an abyss that no theory of history can suture—not even the one Broch reproposed, ever more contradictorily, ever less convincingly, in his very final works of fiction—because it is precisely history that continually recreates that abyss. It is no accident that *The Death of Virgil* closes with the rejection of the fatal continuity of history, as the dying protagonist glimpses a single, profound simultaneity. "Because turned round toward the immensity which he had once left behind him, he saw through it into the immensity of the here and now, looking backward and forward at once, listening simultaneously to what was behind and what was ahead, and the rustling of the past, sunken into the forgotten invisibility, was rising up again to the present moment and became the simultaneous stream of creation in which the eternal rests, the first image, the vision of visions. Thereupon he shuddered and it was a mighty shuddering, almost beneficent in its finality, for the ring of time had closed and the end was the beginning. The images sank down but, preserving them unseen, the rumbling continued."[97]

GOYA'S CANVAS

In the finale to *The Death of Virgil*, Broch's impolitical journey appears to have reached its destination. Whereas in his early works he approached his ethico-political enterprise optimistically, through the question of the philosophy of history (which was to continually rise from the ashes in his final American writings too), with this novel, at last, it appears eviscerated from within, hollowed out by the *force of negation* that pushes the "positive pole" of the political beyond the limits of what can be represented. But this destination also signals another insuperable limit, further attesting to the internal conflict in Broch's work that was never fully overcome. The greater part of the book is in fact dedicated to transcribing this unrepresentable element *beyond* images and *beyond* language (albeit, inevitably, in a representative form), in a hyperelaborated conceptual search for the explication of the inexplicable and the nomination of the unnamable. The result is a sort of formal compromise between a programmatic declaration of undefinability on one hand and, on the other, this declaration's negation at the empirical level by Broch's actual attempts at definition (of terms like "humanity," "solidarity," and "reciprocity"). This is what compromised Broch's endeavor, not the inquiry in itself—which is both unavoidable and liable to result in wildly variant outcomes, as we will see in the final chapter of this book.

The answer to this impasse cannot be found within Broch's work. If anywhere, it must be sought at that work's outer limits; taking the form, as we will see, of a pure *question* in the writings of his great interpreter and friend Elias Canetti (who we could situate, in a position symmetrically opposed to Arendt, "beyond" Broch). There is a cluster of pages in the third part of Canetti's great intellectual autobiography that express, with Canetti's inimitable analytical lucidity, the unbridgeable distance that separates him from his friend (who was in some ways also his teacher), precisely by virtue of their intellectual proximity. Canetti in fact gives the title "The Beginning of a Conflict"[98] to the section that explains, in a way, the recurrent metaphor for Broch within Canetti's "mythical" world: a "big, beautiful bird whose wings have been clipped,"[99] a "hampered flight."[100] Canetti reports an exchange that sheds more light on the conflict in question than perhaps any of the other, more complex conceptual differences between the two (such as their differing judgments on Freudian psychoanalysis). The exchange concerns a critique that Broch leveled at Canetti, in which Canetti's works are said to effect a sort of "intensification" and even an "introjection" of fear (particularly the play *The Wedding*, and the novel *Auto da Fé*): "but you do not threaten people with hell, you paint a picture of hell in this life. You don't picture it objectively, so as to give people a clearer consciousness of it; you picture it in such a way as to make people feel they are in it and scare them out of their wits. Is it the writer's function to bring more fear into the world? Is that a worthy intention?"[101]

Against this typically Canettian method, Broch has a different narrative strategy: an *ethical* juxtaposition of "different value systems, good ones and bad ones," that permits a "compromise" position that can "partly alleviate the fear."[102] The result is what Canetti calls a "comforting" effect—almost a counterbalancing—that lessens the lethal impact on the reader of Canetti's "frightening" literature. The entire gulf between these two authors' "philosophical" conceptions can be found in this "methodological" difference (although in Canetti's case we would need a generous estimation to call it philosophical). It also contains the two writers' radically distinct ways of understanding the relation between the "positive pole" and the "negative pole," to use Broch's terms. Let us hear something more from Broch on this:

> You believe in alarming people to the point of panic. In *The Wedding* you've undoubtedly succeeded. After it came only destruction and disaster. Do you want this disaster? I suspect that you want the exact opposite. You would gladly help to show a way out. But you do nothing of the kind; in both *The Wedding* and the novel, you end cruelly, mercilessly, with destruction. In that there is an uncompromising quality that I have to respect. But does this mean that you yourself have not found a way out or that you doubt the existence of a way out?[103]

Canetti's response to this brings fully to light the ultimate stakes of the difference in question. For Broch's political philosophy, and for the philosophy of history upon which, despite everything, it is still based,[104] "hope"—the "positive pole"—must be sought beyond, *outside of* the negative one. "Good and bad" value systems are juxtaposed so that the contrast leaps out at us. But in Canetti they are made both more complicated and at the same time "frighteningly" simple. The positive pole, and the never-extinguished hope to which it alludes, not only can no longer be positively theorized and represented (as Broch already knew) but is also entirely subsumed by and caged within the negative pole's spectral appearance. Canetti's position amounts to a fulfillment of Broch's—and its overturning. If only the negative is representable (evil, in Broch's parlance, or *power* in Canetti's), then it is only from this evil, and a meticulous analysis of its representation, that the *silence* of the positive can emerge indirectly; in its reflection, or in its echo.

The intellectual extremism for which Broch reproached Canetti has to do with exactly this gesture, by which Canetti condenses the represented world into the negativity that it represents (the "fear" that fills it and ripples its surface) so that the two coincide without remainder. This is also perhaps what Canetti was referring to with his use of the final, intense metaphor he dedicated to Broch, in a speech for the occasion of his fiftieth birthday: that "cruel and radical demand" to be "a dog of his time" and *at the same time*, to "stand against his time."[105] To be against his own time *from within* it. To imprison hope, *all* hope, as Canetti will say of Goya, within the horror of reality: and only in this way bring the horror of reality to the limits of hope:

> Since Grünewald's *Christ* no one had depicted horror as he did, no whit better than it was—sickening, crushing, cutting deeper than any promise of redemption—yet without succumbing to it. The pressure he put on the viewer, the undeviating direction he gave to his gaze, was the ultimate in hope, though no one would have dared call it by that name.[106]

It is exactly this tendency to enclose hope within desperation and read that desperation as hope; to assume death, evil, the negative as the only "field of enquiry;" and to allow hope to speak directly, we might say, without estrangement devices or voices from off stage, that explains Canetti's predilection for the language of "great enemies." This language belongs to those great "negative" thinkers (above all Hobbes, De Maistre, and Nietzsche) who like him, albeit *against* him, preclude any affirmative "escape" from the macabre reality they analyze: "All thinkers who begin with human wickedness are characterized by an enormous persuasiveness. They sound experienced, courageous, and truthful. They look at reality point-blank and never fear calling it by its name. One does not notice until later that it is never total reality. And it would be more courageous to see the germ of another reality in that one without falsifying or beautifying it. But the man who admits that would have to know wickedness better, have it in himself, seek it in himself, find it in himself, a poet."[107]

This aphorism could be paired with another, in which Canetti declares that he would "never really have gotten to know power if I hadn't practiced it and if I hadn't become the victim of this my own practice of it."[108] Together, the two open what is perhaps the most 'obscured' dimension of Canetti's thought, and with it a hidden impolitical turn in his work (which has remained hidden partly because it has never been sought by critics, who have generally been more concerned with tracing utopian implications in the work of an author who in fact makes the anti-utopian a true and proper plane of life). Unlike in Arendt, and sometimes in Broch too, Canetti's impolitical moment does not come as an ultrapolitical "counterattack." The former approach, when faced with an ever more depoliticized reality, remains political by concealing itself as its symmetrical opposite (and thereby redeeming itself, at least in Broch's case). In Canetti, to the contrary, the impolitical concerns the hidden visage, the unexpressed voice, or the forgotten foundation of a reality that is organized entirely within a single political code: power. If there is an author who interprets politically every aspect of psychological, anthropological, and social reality, it is certainly Canetti.[109] But it is exactly because it is so resolute and apparently exhaustive that Canetti's political language opens a semantic void *within* itself, as we have said (never outside or instead of itself), so that every word carries within it the echo of its own opposite. This is why Canetti's language also has a hidden dimension; a silent and entirely negative counterpoint concealed within that part of it that remains unthought (this, incidentally, is typical of a certain Jewish tradition). This negative dimension is carried alongside the conception of history as a sequence of concrete, realized events: "History portrays everything as if it could never have come otherwise. Yet it could have happened a hundred different ways. History is on the side of what has happened, detaching it in a stronger context from what has not happened. Among all possibilities, it banks on the one, the surviving one. Thus history always seems as if it existed for the *stronger*, for what has actually happened; it could not have *not* happened, it *had* to happen."[110] Here what counts is not the presence of all other *possible* histories so much as their *concrete* absence: the victory of the *only* real history, which none of the other possible histories have the power to contest.[111]

This is what gives rise to the two specific features of the Canettian impolitical. First, the rejection of any political-theological dimension, understood as a nexus between the Good and power. It is reality itself, *reality's* history, that in a slightly different sense has a rigidly political-theological structure, as the "*religion* of power."[112] And second, the preclusion of any historical alternative—and still less any redemptive alternative—to the language of power. The reason for this impossibility is not so much that any alternative would necessarily fall prey to the progressive philosophy of history that he considered responsible for the worst misdeeds carried out against man in the name of humanity. Rather, we must be careful to note, it stems from the nature of the language that must belong to any possible *subject* of antipower *as* a subject: a language that is necessarily powerful *in itself.* Here we find ourselves in the darkest reaches of Canetti's discourse. The impossibility of an alternative to the language of power arises, that is, from the identity between power and antipower, dominator and dominated, victim and executioner, that is entailed by the structure of subjectivity. Now, what is radical about Canetti's perspective is that he presents this identity—which has been understood or pronounced by a whole host of thinkers as belonging to the moment of a given historical juncture (from Nietzsche to Broch, to say nothing of earlier thinkers)—as the consequence of a biological law. For Canetti this problem concerns *life*, and more precisely life's ineluctable relation with death. "With the growing awareness that we are perched on a heap of corpses, human and animal, that our self-confidence actually feeds on the sum of those we have survived," wrote Canetti in 1956, "with this rapidly spreading insight, we find it harder and harder to reach any solution we would not be ashamed of. It is impossible to turn away from life, whose value and expectation we always feel. But it is equally impossible not to live from the death of other creatures, whose value and expectation are no less than ours."[113]

The reason that a solution is "impossible" has precisely to do with Canetti's rejection of Broch's split between the two "poles" of the political (the negative and positive), and the resulting coincidence of the semantic axes of good-evil, victim-executioner, life-death. How is it possible to live without death, if life nourishes itself on death? How is it possible to push all the death out of life, if life derives from the indisputable reality of death? This *the* Canettian question. How can one live without doing so by surviving others [*vivere senza sopravvivere*]? How can we achieve the impossible "squaring of the circle"—to use the terms of that decisive aphorism that seems, in the end, to have given rise to all the others? "The satiety of the victor, his voraciousness, contentment, his long digestive comfort. There are many things one shouldn't be, but the only thing one must *never* be is a victor. Yet one is a victor over every person one knows well and survives. Victory is surviving. How can one keep living and yet not be a victor? The moral squaring of the circle."[114] If the circle could be squared, we would then have to be able to live *without* growing, or grow *without* eating: "A man who wouldn't have to eat and yet thrives, who behaves like a human being, intellectually and emotionally, although he never eats—that would be the highest moral experiment conceivable; and only its fortunate solution could make one seriously think of overcoming death."[115] But it is in fact growth that produces life, and eating that produces growth. That is, *it is power that produces the subject: including the subject of antipower.* This is the unavoidable fact that Canetti's language closes within its maw, taking with it any possibility for hope (which is thus denied any kind of utopian space). The *topos* of hope is entirely covered by shadow. But it is covered, at the same time, by the light that the knowledge of that shadow produces: "The humiliating thing about life: ultimately, one accepts everything that one has loathed with strength and pride. One thereby returns to the point at which one started when young, into the same old environment, transformed into it. Yet where is one now? One is in the difficult clarity with which all this is seen and registered."[116]

Although this is the *ultimate* meaning of his discourse, before arriving at this point Canetti nonetheless puts into play a series of defensive strategies or delay tactics concerning the power-subject, or the subject-to-power, that should be noted despite the fact that they will prove to have been ineffective. The principal and most far-reaching of these, already widely discussed in the critical literature (but almost always in a "utopian-liberatory" register), concerns the concept of "metamorphosis" (*Verwandlung*) and all the capacities (for multiplicity, transformation or change) that make it the semantic opposite of power's paranoid principle of identity:

> There are two kinds of people; one kind is interested in the positional aspect of life, the position one can achieve as a wife, school principal, manager, mayor. They keep their gaze riveted on the point they have put in their heads, they can view their fellow men only in terms of such points, and all that exists is a position, anything else doesn't count and is unsuspectingly overlooked. The other kind wants freedom, especially the freedom from positions. They're interested in change; the leap through apertures rather than up. They cannot resist any door or any window, but their direction is always out. They would fly from a throne, from which nobody in the first group, once he were on it, could raise himself for even a millimeter.[117]

There is perhaps no passage that gives a greater sense of the dual possibility—a forking path—entrusted to the choice made by the subject: one is static, conservative, and centripetal, the other dynamic, transformative, and centrifugal. The former strains for the defense of its identity in a paranoid manner; the latter is ready for any opportunity for self-multiplication and metamorphosis. Canetti seems to cast this opposition with such certainty that it conditions his own judgment on the thinkers of the past: "bad writers wipe away the traces of metamorphosis; good writers display them."[118] Aristotle is a predominant example of the first type, because he "excludes human enthusiasm and metamorphosis,"[119] as is Francis Bacon, a typical exponent of the "closed minds" (Bacon is very similar in this respect to Aristotle, "by whom he always measures himself"[120]). What these writers share is an understanding of the world as knowledge, and knowledge as a series of boxes within which everything can and must be systematized: "A thing only need be found to enter here, and it has to remain dead and still inside its box. Aristotle is an omnivore, he proves to man that nothing is inedible once you know how to fit it in."[121]

Canetti compares these "ordering" minds—who created orders of sameness and difference, the catalogue and its exclusions—to "illuminating" ones:[122] Heraclitus and Democritus, Bruno and Spinoza. It is above all Spinoza, with his substitution of the concept of *potere* with that of *potenza*, who is Canetti's true classical antecedent. Whereas power as *potere* concerns the imposition of a limit, an end or a prohibition, power thought as *potenza* requires fluidity, heterogeneity, connection. Whereas the former is mediation, the latter is immediacy, imagination, contingency. This is a distinction between affirmation and negation, exteriority and depth, the body and consciousness. Canetti's famous 1951 aphorism *in philosophos* in fact has to do with his claim that the body cannot be mediated, and thus it belongs not to an ontology of being but a phenomenology of life: "The thing that repels me the most about philosophers is the *emptying* process of their thinking. The more often and more skillfully they use their basic terms, the less remains of the world around them. They are like barbarians in a high, spacious mansion of wonderful works. They stand there in their shirt sleeves and throw everything out the window, methodically and steadfastly, chairs, pictures, plates, animals, children, until there's nothing left but whole empty rooms. Sometimes the doors and windows come flying last. The naked house remains. They imagine that these devastations make it *better*."[123]

It is well known that this emptying procedure, and its related "head without a world" as the title of the first section of *Auto da Fé* reads, is epitomized by that book's protagonist, Peter Kien. As the greatest example of the paranoid power-subject, obsessed with his own project of survival, Peter brings the principle of specialization that marks the modern division of labor to an unusual outcome: a voluntary blindness to all that surrounds him. His erasure and exclusion of what is other to him, whether persons or things, functions toward the conservation and reinforcement of his own individual identity. This amputation of experience in service of the "I" is systematically effected by means of two related mechanisms: the reduction of things to ideas, and the reduction of ideas to a rigidly formalized language that can arbitrarily unify the complexity of reality. Peter's repressive semantics are contrasted—here too merely as an *apparent* alternative—with the liberating ones of his brother George. As Peter is closed and exclusive, so George is open and available for a communicative relation with people and things. This openness allows for an integration between subject and object, and results in a true and proper incorporation and transposition of one into the other. This is best exemplified in the "gorilla" sequence: "In his own consciousness he would gradually draw the separate halves of the patient—as he embodied them—closer to each other, and thus gradually would rejoin them. . . . Thus he lived simultaneously in numberless different worlds."[124] The character of George foregrounds that capacity for transformation that undermines the repetitive and exclusive logic of the subject-to-power: "Countless parts had become second nature to him. His spirit hungered for rapid transformations."[125] Indeed, George responds to Peter's reactive, individualist ideology with a knowledge of the *multitude*—something that is produced by and productive of transformations:

> Of that far deeper and most special motive force of history, the desire of men to rise into a higher type of animal, into the mass, and to lose themselves in it so completely as to forget that *one* man ever existed, they had no idea. For they were educated men, and education is in itself a *cordon sanitaire* for the individual against the mass in his own soul.
>
> We wage the so-called war of existence for the destruction of the mass-soul in ourselves, no less than for hunger and love. In certain circumstances it can become so strong as to force the individual to selfless act or even acts contrary to their own interests. "Mankind" has existed as a mass for long before it was conceived of and watered down into an idea.[126]

This is the point of maximum tension between Peter's uniform world, and George's metamorphic one. Whereas the former *masks* the "multiple" with the "one," the latter *unmasks* the "one" contained within the multitude and vice versa. It is precisely the symmetry that Canetti constructs between these two perspectives that leads us to question whether each really is an alternative to its opposite. It is almost as if the author, considering his characteristic method, placed the two paradigms into opposition only in order to emphasize their complementarity. At a certain point he even has George realize this, when he attests to the failure of his "mission": "Both together, a memory for feelings and a memory for facts—for that is what yours is—would make possible the universal man. Perhaps I have rated you too highly. If you and I could be moulded together into a single being, the result would be a spiritually complete man."[127] George fails in his mission because instead of understanding Peter and thus saving him, he imposes himself upon him, thus losing him. As such, he fails not despite his metamorphic approach, but *because of it*. This decisive point must be underlined. George's approach does not fall short of its aim, *but is completed and is inverted into its opposite*. As such, actualizing his aim ceases to be a strategy for life and is rather the production of death. Canetti thus clearly suggests that metamorphosis is ambivalent—it is vital and liberating, but *at the same time* lethal and destructive—because at the same moment that he puts this realization forward he does not hide the *power* that it inevitably rebirths: "Man must learn to *be* many men consciously and to keep them all together. This latter and far more difficult task will give him the character he imperils with his plurality. Instead of ruling others, he will have to rule over his own personae; they will have names, he will know them, he will be able to order them about. His lust for power will no longer want other people; it will seem despicable to want others when one can be as many people as one controls."[128] Transformation, then, appears not as an abolition of the "lust for power" but as its transferal and *potentiation*. It may be an incorporation, but only within a fresh "subjectification."

It is here that we finally encounter the most tragic but also the most authentic timbre of Canetti's writing, having moved beyond any possible rhizomatic-liberatory interpretation (transformation against identity, multitude against individual, life against death). Rather than conflicting, these terms are made to overlap and enter into mutual reciprocity. This is also clearly visible in the chapter of *Crowds and Power* dedicated to the dialectic of masking and unmasking, which makes power and transformation into synonyms. There, the power of the "divine king" (the custodian of identity) is aligned with—certainly not opposed to—that of the "shaman," the "master transformer."

> The master transformer achieves real power as a *Shaman*. In his séance the Shaman summons up spirits, whom he makes subject to him; he speaks their language, becomes like one of themselves and can command them in a way they understand. When he journeys up to heaven he becomes a bird, when he dives to the bottom of the sea some marine creature; anything is possible to him. His paroxysms result from the rapid sequence of transformations which continue to shake him until he selects from among them the one he needs for his purpose.[129]

But this concept of metamorphosis, which for good reason Canetti approaches with a telling prudence,[130] is constitutively ambivalent. That was clear from the moment Canetti recognized its mutual dependence with the concept of "increase," which relates semantically to the sphere of power: "Thus the strength of the link between increase and transformation cannot be overrated; the two go hand in hand. Once a transformation has become fixed and, in its precise shape, can be cultivated as a tradition, it ensures the increase of *both* the creatures which, in it, have become one and indivisible. One of these creatures is always man. With each totem he ensures the increase of yet another animal."[131] What is finally brought to light in this passage (which, incidentally, allows us to glimpse a much stronger connection with the Freud of *Totem and Taboo* than Canetti would ever have liked to admit) is the bond that links transformation and increase, increase and production, production and transformation, into a chain of reciprocal references, in an equation of "production with transformation"[132] and, therefore, of transformation with death.

It is this same chain that binds the multitude into an unbreakable dialectic with the "I": that powerful subject against which, from another point of view, it also stands opposed. This was already clear in *Auto da Fé*, where the passage that immediately follows George's statement in favor of the multitude allows us to glimpse, in reverse, the other *simultaneous* face of his position: "It foams, a huge, wild, full-blooded warm animal in all of us, very deep, far deeper than the maternal. . . . In the meantime the mass within ourselves is arming for a new attack. There will come a time when it will not be scattered again, possibly in a single country at first, eating its way out from there, until no one can doubt any more, for there will be no I, you, he, but only it, the mass."[133] This other face is perhaps even more visible when George's parable of the termite colony reveals the crowd's true destructive and self-destructive nature, symbolically preempting the end Peter would later meet in the "crowd" of the fire. The fact that the crowd is destructive in no way negates its liberating aspect, because this is its hidden but unmistakable foundation: "Each will be himself, it begins with a hundred or a thousand of them, the madness spreads, *their* madness, a mass madness, the soldiers abandon the gates, the whole mound burns."[134] This foundation can be seen most clearly in *Crowds and Power*, in which the two terms of the book's title are bound into a tight, transformative correlation. Even as they stand opposed, each term continually transforms into the other, right from the book's first pages where the crowd assumes *all* of the attributes of power: growth, longevity, the destructive impulse. This makes the crowd simultaneously (1) the adversary of power, (2) the instrument of power, (3) the object of power, and (4) power itself. The crowd is both the opposite of the "One," the Subject that power manifests, and at the same time its realization *en masse*. It is a new unity that derives from the One, tends toward the One, and *needs* the One as both its leader and its victim. In fact, two interacting movements are at play in Canetti's great work. One transforms power into its opposite, infinitely destroying it as power—*and for that very reason not offering any chance of salvation*, as we may read in the epilogue "The End of the Survivor;"[135] and a second transforms antipower (transformation, the crowd) into a new and ever more powerful power. Canetti's text is locked in the vice of these twin transformations with no means of escape, thus confirming that the scenario the author "fearfully" poses is without resolution. More generally, what is also confirmed here is the self-consciously, helplessly contradictory nature of an opposition to power by any kind of subject—even the subject of antipower, flux, or transformation. This is a problem with the *subject*: It is powerful *as such*, and so it remains complicit with or internal to its own object of critique.

At this point, having dispensed with any optimistic hypothesis about the ends of power, along with every misinterpretation of power's crises as the signs of its definitive dissolution, the question with which we began our discussion of Canetti returns at its sharpest. How can we eat without killing? How can we grow without eating? How can we live without growing? In short: how can we live without surviving? Is it possible to conceive of a subject that is genuinely opposed power—or is power the *absolute* condition of the subject?

4

A POLITICS OF ASCESIS

THE VIENNESE SUN AND THE "PLANT MEN"

A negative answer to the question that closed the previous chapter—is it possible to wrench the subject from the power that predicates it?—will uncover another aspect of Canetti's world. Though peripheral and implicit, and indeed barely gestured to by the author himself, this is nonetheless the dimension of Canetti's thought that will newly redefine the phenomenology of the impolitical. The subject can neither be separated nor saved from *its* principle: power [*posse*]. Power is so deeply enjoined to the very constitution of the subject as to be wholly one with it. In every case it is the *subject* who "can do" [*potere*]—and the subject cannot help but "be able" [*potere*]. It was this nexus between the subject and power—or indeed their *identity*—that would mar the first strategy, that of transformation, set into play in Canetti's writing. Transformation cannot liberate the subject from power, because the subject itself is inextricably entwined with power; whether in terms of multiplication, increase, or *amassment*. To transform into something else, to incorporate something or to allow oneself to be incorporated, is a *summation* of a primary entity together with a supplementary alterity. It means to bind, to connect, to consolidate [*accorpare*]. As such, even when it is given a liberating and antinomic function, this semantics of the body [*corpo*] still implies a process of potentiation. It may emphasize multiplicity, flux, and exteriority as an opposition to the language of power, but precisely in doing so it also augments the subject—by *embodying* it—and therefore so too the power that constitutes it.

In this sense, therefore, the potentiality [*potenza*] of the subject cannot prevent its own fate, which is to eventually become power [*potere*]. Indeed, the more an escape from or alternative to the destiny of power is sought, the more power trails behind such efforts as their shadow. Yet, there is another way of understanding power [*potenza*]: as passion, as suffering, as patience. In short, it can be understood as *passive power.* It is only an "active" conception of power that encloses it within the regime of the power-subject. As long as that conception holds, potentiality will always translate into empowerment, increase, and the production of a powerful subjectivity. It is only when it is approached through passivity that potentiality can attempt to undermine power—beginning with its subject, excavating it from within—thus turning it into its apparent opposite: *impotence* (which is its opposite only from the point of view of activity). "Savour powerlessness, after power, in every phase that matches it precisely; replace every old triumph with the new defeat; strengthen yourself on your weakness; win yourself back when so very lost."[1] Here, in the dialectic between power and impotence that is created by "suffering," Canetti finally finds a space that is not an alternative to the mechanism of power but a withdrawal from it. He does not do so, however, simply by opposing power and powerlessness (there is no question here of an "ethics of weakness") but rather by selecting power's passive inflection, which identifies it with its antithesis.

What is at stake here is a self-negating dialectic that undermines the necessarily powerful subject's most defining features: primarily the will, but also thought.[2] This does not mean a departure or "distraction" from thought, however, but rather a thinking that is so intense, so concentrated, so *attentive* (to introduce an expression we will develop in the course of this chapter) that it absorbs its object within itself. Or a thinking that entirely loses itself in its object, which is the same thing. This is why, for Canetti, "[man] can remain free only by thinking to no avail."[3] If he can withhold from thought any end except the act of thinking itself, or if he succeeds, better still, to think nothing—or think *the* nothing: "A man lives in the belief that everything going through his mind is poisoned and must be avoided forever as of this moment. Reducing all existing things to the known is his only salvation. To protect the unknown against himself, he invents a method of *thinking nothing.* He succeeds in realizing it; the world around him blossoms again."[4] The reason that the world can return to bloom is that in making itself passive through self-reflection (that is, reflection on the absence of the object of reflection), thought—the subject's most distinguishing attitude—creates a void that leaves space for the world. Space for that which is not thought, or for the thought of others—*other* thought. Space for a thought that has reached the point where it no longer wishes to be thought, and therefore resolves its own nihilistic potential by turning it against itself (since it cannot be dispensed with altogether). This is a thought that suppresses itself so as not to have to become oppression: "the true temptation of the thinking man is to fall silent. A thought achieves its highest dignity in silence: it has no further aim. It explains nothing,it does not expand. The thought that silences itself forgoes contact. Perhaps even this thought can kill. But it doesn't know that. It did not wish that. It does not insist on surviving."[5]

So much, then, for the will and thought. We are left with a will to *non*-thought and a thought that does *not* will. But it is doing, action—the active aspect of power, as we have said—that Canetti addresses with his self-negating *intentio* (which is the *intentio*, at least, of this particular reading of Canetti). His impolitical rejection of action lies at the center of a series of aphorisms that gravitate around the synonymic chain act/violate, violate/eat, eat/kill. "Every work," begins Canetti, "is an act of violence, through its sheer mass."[6] Therefore, "it is quite possible that doing and killing can no longer be separated; and unless the world does not care to go under in splendour, human beings would have to wean themselves of action."[7] But there is one passage above all that should be reproduced in its entirety because of its implications for the course of our discussion:

> The slowness of plants is their great advantage over animals. The religions of passivity, such as Buddhism and Taoism, want to help people to a plant-like existence. They may not fully realize this character of the virtues they recommend; but the life of action they struggle against is eminently animal. Plants are not wild; the preparing or dreaming part of their nature is far superior to the voluntative. But within their sphere, they have certain things reminiscent of us. Their blossoms are their consciousness. They got there earlier than most animals, whose actions leave them no time for consciousness. The wisest people, whose time of action is way behind them, bear their mind as a blossom. Plants, however, blossom in large numbers and always anew; their mind is plural and seems to be free of man's dreadful tyranny of oneness. We will never be able to emulate them again in that respect. Oneness has grabbed us, and now we are trapped

forever in its teeth. The scattered works of artists have something of blossoms; only the plant always brings forth the same, whereas modern artists are racked with the fever of variety.[8]

This passage contains all the elements we have outlined up to this point: from the opposition between the "passive" and "volitional" dimensions of *potentia*, through to the resulting opposition between action and consciousness. But to whom does the reference to the "wisest people" allude, within this metaphor of the plant? Can we find an answer to this question in Canetti's text, beyond the general notion of a species on the road to extinction—one of those "plant men" "whose time of action is way behind them"?

I believe I can answer this question in the affirmative, and provide at least two examples. The first is Kafka, whom Canetti was quick to identify as one of those figures "who saw something more important beyond their achievement, something unattainable, so that their achievement seemed to shrink until it disappeared."[9] Contraction and disappearance are indeed the categories through which Kafka manifests the impotence[10] that is the dominant note, the foundational timbre, of his correspondence with Felice Bauer,[11] "rewritten" by Canetti in *Kafka's other Trial.* "The small person as the powerless one is a figure familiar to us from [Kafka's] writings,"[12] whose deepest inclination is to "become smaller, quieter, lighter, until one disappears."[13] Hence, what torments Kafka about marriage is precisely "its ruling out the possibility one's ever becoming so small as to be able to vanish."[14] This explains all those "abnormalities" that characterize Kafka's writing, corroding it from within: his rejection of the upright stance,[15] the assumption of thinness as the condition of existence,[16] and the reduction of the human to animal form[17] perhaps best represented by the story of the mole, which marks the height of Kafka's process of disempowerment: "Through this shrinkage he gained two advantages: he evaded the threat by becoming too diminutive for it, and he freed himself from all exceptionable means of violence; the small animals into which he liked to transform himself were harmless ones."[18] In this withdrawal from the body, this inclination toward the body's complete absence, Kafka experienced perhaps the only metamorphosis that is not also an increase, and the only transformation not subjected to the return of the "form." Not by chance, this operation does not relate to any action—not even to the "intransitive" action of an *escape* from action (which is still an *action* of escape). Kafka describes this transformation "in an observation that might almost come from a Taoist text, [in which he] epitomized what 'smallness' meant for him: 'Two possibilities: making oneself infinitely small, or being so. The second is perfection, that is to say, inactivity, the first is beginning, that is to say, action.'"[19]

The second important figure in Canetti's narration of power's passivity goes by the name of *Sonne*, "so sacred a word . . . luminous, searing, winged, source and (as still believed at that time) end of all life,"[20] around whom the entire world of *The Play of the Eyes* is arrayed. Sonne is a *stellar* figure, mysterious and at the same time concrete, in whom Canetti's powers of representation seem to reach their greatest concentration. Yet, at the same time, they are dispersed by way of a doubling effect, since Sonne is, in fact, situated halfway between two further figures, each of whom mysteriously reflects his character without being simply reducible to him. The first is Karl Kraus. Sonne does not merely resemble Kraus—he *is* Kraus: "It was a likeness and not a double, for when he was standing or walking he had nothing in common with Karl Kraus; but when he sat reading the paper, the resemblance was unmistakable."[21] Sonne is Kraus, but Kraus as seen from a reverse angle—that is, from a point of view in which he does not resemble Kraus in the slightest. Rather, he appears as his opposite: "His face was grave and unlike Karl Kraus's impassive mien."[22] "I felt his concentration as if he *had* been Karl Kraus, but a silent Karl Kraus such as I had never encountered."[23] Sonne, more concretely, is that part of Kraus that Kraus does not know how to be, the part that his presence—or more so his *word*—continually denies. Sonne is what is unheard in Kraus: his *silence*. An unidentified silence, a silence that remains nameless, that finally wrenches Canetti from the tyranny of the word that had until then dominated him:

> I was glad he had no name. For once I knew his name, he wouldn't be Karl Kraus anymore, and the great man would cease to undergo the transformation that I so fervently desired. Only later did I realise that this silent relationship brought about a cleavage. Little by little, my veneration detached itself from Karl Kraus and turned to his silent likeness. My psychological economy, in which veneration has always played a prominent part, was undergoing a profound change, all the more profound because it took place in silence.[24]

As we have said, Kraus is not the only figure who is superimposed onto Sonne on the basis of his *difference* from him. Sonne's "task" is not completed by his negation of Kraus (or his negation of what Kraus in turn negates). Sonne is also associated with another name; this time, however, not through his appearance but rather his voice: Robert Musil. In this case, too, we are concerned with an identification *e contrario*. Kraus's silence is, in Sonne, Musil's *word*:

> It was some time before I saw the connection. Dr Sonne *spoke* as Musil *wrote*. But it should not be supposed that Dr. Sonne sat at home writing things which for some reason he did not wish to publish and subsequently drew on them in his conversations. He did not sit at home and write; what he said came into being while he was speaking. But it was said with the perfect clarity that Musil achieved in writing. Day after day I was privileged to hear chapters from a second *Man Without Qualities* that no one else ever heard of. What he said to others—and he did speak to others, though not every day—was a *different* chapter.[25]

What these other chapters amounted to—what part of *The Man Without Qualities* they would continue—we will see shortly. What must be underlined here is the symmetrical, intertwined relation between Kraus and Musil that Canetti orchestrates under the "mask" of Sonne. We know what it is about Kraus's word that Canetti sought to negate with Sonne's silence: his claim that language can contain every value necessary to ground judgment; the ethical-discursive foundation for language—itself resting on a homology between language and nature—that makes the word a Law that must be imposed and defended; and the speed and force with which his condemnation, contained in phrases sequenced and welded together to form an impassable barrier, was at once also an execution. But through Sonne's *words*, Canetti also rejects something about Musil. Musil is reproached (albeit with explicit and almost awestruck admiration) for his "natural or, one might call it, a traditional attitude toward survival,"[26] his being "a man of solids," always ready to draw boundaries, to distrust "amalgamations and alliances, superfluities and excesses,"[27] his avoidance of "unwanted contacts" and his determination to "remain master of his body,"[28] his ability to relate external events to his carefully constructed and miraculously elaborated plan toward the artistic "fullness" of his "self."

> Musil was chained to his undertaking. True, he had total freedom of thought, but he felt subordinated to his purpose, regardless of what might befall him; he never *forwent* an experience, he had a body, which he acknowledged, and through his body retained his attachment to the world. Though himself a writer, he observed the goings-on of others who called themselves writers; he saw though their futility, and condemned it. He respected discipline, especially that of the sciences, but he did not deny himself other forms of discipline.[29]

Musil thus stands at the polar opposite of Sonne's world: "Sonne, on the other hand, wanted nothing. . . . He was free from purpose of any kind and was in competition with no one."[30] It is this trait that fascinates Canetti, surprising him for the first time at the Café Museum, where he is entirely *hidden* by his newspaper: his absolute *impersonality*. "For one thing, he was so utterly impersonal. He never talked about himself. He never made use of the first person. And he seldom addressed me directly. By speaking in the third person, he distanced himself from his surroundings."[31] What Sonne cannot do is pronounce the pronoun "I." This is a rejection—a dispossession—that involves not only the will (reason directed toward an end, the expansion and projection of the self) but also the body itself: It involves a contraction of the body (with Kafka), a body diminished to the point where it liberates a pure thought: *the thought of thought*. "I knew nothing about Sonne; he consisted entirely of his statements, so much so that the prospect of discovering anything else about him would have frightened me. No particulars of his life were bandied about, no illness, no complaint. He was *ideas*, so much so that one noticed nothing else."[32] Nothing could be noted about him because in the end, "he" no longer existed: he adhered so perfectly to what was other to him as to be fully absorbed by it; turning himself inside-out like a glove, in a bare objectivity: "He seemed the most down-to-earth of men, not because earthly possessions were important to him but because he wanted nothing for himself."[33]

Not wanting anything for himself—or more precisely, wanting himself to be nothing—is Sonne's way of giving himself to others, of living *their* life: not abandoning the world, but annulling himself in it. "Sonne had given up his activity in the world, why I did not know. But he *remained* in the world, clinging to it with every one of his thoughts. He withdrew from action, but he did not turn his back; even in the unbiased justice of his conversation one sensed a passion for this world, and my impression was that his only reason for *doing* nothing was that he wished to do no one an injustice."[34] Here the impolitical theme of nonaction again returns to the fore. Or, more precisely, a "potential" and inactive action: an action stalled in its own potentiality, unable to become activity and so make itself an "act." The more "decided" is this action, the more conscientious—and the more attentive, tense, and vigilant the thought that motivates it—the more that action will be deprived of any effective command or appropriation: an action without desire. Thought immediately turns, here, to the *Ekstatische Sozietät*, the *anderer Zustand* in Part III of the *Man without Qualities* ("Into the Millennium"). These are the chapters, to which we alluded earlier, of which Sonne now seems to speak—despite his distance from Musil (or perhaps precisely as its result).

> In this kingdom, you must keep quite still. You cannot leave room for any kind of desire: not even the desire to ask questions. You must also shed the understanding with which you ordinarily perform tasks. You must strip the self of all inner tools. It seemed to her that walls and columns retreated to the side within her, and that the world was entering her eyes the way tears do.[35]

PASSIVE POWER

The reference to *Gelassenheit* in this passage of Musil's text offers a context within which to gather and connect all the elements of my analysis to this point. From Musil's move "Into the Millennium" to Canetti's silent Sun absorbed in thought, from the Kafka-"mole" to Broch-Virgil, the theme that marks and in its own way unifies all this thought *ohne Eigenschaften* is surely the critique of the proper [*proprium*]. That which is not "proper" [*proprio*] (appetizing, able to be appropriated or devoured) cannot penetrate into worldly language, or the languages of the world. But for precisely this reason, the improper is the point of view from which language can be radically interrogated. Such an interrogation is carried out most explicitly in Virgil's plan to destroy the *Aeneid* (and its eventual restitution to Augustus, which signals that such a plan would be absolutely impossible). Yet it also resonates, and perhaps even more somberly, across the dry, arid passages in Kafka's diaries; within Sonne's acute silences; in the impossible *coniunctio* between

Ulrich and Agathe. That union, had it been realized ("put into action,") would have negated the passive power that for a few brief, shimmering, ecstatic instants seems to save these characters from the image of their *personae* (the *persona* always refers to an image, to representation). It would have meant reintroducing an element of propriety into the void-of-power created by these subjects' (temporary) renunciation of the essence of their own subjectivity—the law [*statuto*] of the proper.

There is a strong objective connection between the structure of the Ego and the modalities of the *proprium*: it concerns law [*diritto*], *Nomos*, as the expulsion of every antinomy from the sphere of discourse. Discourse is a law [*legge*] of noncontradiction, and the greatest, most unnerving contradiction of all would be the denial of the intrinsic relation between "belonging" and the subject. The subject is above all the subject of "belonging," and it is only because of this fact that it is also the subject of inalienable rights. It is not the law [*diritto*] that founds belonging, but belonging that founds the law—even if this belonging is, ultimately, "unjustified." Indeed, law's unjustifiability is constitutive, as is its difference from and opposition to Justice (which is the sphere of radical alterity to the "proper"). This is why the "just" rejection of the "proper" always manifests as a defaulting of the subject that sustains it; the evacuation—always a *self*-evacuation—of the subject's right to an appropriative existence. This evacuation is effected through two related processes, as can be seen in Canetti at his most "extreme": the dissolution of every will to action, or of every desired action, and correspondingly, the concentration of the faculty of thought into a reflection that is methodically deprived of all finality: an *attention* liberated from the subjective by-products of sensation and the imagination.

This is a theme shared by all of the authors I have evoked here—or perhaps it is better to say an inclination (in the true sense of *clinamen*)—and we have already seen how it appears in their work stripped of any literary or purely stylistic register. Yet its most complete and meaningful conceptual elaboration may be found in another contemporary thinker, one who was distant from the others in terms of culture and vocation, but joined to them by numerous concealed threads (perhaps, in an entirely unexpected way, to Canetti more so than the others). This author is Simone Weil. In Weil's writing, all the references, remarks and allusions that seem to cast Canetti's text as a semantic analysis (sometimes, one might even say, more so than he intended), become the explicit objects of a sustained meditation, and undergo their clearest and most radical categorical analysis anywhere in the twentieth century. Weil's interrogation of the metaphysical relation between subjectivity and power is a prime example: "I have power, therefore I am [*je puis, donc je suis*]." "To exist, to think, to know are only aspects of a single reality: to be able to do something . . . what I am is defined by what I can do."[36] The I (the *moi*, more precisely than the *je*) is above all a power. This means that it is constantly expanding—recalling that in Canetti the crowd's "increase" is also an individual impulse—and it finds the presence of others no obstacle to that expansion. When it does, the I cannot help but destroy those others (so that it is not itself destroyed). In this sense, the I is essentially the refusal of that coexistence of beings from whose fabric the world is formed.[37] This coexistence is deprived of its content, denied its objects, by an imagination that transforms its victims into shadows—or equally, into food for augmenting the subject (the imagination, for Weil, is the subject's most "proper" quality): "To live the death of a being," writes Weil in an extraordinarily Canettian passage, "means to eat it. The reverse is to be eaten."[38]

This is the dilemma that befalls the subject—or better, gives the subject its life: to eat or be eaten. Unless, that is, it can add to its repertoire a "diagonal" factor that is capable of shattering the mirror of this dialectic. I refer to the *gaze*, understood as an attitude toward others that is not a matter of appetite. This attitude is partly aesthetic: "One wants to devour all other desirable objects. Beauty is something that one desires without wanting to devour it. We simply desire that it should be."[39] The gaze accepts, consolidates and protects the existence of the other, and for this reason it starkly opposes the self-centered process of ingestion: "Man's great affliction, which begins with infancy and accompanies him till death, is that looking and eating are two different operations."[40] Man must choose one or the other, while being aware that the consequence of this choice will determine the "weight" of his subjectivity: If the choice to eat without looking expands the subject, looking without eating reduces it by just enough to preserve the existence of the other. To look upon the other means to meet their gaze, to make one's perspective commensurate with theirs—and to rob one's own gaze of its centrality (the center is *the* place of the subject): "A man standing ten paces away from me is something separated from me by a distance (ten paces), but also another point of view under which all things appear."[41] The risk of assuming any perspective at all is to end up treating it as the *only* perspective, and thus as a basis for the erasure of all others; to end up understanding the whole universe as a function of that perspective, and therefore to annul the universe as such.

This critique of the *centrality* of perspective is a theme fundamental to the entirety of Weil's reflection, and one that directly conflicts with the tradition of Catholic personalism (we might recall here Guardini's discussion of *Weltanschauung*). Whereas the Catholic person gains its ontologically strong character as the subject of free will from the fullness of its "point of view," Weil's approach will be to reject voluntarism. Or more precisely—according to her characteristic method of pursuing a line of thought until its opposite emerges—Weil allows voluntarism to turn into its apparent opposite: the adoration of Necessity (though not in the Nietzschean sense of the *Amor fati*). This path will take Weil ever further from the voluntarism of Alain (from this point of view—but from this point of view alone, as we will see—Del Noce seems justified in contesting Pétrement's suggestion that Weil's work is essentially continuous with that of her teacher).[42] In fact, it is not enough to say that while Alain's prose is detached, Weil's is more pessimistic and violent (on account of the presence of pain),[43] or that the true (and only) difference between the two involves their conceptions of Grace.[44] These differences are accompanied, or indeed precipitated, by Weil's radical alteration of Alain's epistemological and lexical frame, by which Weil moves from Alain's basically post-Kantian horizon to a post-Nietzschean one (albeit with the many connections that may and in this case do associate the two), or even in some respects one that should be understood as post-Heideggerian. Heidegger too, after all, sets into opposition the Greek and Modern conceptions of the *repraesentatio* of the *subjectum*.[45]

But it is perhaps even more important to note the specific philosophical place, or rather the specific author, in whom the difference between Weil and Alain seems to disappear: Spinoza. It is well known that Alain, who had included Spinoza's *Ethics* in the first-year curriculum of Weil's *khâgne*, reported that there were some of Weil's commentaries on Spinoza "*qui dépassaient tout.*"[46] Her fellow disciples Chateau, Hyppolite, and Pétrement all confirm the matter (albeit with some caveats in Pétrement's case).[47] Weil herself cites Spinoza a good fifteen times in her *Notebooks*, even describing her own meditation as "ultra-Spinozist."[48] In addition to these important historico-biographical factors, however, there are at least two points where the relation between Weil and Spinoza raises important questions of interpretation (indeed the work of both thinkers can technically be classified under the genre of hermeneutics). The first of these concerns the mathematizing nature of Weil's ethics—*ordine geometrico demonstrata*—and the rationalizing (and also abstracting) nature of her conceptual lexicon in general. "But just as the order of the world, in God, is a divine person which may be called the ordering Word, or the Soul of the World, so in us, the younger brothers, necessity is relationship—that is to say, thought in action. 'The eyes of the soul,' says Spinoza, 'are the demonstrations themselves.' It is not in our power to modify the sum of the squares of the sides in the right-angled triangle, but there is no sum if the mind does not work it out by conceiving the demonstration."[49] Seen from this point of view, Spinozan mathematism, understood as a science that privileges *nonrepresentable* relations at a sensory-imaginative level, pushes Weil in a gnostic direction.

But where Weil's relation with Spinoza is even closer is on the question of necessity, which both thinkers identify with the realm of the freedom-will, to the point where the two terms become synonymous. The passages in Spinoza that remove freedom from the contingency of free will and crush it under the rational boot heel of necessity are well known.[50] Freedom in Spinoza does not diminish the necessity of action, on the contrary it presupposes it. For Weil too, the relation between freedom and necessity is no simple opposition. We know that for her, man has no chance of breaking free from the cage of necessity which, seen from the point of view of the supernatural, is identified with obedience to God. What man can choose is simply whether to give his consent to this necessary obedience: that is, whether or not to desire it.[51] From this more objective perspective, disobedience as such does not exist—there is only desired or undesired obedience (which would otherwise be called disobedience). Now, the difference between the two types of obedience is critically important, in that it produces a qualitative distinction between two kinds of necessity. If obedience is undesired, it still remains as a mechanical necessity governing the world materially. If, however, obedience is desired, it is understood as belonging to the laws of the supernatural sphere, despite being objectively identical to its undesired counterpart. It is this second kind of necessity that liberates from an experience of necessity as constraint: "Obedience is the supreme virtue. To love necessity. Necessity and dharma are but one and the same thing. Dharma is necessity that is loved—Necessity is whatever is lowest in relation to the individual—coercion, force, 'harsh necessity'—universal necessity delivers from it. To consider dharma, not as duty, but as necessity, is to raise oneself above it."[52]

Necessity therefore frees itself *from itself*—or from an apparently inferior form of itself. And freedom, then, is something disclosed by necessity's difference from itself. But this difference is only visible because of a necessarily subjective condition that involves the will—or more exactly, its decomposition. In reality, man always experiences necessity as either an obstacle to the will or a chance to satisfy it, and seen from this point of view necessity always has something to do with an exercise of the will. In order to arrive at an objective interpretation of necessity, it must be extricated from the material setting in which it seems rooted, so that it can be understood as a purely ideal complex of interrelated conditions—which is exactly the aim of that science of reality, of all of reality, that is mathematics.[53] Naturally, man has no presence within a necessity that is thought "mathematically" (that is, in the only rigorous manner), apart from the operation by which that necessity is thought. We could even say that the condition by which necessity can be thought is the absolute impersonality of the thought that thinks it: the gradual dispersal of thought into the infinite ocean of reality.

Here the Spinozan nexus between necessity and freedom—a free necessity, and a necessity that frees—clearly leads us to the semantics of "decreation."[54] This theme, too, is Spinozan (bearing the influence of Isaac Luria and Haïm Vital, having come to Spinoza through Herrera). However, it belongs to a Spinozanism that ultimately distances Weil from Alain, because it is increasingly marked by the rejection of the will, if anything bringing her closer to his teacher Jules Lagneau (who was also a Spinozan, though not in the same way as Alain).[55] The modern origins of the term "decreation" are known to specialist scholars. It was abstracted from controversial Cathar and Kabbalistic roots (although we should not overlook Meister Eckhart's corresponding "*entwerden*" [annihilation], which was later revived and transcribed by Sebastian Franck and A. Silesius), and had already been adopted by Charles Péguy[56] (and, albeit differently, by Maurice Blanchot,[57] Stanislas Breton,[58] and Paul Ricoeur,[59] to say nothing of Levinas). Weil's specific and original sense of the term is also clear. For Weil, decreation is an annulment of the "I," or more precisely the decoupling of the pure, transcendental *je* from the sensory, desiring *moi-egoité*, which comes about together with the withdrawal of God in creation, and in order to compensate for that withdrawal.

Even if I cannot engage with Weil's metaphysics at length here, what is clear is the ambivalent (or even oxymoronic) character of her semantics—and of the term "decreation" itself. Decreation is a self-annulling creation, a creative self-annulling. More generally, it is also an act that does not express activity—or rather, it is an activity that is not completed in an "act" but rather remains "potential" (according to the notion of "passive power" that we have already encountered): Weil will in fact arrive at a definition of decreation as a *passive activity*. Her point of contrast remains the sphere of the will, which for Weil is analogous to muscular exertion. This analogy explains why the will finds itself out of place when it has no duty to confront and must follow its natural inclination or vocation: "Actions prompted by our inclination clearly do not involve an effort of will. In our acts of obedience to God we are passive; whatever difficulties we have to surmount, however great our activity may appear to be, there is nothing analogous to muscular effort; there is only waiting, attention, silence, immobility, constant through suffering and joy. . . . This kind of passive activity, the highest of all, is perfectly described in the Bhagavad-Gita and in Lao-Tse."[60]

It is here that Weil's break with Alain's voluntarism becomes a true and proper overturning, precluding the kind of secular morality that had marked Alain's thought (based as it was on the primacy of the will): "It is because the will has no power to bring about salvation that the idea of secular morality is an absurdity. What is called morality only depends on the will in what is, so to speak, its most muscular aspect. Religion on the contrary corresponds to desire, and it is desire that saves."[61] Weil contrasts the will with "waiting" (*attente*) or *hypomonè* (which, together with *tapeinôsis* or humility is one of the two Christian ways to Silence)—a term that can be traced back to *patientia* only with some difficulty.[62] But the most important point, to which Weil will return repeatedly, is that this is a question of an attitude that is "not like any form of activity,"[63] unless, as we have said, we understand that activity as passive. This idea of a passive activity expresses the structure of the kenotic process of decreation in the most contradictory way—and therefore for Weil the most truthfully. It is thus not surprising that with its antinomic constitution, this concept subsumes the triad of categories that sustains Weil's metaphysics: attention, desire without object, and inactive action. The "active" part of waiting, so to speak, is "attention" (although any attempt to specify it philosophically necessarily betrays Weil's intention). This attention should in no way be confused with a quietist stance, as it is by Del Noce,[64] or with an inertia of any kind. It is on the contrary a sort of active passivity, whose active aspect is attention—which is to say, a suspension of thought that empties thought out and renders it permeable by its object. It is precisely "empty, waiting, not seeking anything, but ready to receive in its naked truth the object that is to penetrate it."[65]

Attention is clearly an entirely negative exertion, but still one that requires energy. This energy is desire (to move to the second category in Weil's triad), but a desire that is utterly deprived of its object (otherwise it would be the surest way to expand the *moi*). In order to achieve this deprivation, it is not enough to do away with individual objects of desire, because it is the very *structure* of directed intention that must be suspended. However, since at least one part of the will remains active—and even highly alert—this should not be considered a stalled state of pure indifference (whose precise equivalent could be found in the concept of *indifférence* in another "Spinozan," namely Fénelon). This active part coincides with divine will; which is to say, the necessity that actualizes it (or that it *is*). At this final, unifying point the third category of the triad comes to the fore: "inactive action" [*azione non agissante*]. This category requires particularly careful analysis, because it leads us directly into a consideration of our most immediate problem: Weil's reflection on the political—or rather, the impolitical. First, however, a general observation: the problem of action is a topic of great importance to Weil from the very outset (we need only recall her continual interest in the theme of work). Right from the start, that problem finds a connection to the question of thought. Any thought, any consciousness, any philosophy that wishes to penetrate reality—but, as we will see, also any *language*—must *in time* become action: "Philosophy (including problems of cognition, etc) is *exclusively* an affair of action and practice," reads one of the final pages of *La connaissance surnaturelle*.[66]

This idea seems almost Marxian, and Weil rightly identifies it as a "philosophy of praxis": true thought must find its fulfillment in action. There is nothing particularly novel up to this point. But—and here is the internal vortex that often seizes Weil's concepts—this relation still holds true, even if its order is reversed. For Weil, action itself is part of how one knows the world, and in its most general (and purest) form it is even *at one* with thought.

This theme goes as far back as her third school *topo* dated April 1926, titled "That the Only Action Is Thought": "Action cannot be distinguished from thought. Indeed, as soon as there is freedom there is also perfect consciousness, with no trace of lack nor any possible uncertainty."[67] Despite being such an early text, this passage clearly signals the direction Weil's reasoning would take in her mature years, where the transmission of action into thought (or its absorption into thought, so to speak) will mark the passage from a personal-subjective plane of discourse to an impersonal-objective one. It is this path—one we know well—that leads to Weil's elision (or better, transformation) of the will into necessity, which can be seen in her affirmation that one need not act every time it is possible, but only when it is necessary: "By analogy, to discern the cases where, although things do not appear in this clear fashion at first sight, the possibility implies a necessity. To act in these cases and not in the others."[68] In conforming to necessity, man evidently loses everything personal that is left in him. When the spirit acts on the basis of necessity, not only has it no further need for the ontological support of the *moi*, but it must dispense with it as it would any unwieldy baggage. What might it mean to act in such a way as to dispense with one's subjectivity, if not to act in a state of *passivity*? Indeed, inactive action is eminently passive action:[69] "Acting not *on behalf of* a certain object, but *as a result of* a certain necessity. I am unable to do otherwise. This is not action, but a sort of passivity. Non-active action."[70]

With this, all of the categories presupposed by the concept of passive power—which has constituted a kind of semantic chase that has guided this discussion—are finally made clear. An action that is necessary is always passive. It is, nevertheless, still an action: a "power" [*potenza*], something that is not indifferent to reality. On the contrary, to the imaginary "I," it is the only thing that is real (the "I" who imagines and is imagined as real). The notion that there is a relation between passivity and power *within* action, or that action *is* a passive power, is found even in Weil's first writings of November 1925. In "Le conte des six cygnes dans Grimm," Weil considers the story of six brothers turned into swans by their stepmother and returned to human form by their sister. In order to perform this feat, the sister must sew six shirts made from white sea anemones and remain silent for six years. As Weil writes of the tale: "To act is never difficult: we act too much, and we are continually losing ourselves in disorderly acts. To sew six shirts from anemones and stay silent: this is our only way of acquiring power."[71] To act in silence, to act passively, to act *in not acting* is the only way to acquire power ("the only force and the only virtue is to refrain from acting"[72]). In light of this passage, an otherwise incomprehensible text from Weil's sixth notebook becomes clear: "The Word—*purely* powerful, *purely* passive. Has done everything from the beginning; the lamb slain from the beginning. Man: mixture of power and passivity. Being a creature, a partial being, can only find purity in pure passivity."[73] Here, with this power *in* passivity, and this passivity *for* power, we are a long way from the power of the modern tradition—but we are equally far from any notion of escaping it by way of "weakness."[74] Weakness is man's *force*, just as necessity is man's *decision*—a necessary decision. But if decision is necessary and if action is inevitable, how can decision not be a part of the "desiring machine" that naturally orients it to the increase of the "I"? In other words: On what specific basis can action-decision become necessary, activity become passivity, and the act become potential?

The clearest answer to this question, which is *the* question of Weil's political philosophy, is contained in the parable of Arjuna from the *Bhagavad Gītā*. "The four estates were created by me, divided according to constituents and actions," says Krishna to Arjuna. "Although I alone am the one who did this (*kartāram*), know that I am an eternal non-actor (*akartāram*). Actions do not taint me. I have no desire for the results of action (*phala*). Whoever understands that I am like this is not bound by actions."[75] Weil's response to the preceding question will be that we can identify the point of difference through the distinction between "renunciation" and "abandonment." This distinction is certainly present in the *Gītā*: "Seers understand renunciation [*samnyāsa*] as the rejection of actions motivated by desires; the discerning describe abandonment [*tyāga*] as the giving up of the results of all actions."[76] Here, just as in the *Gītā*, Weil intends to substitute *samnyāsa* with *tyāga*, meaning that she would substitute abandonment for renunciation. This is truly a decisive point for grasping the specific impolitical sense of Weil's thought. To abandon the fruit of one's actions in no way means to renounce action—this is in fact the cross, but at the same time the salvation, inscribed into Arjuna's destiny: "You are qualified simply with regard to action, never with regard to its results. You must be neither motivated by the results of action nor attached to inaction."[77] That Arjuna should not enjoy the fruits of his action does not change the fact that he must act—and as *efficaciously* as possible. Weil's work is without any tendency to an aesthetics of action—action only for action's sake (she always forcefully rejected the logic of gratuitous action)—or any kind of Kantian formal duty devoid of content. Act one must, and *effectively*, too. Thus Weil will affirm: "Nonviolence is only good if it is effective. Hence the question put by the young man to Gandhi concerning his sister. The answer ought to be: use force, unless you happen to be such that you can defend her, with as much probability of success, without resorting to violence; unless you radiate an energy (that is to say, a potential efficacy in the strictly material sense) equal to that contained in your muscles."[78] This is why Arjuna must fight. He must do so "passively," without personal reward, but he *must* fight—his destiny requires it. His destiny is part of a necessity that his decision must acknowledge, with a passion that does not give way to pity: "That is where Arjuna is wrong. The action of engaging in battle was in accordance with the light which was within him, since he prepared to carry it through resolutely. He ought to have stuck to his decision so long as he had not received more light; otherwise he could only fall to a lower level, not rise to a higher one. For that pity which enters into him through the visual senses and sweeps away his energy—it is not in that fashion that the light comes to one."[79]

"THERE IS NO FORCE BUT FORCE"

The fact that these passages belong to the final phase of Weil's writing—both chronologically and semantically—is significant for a more holistic understanding of her work. At the very least, it strongly calls into question a traditional interpretative *topos*: the idea that Weil's early interest in the political is dulled over time to the point where it disappears altogether, to be replaced by the more exploratory field regarded as her true and proper vocation, typically defined as mystical. Setting aside the different and even opposing views of this development offered by Marxist critique on one hand and Catholic critique on the other (negative and positive respectively), what all these accounts share is a common hermeneutic model: the identification of Weil's passage (if not a leap) from an attitude of "realistic" acceptance of the political to a register that is ever more markedly "unrealistic," "idealistic," and precisely "mystical."

It seems to me that this mapping—which depends, it should be noted, on a wholly inadequate definition of the "mystical"—ought to be reconsidered from start to finish. Not because there is no evolution or even rupture in Weil's intellectual itinerary, nor because such a rupture fails to trigger any change worthy of our attention in her conceptual lexicon, but rather because this rupture's consequences are the opposite of those just outlined. With the passage of time, not only in the first phase, but also with the passage to the second ("mystical") phase, Weil's political language becomes not *less* but ever *more* realistic—to use a category of the European political philosophical tradition that may not be wholly appropriate here. Of course, this means that something does change. But it is certainly not Weil's interest in the political, which is perfectly healthy right up until the final months before her death. Nor does it concern her analytic precision, which if anything becomes drier, as we have said, more biting and deliberately "Machiavellian"—as various texts from the 1940s, and before those the rightly famous text on the *Iliad*, clearly demonstrate.[80] What changes is rather the place where her reflection finds its footing. It is no longer situated within the political, but outside of it. Critically, not only is this shift not "recessive" (in the sense of making Weil's focus on the political conceptually or semantically weaker), but on the contrary, precisely thanks to its new location outside the political her gaze becomes stronger and more intense; capable of regarding her object, which is now *external*, with an even sharper focus.

Otherwise, if Weil's "impolitical" choice had made her political object less clear, we would have to limit the worth of her "political philosophy" to her writings of the very early 1930s. The thematic substance of that work, though Weil interpreted it rather personally, does not stray from the intellectual milieu common to the French political culture of opposition at the time (an opposition to the labor movement's official party and trade union). On the contrary, it is Weil's gradual distance from that context around the middle of the decade, and then her outright difference from it, that results in the most original period of her political reflection. This divergent tendency, which we see clearly in the great 1934 essay on the "Causes of Liberty and Social Oppression," is already present in the three articles that precede it: on the situation in Germany, the (ever more improbable) proletarian revolution, and war. In fact, what is striking about these essays is the *non-dialectical* way Weil constructs her problems (besides, that is, the fact that she addresses the canonical themes of the revolutionary left as it was represented by Souveraine, Louzon, Monette, Laurat, and Lazarévitch—themes like the degeneration of authority in the soviet revolution, the risks of abundant bureaucracy, and the critique of the notion of progress and Marxism in general). Weil considers that each of the contradictions she identifies cannot be solved, starting with the problem of the all-pervasiveness of the political,[81] introduced in the first of these essays ("L'Allemagne en attente"), and the stalled situation that paradoxically results from it:

> This energy remains latent. In a situation like this one, which seems to correspond perfectly to the very definition of a revolutionary situation, everything remains passive. The observer, struck by the convergence of all thought toward the problem of the political, is at the same time even more vividly struck by the absence of any agitation, of passionate discussion in the streets on the trains, of readers who anxiously throw themselves into their newspapers, of actions hastily planned or even merely discussed. This apparent contradiction gives the essential character of the situation. The German people are neither discouraged nor asleep; they are not detached from action; and yet they do not act; they are waiting.[82]

What they are waiting for, or rather what it is that awaits them, we now know only too well. But Weil herself seems more than merely to glimpse it when she moves to examine the deepest causes of this state of paralysis. The paralysis, the inertia, the weakness of the German populace—a key notion that came to occupy an ever more important role in the texts that would follow—is but a countereffect or mirror image of the meeting of certain *forces* that tend to neutralize each other. First among these is the National Socialist movement, which was made up of an amalgam of intellectuals, petit bourgeoisie, and employees and farmers, and held together by a patriotic and anticapitalist sentiment toward their victors: "In reality, what attracts them [the German workers] to the National-Socialist movement is, as in the case of the intellectuals and the petit bourgeoisie, that they feel its power. They do not realize that this force feels so powerful only because it is not theirs, it is the force of the dominant class, their 'capital' enemy. And they count on this force to compensate for their weakness and, even without knowing how, to realize their confused dreams."[83] The second force is the Social Democratic party, with its reformist unions cultivated *within* the same developmental process as capitalist society, and for that reason taken with its force, as if hypnotized by it: "the more the capitalist economy was shaken by the crisis, the more the trade unions (who, as always, take their own development as their highest aim rather than the rendering of services to the working class), cowered behind the only stabilizing force, the power of the State."[84] Finally there is the Communist Party, made impotent by its dependence on yet a third force, namely the Russian bureaucratic dictatorship, which "plays" the party in its own interests. Stretched between these three opposed and domineering forces, and constituted at the point where they converge, the German workers' movement finds a perfect state of inertia.

This is Weil's initial, powerful, panoramic view. Initially concerning only the situation in Germany, soon enough it would extend across the entire map of European politics (and then modern politics at large), and at the center of this map lies the question of force. This force is *external* (force is always, in the final analysis, external). The Communist Party is weakened—it would be better to say annihilated—by its subjection to the external force of the new Soviet state. Not coincidentally, this state will become the object of analysis in the second of the three essays referred to earlier ("Prospects: Are we heading for the proletarian Revolution?"). Here, too, what matters most to our discussion is not a detailed reconstruction of the downward spiral of the Soviet state, which according to Trockij's enduring judgment moved beyond mere defects that could have been corrected and into something absolutely incompatible with a workers' state (via the suffocation of any internal critique, its becoming a single-party state, the supremacy of the bureaucratic-administrative machine, and the rise of an omnipotent police). More important, in this essay Weil identifies a completely new system of oppression with respect to those that had come before it, based as they were on an armed force or on wealth transformed into capital. Instead, this new system was wielded in the name of *function*: that is to say, the very force of production.

In the name of rationalization and specialization, the new system of oppression suppresses that category of worker who still manages his or her own work. It is thus able to divide the factory between those who execute work without directing it and those who direct it without executing, but now with the addition of a third actor: the growing bureaucratic-administrative caste that has every interest in keeping consumption subordinate to production, and, moreover, in directing production toward the needs of war.[85] Once she has made this chain of deductions, war will become one of the constant figures in Weil's analytics. But it is even more important to note that war will be tightly connected to all the other elements of the system, making it a domestic political phenomenon more than an event of foreign policy.

This shift in interpretation, which is at odds with both the French post-revolutionary and Marxist traditions, becomes clear in the 1933 essay "Reflections on War." Here not only her analysis of the event of war but the entirety of Weil's political philosophy seems to be forced, with no prospect of return, along a tightrope without a safety net. Clearly visible here is the particular feature that distinguishes contemporary war from every previous kind of conflict and connects it, by two threads, to the structural features of production. On one hand, war is merely the continuation of political economy, and more precisely the politics of competition (not of politics in general, as Clausewitz had maintained). On the other, the entirety of political economy is *productively* oriented to war: "In this inextricable mixture of the military and the economic, where arms are put at the service of competition and production at the service of war, war only reproduces the social relations that constitute the structure of the regime, although to a considerably higher degree."[86] But something more defines modern war, and that is the combatants' absolute subordination to the instruments of battle. The technical threat of the "machine" rears its head again—and in such a way as to radically highlight its potential for annihilation, since "the war of one state against another is immediately transformed into a war of the state and military apparatus against its own army."[87]

Here we are again at the edge of a contradiction that can be resolved neither within the "war system," nor, crucially, outside of it—not even by invoking revolutionary war, the people's war that is at least theoretically a war without officers. Weil clearly declares that revolutionary war, again entirely at odds with the historical culture of the left, is the "tomb of the revolution." This explains why every revolution born of war or that occurs during the course of one—such as the Soviet revolution—cannot help but be corrupted, or come to blows with itself: "It seems that a revolution involved in a war has only the choice of succumbing to the deadly blows of the counterrevolution, or of transforming itself into a counterrevolution though the very mechanism of the military struggle. The prospects of revolution seem therefore very limited, for can a revolution avoid war?"[88]

Weil will immediately take up this rhetorical question—which is of course really an affirmation—in the important essay published the following year. This essay is truly a limit-point, in the sense that it is constructed at the limits, and *from* the limits, of the political. Though it is still anchored by political categories, the essay nonetheless looks toward their imminent overcoming. Or better, their deepening, in that the essay strikes at the very roots of political anthropology in a way that cannot help but recall Broch or Canetti, and particularly Canetti, whose dialectic of the survivor's annihilation and self-annihilation is echoed almost to the letter by the analysis of the mechanism of oppression, already introduced in Weil's previous essay, that is this work's "negative soul." Here, however, we see the extreme effects of this analysis, which strikes at the nature and essence of privilege (be it social, economic, scientific, or technical) while also getting at something deeper, something presupposed by the inequality of conditions themselves. That is, power [*potenza*], and the struggle that it unleashes: "Nevertheless, privileges, of themselves, are not sufficient to cause oppression. Inequality could easily be mitigated by the resistance of the weak and the feeling for justice of the strong; it would not lead to a still harsher form of necessity than that of natural needs themselves, were it not for the intervention of a further factor, namely, the struggle for power."[89]

What makes this struggle so Canettian is the fact that "power contains a sort of fatality which weighs as pitilessly on those who command as on those who obey."[90] As Weil continues, "it is insofar that it [power] enslaves the former that, through their agency, it presses down upon the latter."[91] This "fatal" situation comes about because of the growth of power: For those who hold it, power's growth is a necessary condition for keeping it, and one cannot retain power except by defeating those who resist it. This produces a vicious circle in which "the master produces fear in the slave by the very fact that he is afraid of him, and vice versa."[92] The only way to break the circle is to suppress inequality, which is impossible because it is unnatural. Or, to establish a power that is capable of arriving at a stable equilibrium between those who command and those who are commanded. Yet—and here the contradiction folds back on itself—that is possible only by dispensing with the "active" sense of power that is critiqued by the entire tradition of *potentia passiva*:

> But men are essentially active beings and have a faculty of self-determination which they can never renounce, even should they so desire, except on the day when, through death, they drop back into the state of inert matter; so that every victory won over men contains within itself the germ of a possible defeat, unless it goes as far as extermination. But extermination abolishes power by abolishing its object. Thus there is, in the very essence of power, a fundamental contradiction that prevents it from ever existing in the true sense of the word.[93]

What Weil's analytical excavation brings to the surface is power's most surprising feature: that its existence is impossible. Or to put it even more clearly, that power's *nonexistence* is something "real"—the fact that it belongs to the world of the *imagined*, which for Weil, as a Spinozan,[94] corresponds to the sphere of nonbeing. Power [*potenza*] cannot exist in relation to the category of possession. It is impossible to *possess* power, and thus to stably constitute it as *one's* power [*potere*], because "there is never power, but only a race for power, and . . . there is no term, no limit, no proportion set to this race, neither is there any limit or proportion set to the efforts that it exacts; those who give themselves up to it, compelled to do always better than their rivals, who in turn strive to do better than they, must sacrifice not only the existence of the slaves, but their own also and that of their nearest and dearest; so it is that Agamemnon sacrificing his daughter lives again in the capitalists who, to maintain their privileges, acquiesce lightheartedly in wars that may rob them of their sons."[95]

In referring to Agamemnon's destiny, which Weil quickly generalizes to include all of the Greeks (who fight a war "without object"), Weil moves her discussion onto a discursive terrain so radical and extreme that none of the following pages of "Reflections on War" can retrieve it, nor even those of the seemingly more constructive "Theoretical Picture of a Free Society"[96] (as is clear enough from the fact that, certainly not by coincidence, the essay was not published). And indeed, the last pages of Weil's writings that can still be said to use a properly political language in some way—the last before the "mystical" turn that will ultimately lead the author to the impolitical "politics of ascesis" of the final years before her death—is entitled precisely "Ne recommençons pas la guerre de Troie."[97] Here the illusory, mythic, and phantasmatic character that Weil had already identified in the very foundations of power is extended to the entire political universe. In "Critical Examination of the Ideas of Revolution and Progress," Weil discussed in detail the potentially transformative outcome of revolution, emphasizing the cyclical-restorative nature that is implicit in its ultimately conservative ancient etymology.[98] And in the subsequent fragment, "Meditation on Obedience and Liberty," there is an analytics of the multitude that is close to the one that Canetti would later elaborate. Weil responds to Etienne de la Boétie's monumental and still unanswered question about the "voluntary" character of servitude by affirming that the supposed power of the multitude is something purely imaginary: "Number, whatever our imagination may lead us to believe, is a weakness. . . . The masses are not in subjection despite the fact of their being number, but because they are number."[99] But in "Ne recommençons pas" there is a true and proper qualitative shift in the way Weil renders traditional political categories insubstantial and deprives them of any deeper meaning. The Trojan War—or any war—has no objective, and thus no possible measure, proportion, or comparison. And being unlimited, war is devoid of any rational existence (which for Weil is the only justifiable one—here, too, she is Spinozan). The real reason we cannot hope to understand war's motivation is not, as a traditional Marxist reading would have it, because it is veiled by official ideologies or obscured behind something else. Rather, it is because war, essentially speaking, does not exist. It is an empty vessel, similar to all those watchwords, those true and proper imaginary "monsters," that populate our political universe: war, revolution, progress, democracy. "On inspection, almost all the words and phrases of our political vocabulary turn out to be hollow."[100]

We spoke of a qualitative leap. Clearly, what had until this point been a specific critique of established contents—or rather vessels—of the political, now appears to be Weil's distancing herself linguistically and terminologically from the political. Her corrosive impulse, her analytical acidity, is now directed at the entire language of the political—or perhaps more accurately, the political *as* language. There is no political except in language: but this language lacks all rational legitimacy. It is filled with a void that is capable of contaminating and thus annulling everything around it, including the space in which it is exercised: "The struggle between the opponents and the defenders of capitalism is a struggle between innovators who do not know what to make and conservatives who do not know what to conserve; it is a battle of blind men struggling in a void, and for that very reason it is liable to become a war of extermination."[101] It is this situation that will generate an *impasse* in Weil's work, and soon enough also in her life: the inhospitable "quinquennial of death" that she would inhabit between 1938 and 1943. Her disjuncture from the political comes with and from this impasse, and although it remained squarely in view, at the center of her thought, she was by now at the political's outer margins. What is at stake for Weil is *neither* participation in the political *nor* indifference to it, as the closing of the "Meditation" suggests: "Such a state of things results in profound and irremediable spiritual torture for every man with the public welfare at heart. Participation, even from a distance, in the play of forces which control the movement of history is not possible without contaminating oneself or incurring certain defeat. Nor is it possible, without great lack of conscientiousness, to take refuge in indifference or in an ivory tower."[102] Here we are at the confine that separates the political from its own unrepresentable foundation: the threshold "bordering" (*côtoyer*) the political,[103] to use Weil's 1942 term for her own past activities. It is this threshold that will allow the unrepresentable foundation to cast new light onto that which *simply exists.*

THE SOVEREIGNTY OF SOVEREIGNTY

Undoubtedly, it is the unrepresentable nature of this last element that foregrounds the aspect of Weil's thought that is most able to reveal the paradigm and meaning of her discourse as a whole. In the theme of anti-idolatry, the whole of Weil's conception of history and the political comes together into a single impolitical gesture—so much so that one could even say that the (impolitical) critique of the political coincides, in Weil, with a critique of idolatry. This critique, as we have said, pervades the entire spectrum of (often obstinately one-sided) positions that Weil took on the grand themes of history and ancient and modern philosophy, especially the continual debate with Marx that is the implicit (but often also explicit) backdrop to most of her writing.

The critique can be seen above all in the important essay of 1934, where Weil summarizes and condenses its key elements. The central operation here is Weil's replacement of the Marxist antagonism between labor and capital for that between the technical-bureaucratic apparatus and the workers' labor power. In addition, here Weil will reject any prepackaged philosophy of history, and more generally any attempt to reduce the conflicts of power to a struggle between classes—especially at the expense of equally important dynamic factors such as war, for instance. But none of these critiques, which share many elements with the anti-Marxist front of the time, expresses the unusual philosophical and metaphysical sense of Weil's opposition to Marx. What gives rise to that opposition? The answer is essentially Platonism, which, at least according to Weil, is rigidly dualistic. Paradoxically, on the question of Weil's political realism, some have noted that this same element also explains her *attraction* to a Marxian paradigm (which in another sense is also Machiavellian). What unites Marx and Plato is that each identifies the sense of *necessity* that weighs upon social reality. Yet this same sense of necessity, more than anything else, also separates them: while for Plato social reality does not exclude but rather *requires* the existence of another, supernatural reality (which is politically unattainable in its perfection but not for that reason any less real), in Marx social reality remains the only reality that can be thought. So, continues Weil, Marx is bound to incorporate the Good expressed by the emancipatory completion of the historical process within reality. This is surely the critical point. In order to be able to make use of the Good's subsumption into history, Marx necessarily falls into idolatry, since he assumes that the material world can be perfected (thus converting evil to Good). In other words, Marx confuses the level of the supernatural with that of the necessary. This, for Weil, is exactly the definition of idolatry—the highest sin—which "consists of introducing what is unlimited into a domain that is essentially finite."[104]

From this point of view Weil eschews the common understanding of idolatry, which identifies it with polytheism. Not only does she find that definition unsatisfying (polytheistic religions exist that are not idolatrous, for example in ancient Greece, as well as monotheistic ones that are, such as Judaism)—but she regards such a definition as itself being a product of idolatry because it interprets the relation between the One and the many in terms of power and not the Good. "The religions which have a conception of this renunciation, this voluntary distance, this voluntary effacement of God, his apparent absence and his secret presence here below, these religions are true religion, the translation into different languages of the great Revelation. The religions which represent divinity as commanding wherever it has the power to do so seem false. Even though they are monotheistic they are idolatrous."[105] When power is confused with the Good—or worse, when the Good is understood in terms of power—one necessarily falls into idolatry. This can happen in the religious sphere, and it is a risk for certain religions in particular as we will see more clearly soon, but also, spectacularly, in the social one. Weil makes this point so insistently that she will end up defining the social itself as essentially idolatrous, characterizing it in terms of an absolute necessity: "Lacking idols, it often happens that we have to labour every day, or nearly every day, in the void. We cannot do so without supernatural bread. Idolatry is thus a vital necessity in the cave. Even with the best of us it is inevitable that it should set narrow limits for mind and heart."[106]

The fact that Weil casts the social as idolatrous is highly significant (always in relation to Plato's image of the "social beast," but, paradoxically, in some ways also Marx's and even Mannheim's conception of ideology), because this diagnosis is the driving force behind the impolitical turn of her final works. If the individual can at least theoretically escape the temptation to idolatry by virtue of the supernatural, then society, the "we," is condemned in principle: "The social domain is unreservedly that of the Prince of this World"; and more "on account of the ersatz form of good which it contains than on account of the evil which sullies it."[107] Weil forcefully underlines this point. Evil is not so much the evil that is manifested as such, but the evil that is presented in the clothes of the Good: it is the *confusio*, the *coniunctio*, of Good and evil. When the social is made absolute and then given to man as his specific place, we are obliged to interpret the social in terms of the Good (whether as a present or future Good), through that idolatrous machine that is the idea of Progress, and more generally, History. The Good is incorporated into the social when the social is understood as the *only* level there is—which is to say, the level outside of which it is not possible to establish *relations*. If there is one concept that Weil poses as the polar opposite of the idolatrous phenomenon, it is this concept of "relation": "It is the social which throws the colour of the absolute over the relative. The remedy is in the idea of relationship. Relationship breaks its way out of the social. It is the monopoly of the individual. Society is the cave. The way out is solitude."[108] An idolatrous stance typically understands things in isolation from their relation to what is external to them. That is why only putting apparently separate phenomena back into relation can at least reduce, if not eliminate, the degree of idolatry in everyday life.

This may seem to contradict what Weil saw as the need not to confuse the necessary and the Good. On the contrary, it is the direct consequence of that need. Here we must proceed carefully. Weil's stance, which favors the institution of relations *without* confusing these two levels, is diametrically opposed to the typically modern position she believes was brought about by secularization: the tendency to separate the profane from the sacred, and at the same time to confuse the religious and the political—a tendency that finds its completion in totalitarianism. These two processes not only occur together, but they are also mutually dependent in the sense that it is the separation or lack of relation on the first of these levels that creates the confusion on the other. As such, the crisis of relation results in a failure to distinguish. Let us see how. Weil does not criticize the secular for the distinction it might make between the religious and the political (which as we have just said is a necessary distinction), but for the modern interruption of the relation between the public and the private. The result of this interruption is the complete privatization (and appropriation) of the collective good within the sphere of the individual. Totalitarianism emerges precisely to address this phenomenon of the absence of any cohesion between private and public good—or, as Weil has it, between natural and supernatural needs—and totalitarianism is thus a kind of maleficent mending, the formation of an idolatrous conjunction between the political and the religious. Its power lies in its perverse ability to idolatrously fill the void of relations left by modern secularization, which was enacted politically by totalitarian deracination itself (this is the crux of Weil's analysis of fascism in *The Need for Roots*).

Yet not only modern secularization produces this void—or rather, it was not the first have done so. Implicit in the notion of secularization, which Weil does not refute methodologically or hermeneutically, is the idea that the modern only transposes, transforms and completes elements already implicit at the origins of Christianity which essentially belong to the history of Judaism. This history then merged with that of Rome, marking the passage from "divine pedagogy" to "political theology." It is often observed that Weil reserved a radical, stubborn, and certainly partisan negative judgment for Judaism (despite all the Jewish aspects of her own training).[109] Her judgment is a symptom, if not the consequence, of her Catharo-gnostic inclination—to such an extent that her sympathy for Marcionism seems to be motivated by the fact that Marcion distanced himself from the Old Testament.[110] What in fact likens the Cathars to the Gnostics, as Weil noted approvingly, is a conception of the difference between God and world that understands the presence of God as his absence from the world; the world being dominated, as we know, by diabolical powers and forces. These powers are diabolical *insofar as they are powers.* Unlike these powers, unlike the power of the world and the world as power, God is essentially and purely Good.

This is where Weil's obscure difference from Judaism is most marked. The Jewish God's fundamental attribute is omnipotence, making for a heavy, natural, and collective God. Not even his monotheistic nature can redeem him for Weil. On the contrary, the Judaic principle of monotheism originates precisely in the unification of the Good and evil within the idea of God, the unification of the Good and the necessary, the Good and power. This leads directly to idolatry—the identification of God with the Beast, and thus a God who is the founder and conqueror of states. This is not just idolatry, moreover, but idolatry of the very worst kind, because it is manifested in an apparently *anti*-idolatrous form that replaces the image or wooden idol with the idol of the Nation, the State, the Race: "The true idolatry is covetousness (πλεονεξία, ἥτιζ ἐστιν εἰδωλολατρεία *Col.*, III, 5) and the Jewish nation, in its thirst for carnal good, was guilty of this in the very moments when it was worshipping its God. The Hebrews took for their idol not something made of metal or wood, but a race, a nation, something just as earthly. Their religion is essentially inseparable from such idolatry, because of the notion of the 'chosen people.'"[111] There is no need to comment on these expressions here, though when they were written they were nothing short of inconceivable (from the pen of a Jew, no less). What concerns us is to make sense of their radically anti–political-theological significance. Idolatry, in Israel, coincides with political theology, and political theology can be its only logical consequence (again in the sense of an evil *coniunctio*): namely the connection that the Jews institute between disgrace and sin (and correspondingly, between good fortune and virtue).

> Among all the books of the Old Testament, only a small number (Isaiah, Job, the Song of Solomon, Daniel, Tobias, part of Ezekiel, part of the Psalms, part of the Books of Wisdom, the beginning of Genesis . . .) are able to be assimilated by a Christian soul, together with a few principles scattered here and there throughout the others. The rest is indigestible, because it is lacking in an essential truth which lies at the heart of Christianity and which the Greeks understood perfectly well—namely, the possibility of the innocent suffering affliction.[112]

This reference to the Greeks exposes another of Weil's differences from the Judaic paradigm. Whereas the Greeks admitted that divinity is external to the notion of necessity, and in some ways even subordinate to it (as Zeus's conduct in the *Iliad* attests), Judaism's notion of the chosen people binds destiny on earth to a divine will. The ultra–political-theological Jewish stance, posing a direct and inherent link between God and the people (the God of the people, even more so than the people of God), is the direct consequence of the other great difference separating Israel from Greece (and from most of pagan antiquity). That is, the refusal of the Mediation (the Incarnation and the Passion) of the figure of Christ. The rejection of

Christ—and thereby the rejection of the evangelical message—is part and parcel of the Jewish conception of God. Weil writes: "Israel chose the national God and simultaneously rejected the Mediator; it may, at one time or another, have moved towards true monotheism, but it always fell back on, and was unable not to fall back on, the God of the tribe."[113] It is precisely this choice that would go on to heavily influence the often fanatically intolerant teaching, and especially action, of the Catholic Church—the *anathema sit.*

But between these two political theologies, the Hebrew and the Catholic, a third stands as a powerful secular support for future political theology: the national and imperial political theology of Rome. Rome is where the political-theological seed (first sprouted in Israel) finds its most clement terrain, growing and reproducing itself along a course that moves through the French state of the eighteenth and nineteenth centuries, finally arriving at Hitler's totalitarianism.[114] Rome, accordingly, is the object against which Weil's entire impolitical meditation is directed.

Like her stance on Israel, it is generally accepted that Weil's judgment on Rome was highly "partial" (in the sense that her choice of ancient and modern sources was both limited and partisan: Polybius, Diodorus Siculus, Caesar, and Appian of Alexandria; Chateaubriand, Michelet, and Duruy). But here, too, more relevant is the category at the epicenter of her discourse. This epicenter, which moves among the three strands of Weil's "prosecution" of Rome—force, prestige, and propaganda—comes to light most fully as the connection between law and violence realized in the figure of the *proprium*. This is what Rome inherits from Israel and transmits, bolstered by its Roman juridical framework (which is both juridico-theological and juridico-political), to Western Christendom: "In the texts dating from before the exile, Jehovah's juridical relationship to the Hebrews is that of a master to his slaves. They had been Pharaoh's slaves; Jehovah, having taken them out of Pharaoh's hands, has succeeded to Pharaoh's rights. They are his property, and he rules them just like any ordinary man rules his slaves, except that he disposes of a wider range of rewards and punishments."[115]

Rome strips Jehovah of his slaves—hence the Romans' hostility to the Jewish God—but keeps them in the same condition, as *appropriated things*: "From the time of Augustus, the Emperor was looked upon as the master of all the inhabitants of the Roman Empire in the sense of an owner of slaves."[116] It is unsurprising that "the Romans," who "regarded slavery as the basic institution of society" (as did Aristotle, whom Weil detested along with his disciple Aquinas,[117] further marking her affinity with Canetti[118]) found "nothing that might prompt their hearts to say no to a man who claimed to have an owner's rights over them, and had victoriously upheld that claim by force of arms."[119] The structure of the *proprium* is rooted in the power of arms. But more important to understanding the political-theological figure that emerges from the *proprium* is that the force of arms is rooted in law [*diritto*]. It is the force *of* law. This makes plain the idolatrous nature of Rome's public cults, just as it makes plain the *historical* power of Roman law: Law as power and, *at the same time*, as myth. "A sovereign right is the right of property according to the Roman idea, or any other idea essentially similar to it. To ascribe to God sovereign rights without obligations is to turn him into the infinite equivalent of a Roman slaveholder."[120]

Weil's opposition between law and obligation connects this passage to a wider field, traversing the entire thematic palette of her final writings from *The Need for Roots* to the London essays. Where *The Need for Roots* opens with the affirmation that "The notion of obligation comes before that of right, which is relative and subordinate to it,"[121] the essay on "the person and the sacred" subjects the concept of law to such a powerful critical "bombardment" as to dispel any "aura" conferred upon it by the Western juridical tradition. Weil situates law squarely in the middle of a line that connects the market to force: "The notion of right is linked with the notion of sharing out, of exchange, of measured quantity. It has a commercial flavour, essentially evocative of legal claims and arguments. Rights are always asserted in a tone of contention; and when this tone is adopted, it must rely upon force in the background."[122] Law [*diritto*], Weil means to say, is always *partial*—the law of the part, and perhaps even *of the party*, which, incidentally, explains the aversion to political parties in the late phase of Weil's thought in particular.[123] Law is never the law of the *whole*. The whole has no need for the law, because law is a *just division* (like the individual, however, the whole may have need of Justice). But, and here the notion of *jus* begins to contradict itself, this division can be just only if the parties that have a claim of right also have equal power. Otherwise the result will necessarily be unequal because the stronger party will naturally acquire a greater right.

At the conclusion of this typically Nietzschean reasoning, Weil links law to force. Without force, law "will be laughed at."[124] "By the nature of things, the person is subdued to the collectivity, and rights are dependent on force,"[125] even if force in turn requires juridical legitimation, according to the mythical structure we have already mentioned. That force and the market, violence and propriety, would be the perfectly complementary poles between which the chain of *nomos* unravels, Weil demonstrates by noting the two subjective entities to which law fundamentally refers: the collective (not in the sense of the whole, but always the part: the collective part, the partial society) and the person. Law is always in the final instance *personal*, just as the person is in turn a person *by law*, which is the assumption that underpins the entire tradition of Catholic personalism. This tradition, not by coincidence, is shot through with juridical culture, from Mounier[126] (whose *Déclaration des droits des personnes et des communautés* is from 1942) to Maritain (whose *Déclaration des droits* is from the same year), who Weil will cite for his strongly political-theological "Roman" formula: "The notion of right is even deeper than that of moral obligation, for God has a sovereign right over his creatures and he has no moral obligation toward them (though he owes it to himself to give them what is required by their nature)."[127]

We can see that law and the person are in a mutually constitutive relation, given that just as the law is tightly bound to the notion of propriety, so too is the "person," notwithstanding the spiritual meaning of the term. (Weil, as we have said, was frequently involved with the journal *Esprit*; but her rapport with Renouvier and Laberthonnière, as well as Denis de Rougemont,[128] who was a militant of the *ordre nouveau*, also bears thorough investigation in this regard). Unlike the body, which cannot be separated from the "I," our person is something that in the final analysis we *possess*, like an trait, a character, an ability—all nonessential things that we may hold on to, but also lose. As such, Weil will affirm that "if a child is doing a sum and does it wrong, the mistake bears the stamp of his personality. If he does the sum exactly right, his personality does not enter into it at all."[129] The person is the principle of imperfection. Thus—and this is the point to which Weil's reasoning leads—the person cannot be sacred. If there is something sacred in us, it is on the side of the impersonal: "So far from being his person, what is sacred in a human being is the impersonal in him."[130]

All of Weil's work from this period hinges on the concept of the impersonal. It is the "positive" notion that Weil will pose against the political-theological semantics of the person. The fact that this "positive" is set down in necessarily negative terms—the terms of the impersonal—is the result of the rigorously impolitical nature of Weil's critique of the political as it appears in all of her essays from that period, including those considered vainly "constructive" (in addressing everything from political parties to representation and majoritarian democratic rule). Her critique can in no way be understood as affirming the political, except as part of a critique of the person-law-violence triad and its reemployment in the language of "historical development": the supremely idolatrous myth of Providence as the *personal* will of God. Providence, as the historical form of "divine pedagogy," is nothing other than the collectivization of the metaphysics of the person, that is, its extension into "becoming." Becoming is the word [*verbo*] of the law. Not only in the sense that the law becomes historically, but also in the sense that every phase of becoming can be juridically normalized, made susceptible to the norm. It is exactly this profound admixture of law, history, and theology that lies at the heart of the Catholic concept of Providence. The true object of the political-theological myth of Providence is to make becoming juridically governable, in all its norms and exceptions. What is mythical, in the historical unfolding of Providence, is that the force with which it is woven is reduced to law [*legge*], order, and form. Political form and theological form meet and legitimate each other in turn in this veneration of contingency. Indeed the Law [*diritto*] feeds on contingency: "The notion of rights, being of an objective order, is inseparable from the notions of existence and reality. This becomes apparent when the obligation descends to the realm of fact; consequently, it always involves to a certain extent the taking into account of actual given states and particular situations."[131] But the law's contingency is always conducted back to *nomos*, *logos*, the state, so the law's becoming in fact bears the state's idolatrous will.

The other side of Weil's dialectic of law's "conditions" is the unqualified nature of obligation: "This obligation is an unconditional one. If it is founded on something, that something, whatever it is, does not form part of our world. In our world, it is not founded on anything at all. It is the one and only obligation in connexion with human affairs that is not subject to any condition."[132] Just as the law belongs to the order of the person, obligation belongs to the order of the impersonal. This (and this is the most difficult point to fully grasp) is in no way different from the order of Providence, but this "in no way" is, at the same time, in *every* way. It is the *same* order seen in reverse: with one's gaze suspended in the void and one's ear trained to its silence, or to the cry of someone who is unwittingly struck by its force. From this perspective, that same force appears simultaneously to be "indeterminate" and "limited": "Brute force is not sovereign in this world. It is by nature blind and indeterminate. What is sovereign in this world is determinateness, limit. Eternal Wisdom imprisons this universe in a network, a web of determinations. The universe accepts passively. The brute force of matter, which appears to us sovereign, is nothing else in reality but perfect obedience."[133] In these final pages of *The Need for Roots*, the combination of discerning "realism" and extreme "mysticism," which as we have seen marks all of Weil's final works, now reaches its highest form (what is mysticism if not a complete realism? It is the being of *what there is*): "On this earth there is no force but force. That could serve as an axiom. As for the force which is not of this earth, contact with it cannot be bought at any lesser price than the passing through a kind of death."[134]

This "kind of death" is Justice, which resembles death because it is not of this world. *In this world* it is unreal. But it *is* also real: "Where force is absolutely sovereign, justice is absolutely unreal. Yet justice cannot be that."[135] The reason Justice cannot be absolutely unreal is because force is not *absolutely* sovereign. As something unreal, Justice cannot fight against force—nor even meet it. But as something real, it extends in an infinite line that force can never cross. Insofar as it is unreal, Justice is nothing other than force. Insofar as it is real, it is force's own limit: "Every visible and palpable force is subject to an invisible limit which it shall never cross. In the sea, a wave mounts higher and higher; but at a certain point, where there is nevertheless only space, it is arrested and forced to redescend. In the same way, the German flood was arrested, without anybody knowing why, on the shores of the Channel."[136] This "certain point" is not a force other than force—it is force itself having reached its own limit. Neither Providence nor any other "other" force can counter force from outside of it, except that inherent and therefore unmovable limit that *determines* it, like the insurmountable barriers that prevent the water from submerging the land. These limits, which are the invisible face of Necessity, are "without substance and yet harder than any diamond."[137]

This is why force is *not* absolutely sovereign: because it, too, is subject to a necessity whose force is more powerful than any force. The other name for this necessity, capable of sovereignly overpowering any force, is Justice.

Its anonymous face is impersonal, and yet more sovereign than every other sovereignty. It is the sovereign of sovereign power: "justice is the sovereignty of sovereignty," reads an ancient Indian myth. "This is why the weak's justice surely awaits the very powerful, as if by royal decree."[138] This is the mystery of Justice. It is stronger than force, but its force consists in nothing but waiting for what is necessary. Justice is waiting—and thought. Thought, too, can be more powerful than force, *if* it is stronger than the "I," if it is a thought that loses itself in the Necessity of that which is not I. This necessity appears in a flash, and can be grasped only in the void that thought draws out from its own flesh: "This sensible universe in which we find ourselves has no other reality than that of necessity; and necessity is a combination of relations which fade away as soon as they are not sustained by a pure and lofty concentration on the part of the mind. This universe around us is made up of mind materially present in our flesh."[139] Force, then, will vanish in the unfolding of Necessity. It will cede to the "passive" power of the limit: hidden but alive, mute and yet intense, immobile and yet capable of movement, like the "impalpable and weightless" light, which, "in spite of gravity, makes the trees and the blades of corn shoot upwards."[140]

5

THE COMMUNITY OF DEATH

THE CRITIQUE OF PRESUPPOSITION

George Bataille's reading of *The Need for Roots*, published in a 1949 article in *Critique* (to take up exactly where our discussion of Simone Weil has left off), functions through the intersecting logics of negation and of appropriation.[1] These are not two different procedures for Bataille—the negation of one aspect of Weil and the appropriation of another—but rather a single operation. The Weil who Bataille appropriates, assimilating her point of view and unifying it with his own, is the same Weil he rejects. How can the Weil who Bataille accepts also be the one he negates, and vice versa? The answer is that negation—critical demolition—is Bataille's specific method of achieving identification. This ambivalent relation seems to define the entirety of the brief but intense rapport between the two writers. Both were collaborators on *La Critique Sociale* and were united by a common critical stance on the communist orthodoxy—as well as by their unique interpretations of other highly significant political matters, like the rise of fascism in Europe and the "semantics" of the state.[2] Nonetheless, in a letter to the Democratic Communist Circle (into which she had been invited by Bataille), Weil was able to speak of "totally opposed" points of departure and "entirely opposite methods."[3] In her reply to Bataille—who, reviewing Malraux, had written that "in *Man's Fate*, the revolutionary value bears an unusual negative aspect that is produced in an atmosphere of death"[4]—Weil remarked drily that "one cannot be a revolutionary if one does not love life. . . . The revolution is a struggle against all that forms an obstacle to life. It has no meaning except as a means; if the end pursued is in vain, the means loses its value."[5]

Bataille's own reply would not be long awaited. It came, as is well known, in the form of an imaginary (but not far-fetched) portrait of Weil, drawn through the character of Lazare in *The Blue of Noon*. Here the two continue to mirror each other, reversing each other's positions: where Weil had rejected death as an appropriate category through which to view the revolution she identified with life, Bataille, through Lazare, distances Weil from life in order to reassign her to death: "everything about her—her jerky sleepwalker's gait, her tone of voice, her ability to spread a kind of silence around her, her hunger for sacrifice—helped give the impression of a contract she might have drawn up with death."[6] Quite apart from her name, Lazare has the appearance of a corpse, and throughout the course of the novel "macabre," "funereal," and "cadaverous" will be the adjectives that describe her. Yet, we must be careful to note, this is not an unambiguous or single-faceted depiction. As I have suggested, although Lazare bears the negativity of death or filth (Lazare is above all "dirty" [*sale*]), this does not mean it is impossible to understand her representation as positive—on the contrary, that is perhaps its hidden motivation. What in fact fascinates Bataille about Lazare is her "monstrous" quality, which in Bataille's well-known idiom belongs to the sphere of the sacred. Indeed, Henri is taken—even "obsessed"—with the "stench of an infirmary" that follows Lazare, that black "bird of ill omen":[7] "For a moment I wondered if she weren't the most humane being I had ever seen. But what was approaching me was also a monstrous rat."[8] This formula, "But . . . also," expresses the unresolvable contradiction that functions to identify Henri-Bataille with the negative quality that emanates from Weil-Lazare.

This same contradiction takes us back to Bataille's 1949 article, where Bataille abandons all literary fictionalizing and lays bare his logic. Yet this will do nothing to reduce the ambivalence—the duality of register—of his relation to Weil. Consider first the semantics of Bataille's critique, which, though this time they are positive, again invert it from within: "ardent character," "extraordinary tension," "amorous passion," and further, "lucidity," "daring pessimism," and "extreme courage." These characterizations only *seem* to contradict Bataille's description of his Lazare—the "fatal side" (*côté néfaste*) and "marvelous will to inanity" that describe her deathly nature. Rather they are the result of that nature—just as for Bataille it is from Weil's "indisputable ugliness" (*incontestable laideur*) that her "true beauty" (*véritable beauté*) derives.[9] This is not merely a matter of appearances, however.

There is something more in the obsessive fascination that Weil held for Bataille, something belonging to the philosophical sphere that concerns Weil's "will to inanity," her "excess," and the absolute extremism that she harbored right up to death (as Bataille would not fail to observe).[10] In fact, no sooner than Bataille has identified these elements, he makes explicit his ambivalent repulsion and attraction (a repulsion that attracts) and amplifies it in the notion of *completion*: "it is good method," writes Bataille, "to extract from an author a truth that escaped her. . . . If a search for the good is truly thorough and impassioned, it can find itself lost on a path, without a full awareness of where it is being taken. Seeking my own path, I can become interested in the seduction experienced by one who believes they follow the opposite path. The confluence of wholly opposed spirits can have a probative value."[11] This is no simple, natural coincidence of opposing factors. It is rather an appropriation that is able to complete its own thought via the wound it deduces in that of another, and at the same time, complete that other with the truth it causes to flash within its own. Such an appropriation is capable of opening another's discourse so as to wrench out its unwitting heart, or of separating that discourse's conclusions from its origin, so as to pit that origin against its own conclusions.

Setting aside for a moment the 1949 article with which we began, what exactly is the "origin" of Weil's discourse that Bataille appropriates—or rather, feels was always also his own? What is it about the thought (and not only the figure) of Simone Weil that so attracts Bataille? In the previous chapter we recognized the absolute centrality of an anti-idolatrous stance to Weil's analytics, which manifested in her continual opposition to the Roman and Catholic concept of the "person," and, even more strongly, to Providence as the personal action of God. In fact, these are only her first step toward an even more risky denial, one that is altogether unacceptable from a theological perspective: her denial of God as *presence*. An entire section of *Gravity and Grace* appears under the title "He Whom We Must Love Is Absent."[12] This proposition should be read entirely literally, as Weil repeatedly makes clear throughout the *Notebooks* with the recurring idea that we must "believe in a God who is like the true God in everything, except that he does not exist, for we have not reached the point where God exists."[13] Here, with the idea of a nonexistent God, Weil's antitheological stance is at its most extreme. What she rejects with this notion is the possibility that the divine presupposition could ever be made logical by way of the *theo*-logical. It is thus unsurprising that Weil's atheological path leads her to a kind of atheistic or irreligious mysticism, which she herself knew when she wrote that "religion in so far as it is a source of consolation is a hindrance to true faith; and in this sense atheism is a purification. I have to be an atheist with that part of myself which is not made for God. Among those in whom the supernatural part of themselves has not been awakened, the atheists are right and the believers wrong."[14]

This is certainly not the only current of Weil's thought, and as her Catholic interpreters have brought to light, its others may move in contrary directions. Even so, that she would take such a position could not have gone unnoticed by the author of the *Summa Atheologica*. Yet, this is only the first conceptual similarity between the two. It is joined by a further, surprisingly problematic one, which also concerns Weil's critique of idolatry—understood as the confusion between the Good and power. Read on its face, this critique can only mean that it is not *possible* to *do* Good. As something purely supernatural, the Good is not within our power—and whoever believes it is falls into the most classic form of idolatry. Idolatry is, in fact, an evil disguised as good. But this, then, means two things. First, that the Good as such is impossible, even if man *must* practice this impossibility: "All true good carries with it conditions which are contradictory," wrote Weil. "And as a consequence [it] is impossible. He who keeps his attention really fixed on this impossibility and acts will do what is good."[15] Seen from this point of view, Weil's thought is a thought of the impossible (though in a different way from Bataille): "That action is good which we are able to accomplish while keeping our attention and intention totally directed towards pure and impossible goodness, without veiling from ourselves by any falsehood either the attraction or the impossibility of pure goodness."[16]

This notion has a second, even more subtly Bataillian consequence, which requires great care in its articulation. Since we must always remain conscious that the Good is impossible, so as not to confuse good with evil (and so mistake evil for good) it is also necessary to *desire evil*. Weil begins from the anti-idolatrous presupposition that good resembles evil more than it does true Good: "good considered on the level of evil and measured against it as one opposite against another is the good of the penal code order. Above there is a good which, in a sense, bears more resemblance to evil than to this low form of good."[17] She continues in an ever more hazardous direction: "evil has to be purified—or life is not possible. God alone can do that."[18] In fact, God is loved precisely for the evil that his presence guarantees: "We have to love God through evil as such: to love God through the evil we hate, while hating this evil: to love God as the author of the evil which we are in the act of hating."[19] Finally, in Weil's third notebook, the two "Bataillian" threads of Weil's thought combine—the notion of the impossible and the productivity of evil—with an incredibly intense result: "*Impossibility* is the sole gateway leading toward God. (To posit the contradictory. To want the impossible. To love evil). We must love evil as such."[20] At this point we may still be within the orbit of Weil's formulation of the Lord's Prayer, but we are truly within a step of Bataille's atheistic reversal: "O my father, you, on earth, the evil which is in you delivers me. I am the temptation of which you are the fall. Insult me as I insult those who love me. Give me each day my bread of bitterness. My will is absent in the heavens as on earth. Impotence binds me. My name is lackluster."[21]

By now it should not be too difficult to understand the reason for the otherwise inexplicable attraction that, despite everything, drew Bataille obsessively toward Weil. It has to do with this negative *intentio*—her rejection of every affirmative representation of the Good—that in the end makes Weil see the good as necessarily belonging to evil. Yet, as we have already said, this conceptual and linguistic convergence between the two can only appear through their extreme divergence. What produces that difference? At what point in their state of accord does it reemerge? Bataille locates this point in the idea of "obligation," a notion that, according to Bataille, drags Weil backwards along the trail of an old morality that is by now impassable.[22] As we have seen, Weil invokes the concept of "duty" [*obbligo*] to oppose the idea of right [*diritto*], and duty is therefore the positive basis on which she refounds the sociopolitical sphere, which is the explicit aim of *The Need for Roots.*

Bataille's argument strikes against exactly this re-foundational, constructive, deontological aspect in Weil, contending that her text—having begun with a negative critique of an ethico-political language that she rightly recognized as idolatrous and impositional—comes to impose values of its own, thus itself becoming a direct affirmation. "Sometimes—for example, in *The Need for Roots*, or when she touches upon obsessional subjects," wrote Blanchot of Weil, "the affirmation stiffens and hardens to the point of becoming an empty force: then certitude, no longer abiding in its inaccessible firmament, descends to coerce rather than persuade us; and so the intolerance of spirit begins."[23] With this point, Blanchot—as close to Bataille in his judgment as ever—draws attention to those illiberal or even authoritarian elements in *The Need for Roots* (but also in the London essays) that work according to the logic of "rootedness"—a concept that contradicts the inherently deracinating aim of Weil's work. A rootedness in the earth, and in tradition, but above all in the past—albeit not in the sense of restoring that past, but instead receiving its spiritual "emanation."[24]

This shall we say "conservative" stance in Weil's work was interpreted by its critics, above all its Marxist critics, as her unconscious reversion to a moderate or even Petainist political position. But such an interpretation wrongly gives a politico-biographical complexion to what is, in fact, a conceptual contradiction entailed by the idea of "relation"—which, as we have seen, serves as the positive undergirding of Weil's critique of idolatry. Relation (bridging, or *metaxù*) is opposed to all false absolutes. It gathers divergent levels of reality and puts them into a rapport with each other: the natural with the supernatural, the necessary with the spiritual, the political with the sacred. The problem is that this combination of truth and the political in some ways interferes with the anti-idolatrous stance from which the very idea of relation arises. For Weil, the historical instances where such a combination miraculously occurs are extremely rare (one is the Spanish conspiracy against Venice, another is Catharism at the time of its destruction). It is this idea of the "exception" as such that is in subtle contradiction with the rigorously dualistic point of view from which it emerges. Where such an exception manifests, it is as if there is an analogical and representational operation (which is categorically Catholic) whereby a presupposed *image* of a supernatural equilibrium is reflected onto the political equilibrium. In other words, Weil's position implies there is a point at which the temporal and the eternal, the political and the sacred once again come to touch. It is this political-theological residue that promises the possibility of ethically refounding a city not through the necessarily conflictual terms of the *civitas* (the relation between interests), but the holistic ones of the *polis* (Justice and Faith).

What is important here—as Bataille clearly realizes—is that Weil's reversion to a concern with refoundation is not a simple residue within the otherwise radical negativity of her work, nor a sudden backlash against it.

Rather it is precisely that work's consequence, in that it is the result of her dualistic perspective (indeed, a good part of Weil's thought ends in counterposing a positive to a rejected negative). Seen from this point of view, it makes no difference whether this positive is made explicit (as in *The Need for Roots*) or is simply presupposed (as is the case elsewhere); or whether God and the duty that pertains to him are directly evoked or are left silent. In every case, the discussion slides into a self-founded affirmation, so that Weil's impolitical critique of the political turns into a new political program (represented, in this case, by the holistic community capable of putting down roots).

The entirety of Bataille's *Inner Experience* speaks to this point so insistently that it can be read, objectively, as a reply to Weil's "mystic" thesis (that is, without the author having subjectively intended it as such). It is generally known that the question of the "mystical" in Bataille is highly complex. Not only was he too defined as a "*nouveau mystique*,"[25] but Bataille declares his own mystical leanings at the outset of *Inner Experience* ("By *inner experience* I understand that which one usually calls *mystical experience*"[26]); leanings that are further attested by his frequent references to Meister Eckhart, Saint Ignatius, Teresa of Avila, and above all Angela of Foligno. It should not surprise us, then, that Bataille would seek to protect Weil's mystic dimension and, so to speak, bring it to completion.[27] Despite this generally positive attitude to the mystical, there is nevertheless something about it that Bataille radically refutes. We could summarize it thus: the mystical (at least in the sense in which Weil was mystical), though conceived as theology's polar opposite, is destined to fall prey to theology because it retains a dualistic presupposition. If there is a central argument in the inextricable tangle of extreme thought in *Inner Experience*, then it is the destruction of this presupposition—and, it could even be said, of the presupposition as such—as the mechanism that binds "being-there" to something unimaginable and unsayable, and therefore external.

We can frame this problem from another point of view. The mystical is *limited* by knowledge of the end to which its experience tends, as well as by the very fact of this "tending"; and this effectively re-defines it as a project (albeit in a negative form). As such, a mystical method is always a method of salvation and not of perdition, since one loses oneself only in order to be saved. In this way, ascesis can be said to have an inevitably constructive [*progettuale*] aim: "If ascesis is a sacrifice, it is only so *in a part* of itself which one loses with an eye to saving the other,"[28] and this is why Bataille will say that the ascetic "imagines no way of living outside the form of a project."[29] As a result, for Bataille it is necessary to overcome ascesis insofar as it is the *work* of redemption, together with the "attention" that, for Weil, is its essential vehicle: "It is true," admits Bataille, "that in it, I lose myself, I gain access to the 'unknown' in being, but *my* attention being necessary to plenitude, this self attentive to the presence of this 'unknown' only loses itself in part—it can also be distinguished from it."[30] The decisive point, however, has to do with the "limiting" nature of presupposition. It is this presupposition that requires that the mystical be completed in its *own* end, which is not declared but rather presupposed by the movement it brings about. If the mystical always already *knows* what it constitutes as such, it evidently cannot become that nonknowledge to which Bataille turns as the only form capable of overcoming subjectivity.

Weil's radical critique of the subject-person is by now familiar to us, as it certainly was to Bataille. We are aware, too, that through "attention," which for her was a particular type of "inner experience," Weil would propose a kind of objectivization of subjectivity: the subject's adhesion to the pure necessity of things, through which it consumes itself as the subject of the will. But this is effective *only* in relation to the subject of the will, and not the subject of consciousness or of knowledge. In this sense, too, Bataille "completes" Weil's message, transforming it in the process: the limits of subjectivity, the metaphysical statute of the *subjectum*, can be breached only if we lose the subject *qua* the subject of consciousness, and convert its knowledge into an absolute nonknowledge. "Experience attains in the end the fusion of object and subject, being as subject nonknowledge, as object the unknown,"[31] and as such the most important context for Bataille's contestation of Weil's notion of the "limit" is that of the relation between subject and object. (This is also a critique of Weil's Gnosticism—albeit from a position that is not wholly immune to Gnostic influences itself. It would be interesting to compare Weil and Bataille on this matter, since they correspond, to some degree, to Gnosticism's two great branches: the ascetic and the libertine.) The suppression of the subject—not, with Weil, by its withering, but by the ecstatic destruction of its constitutive limit—is the "only means of not resulting in the possession of the object by the subject, that is to say in avoiding the absurd rush of *ipse* wanting to become everything."[32]

Here subjectivity's nihilistic character is laid bare, and by contrast, so is Bataille's anti-nihilistic orientation. The subject extends itself through the will to power, which is revealed in the representative function through which the subject masters the object by representing it as a being (either as a "thing" or as "existing," as Bataille writes). "Subject, object are perspectives of being at the moment of inertia, that the intended object is the projection of the subject *ipse* wanting to become everything, that all representation of the object is phantasmagoria resulting from this foolish and necessary will (that one postulate the object as thing or as existing matters little), that one necessarily ends up speaking of communication by grasping that communication pulls the rug out from under the object as well as from under the subject (this is what becomes clear at the summit of communication, when there is communication between subject and object of the same type, between two cells, between two individuals)."[33]

In this passage, Bataille makes a seamless transition from the rapport between subject and object, to that which exists between two subjects (although to be completely rigorous, we ought no longer use the term "subject" here). The relation between subjects is where Bataille is most concerned to contest the notion of the "limit" (which also has to do with representation). Or not so much contest the limit as *invert* it, so as to emphasize not the separation or exclusion between subjects, but their *connection*. In fact, the term "connection" is also inexact, since the things that are connected do not form a single identity but remain as two differences (which are different, above all, from themselves). The term does vindicate, however, the particular self-other relation that Bataille expresses with the term "communication" (or, more intensely, "community"): "in experience," he writes, "there is no longer a limited existence. There a man is not distinguished in any way from others: in him what is torrential is lost within others. The so simple commandment: 'Be that ocean,' linked to the *extreme limit*, at the same time makes of a man a multitude, a desert."[34] Here the question of the limit returns, showing itself as the true conceptual crossroads of Bataille's analytics as a whole—and the point of their transmutation. The limit is both placed within the subject (or what was once the subject), thus fragmenting any subjective identity; and at the same time it is reversed, since its subjects *share* [*condivisione*] (as I would translate the French word *partage*) a *continuum* that is taken out of the dialectical difference of subjective identity, and returned to absolute difference (a difference that is no longer in the service of presence). What Bataille means by this *continuum* it is not easy to say. To be within the continuum is a *reversal* of the leap beyond the Open, beyond life's indistinction, beyond the splendor of the sun: it is to be situated within the boundary that is typical of *Homo faber* or productive man (the boundary that identifies us and separates us from objects—including those objects that are other subjects). Yet, at the same time, it is also the rupture of any binary principle of opposition.

Considering that we arrive, at this point, at something that cannot be made the subject of discourse, it could be said that the fundamental categorical object of our discussion has been overcome: that is, the impolitical and its distinction from the political. Not in the sense that we have either "transcended" or "realized" our object, but rather that the impolitical has been grasped and hollowed of its own negativity. A consideration of this point will offer us another way to approach Bataille's difference from Weil and her impolitical critique of political theology. Weil's critique, which Bataille otherwise completely accepts, is not sufficient: As *The Need for Roots* demonstrates, it risks becoming an equally authoritarian form of constructive project. Yet importantly, Bataille never counters that constructive aspect with a nihilistic turn to impotence, but oddly enough—especially for those who are used to taking the term in a certain way—he addresses it with what he describes as the "spirit of decision": "nevertheless, I wish to say that I in no way oppose to project a negative mood (an ailing listlessness), but the spirit of decision."[35] "It is only if I pronounce this principle: 'inner experience itself is authority,' that I emerge from this impotence. Intelligence had destroyed the authority necessary for experience: by deciding the issue in this way, man has once again at his disposal his 'possible' "[36] (which means, as Bataille intends it, the *impossible*). It would be wholly mistaken to understand this decision in a classical, shall we say Schmittian sense. We could cautiously suggest that it is Heideggerian, but above all it refers to the incision—the *sharing*—that lacerates and "decides" the very subject of decision. This is not therefore a question of reviving the old political lexicon Weil had already criticized; but nor does Bataille simply come to rest within the borders of the impolitical. It seems that the very opposition between the "political" and the "impolitical" no longer holds, having been abolished by a short circuit between the two terms that incorporates them but also preserves their heterogeneity. Rather than "limiting itself" to posing them in opposition, such a fusion also recognizes that they have always been essential to each other.

This is a profound linguistic conversion, and it pushes thought beyond a simple conflict between conceptual alternatives. Jacques Derrida refers to this same rupture of symmetrical opposition when he writes: "the sovereign operation, the *point of nonreserve*, is neither positive nor negative. It cannot be inscribed in discourse, except by crossing out predicates or by practicing [*sic*] a contradictory superimposition that would then exceed the logic of philosophy."[37] As Derrida will go on to say, "Such a rupture of symmetry must propagate its effect throughout the entire chain of discourse. The concepts of general writing can be *read* only on the condition that they be deported, shifted outside the symmetrical alternatives from which, however, they seem to be taken, and in which, after a fashion, they must also remain."[38] I would say that the binary alternative between the political and the impolitical undergoes this same displacement in Bataille's thought—and an equally intense rupture of symmetry. Such a rupture does not lead us back to classical politics, which was itself based on oppositional symmetries (friend and enemy, order and conflict, etcetera), and it equally avoids the symmetrical negativity of the impolitical. This fact is the key to understanding the notion of decision in Bataille. In *Inner Experience*, decision will be the place where "the fate of the man to come is at stake . . . each time a tragic disorder demands a decision without delay."[39] But instead of being outlined by the dazzling light of a choice of destinies (which is, if anything, the choice *of destiny itself*), decision is draped in the opaque colors of the night: "Without night, no one would have to decide, but in a false light—undergo. . . . There is a secret in decision—the most intimate—which, in the end, is found in night, in anguish (to which decision puts an end)."[40] With this reference to the night—which, of course, is not symmetrically opposed to the day, but as Zarathustra taught, "is also a sun"[41]—we introduce the question of community, to which our analysis must, in the end, be addressed.

THE BOOK OF THE SAGE AND THE SWORD OF ALEXANDER

Before doing so, however, we must take a detour through the semantic space—it is more a void than something substantive—that in our time is both community's horizon and its logical precondition: the theme of the "end of history." In its various forms—which had contrary meanings, as we will see—this notion received particularly concerted attention in the France of the 1920s and '30s. Its profound philosophical nucleus was then unearthed and brought to the surface in the 1960s and '70s—not only in the sense that it came to light, but also in that it was rendered more and more superficial, to the point of its evaporation in the stylistics of the postmodern. Its philosophical core can be traced back to Alexandre Kojève's legendary reading of Hegel's *Phenomenology,* which is commonly recognized as the centre of not just a new interpretation of Hegel, but also of the most significant Hegelian experiences of that period.[42]

We will approach Kojève's text through the most involved and involving of these—and with all the circumspection due to a discourse so vast and powerful as to situate "he who receives it within the void of a dark night whose howling wind prevents [its] words from being heard."[43] In his commentary on Kojève's commentary, Bataille's voice, which adheres to Kojève's text just as closely as Kojève's does to Hegel's, will, in the end, depart from both in exactly the same way: that is, Hegelianly (which is the destiny that befalls all post-Hegelian thought). But what is it about the Hegelian architext that prevents "[its] words from being heard"? What is its unheard and violent truth? Bataille provides a ready answer. It is "that night, that empty Nothingness" of humanity, that constitutes the "'central and final idea of Hegelian philosophy,' which is 'the idea that the foundation and the source of human objective reality (*Wirklichkeit*) and empirical existence (*Dasein*) are the Nothingness which manifests itself as negative or creative Action, free and self-conscious.'"[44] It is this principle, the idea that "Action is Negativity, and Negativity Action,"[45] that gives Hegelianism its dual character as a philosophy of death and of atheism. It is a philosophy of death because in negating the Nature of which he is a part, man is present within that Nature "like a night within light, like an intimacy within the exteriority of those things which are *in themselves*—like a phantasmagoria in which nothing takes shape but to evanesce, nothing appears but to disappear, where nothing exists except absorbed without respite in the *annihilation* of time, from which it draws the beauty of a dream."[46] It is an atheist philosophy because in it humankind has taken the place of God and anthropology that of theology. Of course, whereas in theological tradition spirituality is understood in an exclusively transcendental sense, for Hegel the spiritual being is necessarily temporal and finite. This brings us back, along a circular path, to the work of death. Without death and the agony of death, man would fall back into an animal life. It is only negativity—as the fear of *and* desire for death—that throws man into the movement of history, thus modifying man but also history itself. "Only history," concludes Bataille, "has the power to finish what is, to finish it in the passage of time. So the idea of an eternal and immutable God is in this perspective merely a provisional end, which survives while awaiting something better. Only completed history and the spirit of the Sage (of Hegel)—in whom history revealed, then revealed in full, the development of being and the totality of its becoming—occupy a sovereign position, which God only provisionally occupies, as a regent."[47]

In this way, the question of the Negative is joined to and completed by that of the end of history. What we must underline here, however, is that this end is in fact presupposed by everything that had been said up to that point. Without the end of history (in the event that history were to go on), the entire coherence of the discourse would be called into question, since it has meaning only insofar as it is completed. Indeed, for Hegel the Absolute can never be discovered at the beginning, but only when the entire process is concluded. Although it is true that what is revealed is the Beginning, such a revelation can occur only at the end: "The *end* of the 'movement' is therefore also *Identity*, just as its *beginning* is. It is just that *at the end*, Identity is *revealed* by the Concept. 'Movement,' or rather History, which, after all, is the process of the revelation of Being through Discourse, *reaches* its beginning only at the end: only at the end of History does the *Identity* of Man and of the World exist *for* Man (or exist insofar as it is revealed by human Discourse). History, having had a *beginning*, necessarily also has an *end*: and this *end* is the discursive revelation of its *beginning*."[48]

We must be careful to note—since this is exactly where Bataille's perspective will differ—that for Kojève, this End is absolutely definitive and cannot amount to a new beginning. As Kojève writes: "In fact, the revealed identity of Man and World *suppresses* the Desire that is precisely the *beginning* of History, of Man and of Time. The circle of Time can only be run once; History ends, but it never begins again; Man dies and cannot be revived (at least, not as Man)."[49]

At this point, once any possibility of a return to the past has been precluded (along with any advance into the future), Kojève shifts his attention to posthumous time; the time without time that the end of time produces. This is above all the time of truth, just as history is the time of error. Only man can preserve error—and only Error can preserve man. When there ceases to be error, when error is transformed into truth, when "the perfect conformity of Reality and Discourse is realized, when, that is, Man can no longer *err* because no longer having any Desire he no longer transcends factual givens, then History ceases."[50] Historical time is succeeded by the time-without-time of Wisdom, which is destined by the conclusion of Desire and Action. It is not that the sage forgets Desire and Action—on the contrary, it is only their memory that makes him a true sage, capable of "overcoming the final stage that yet separates *philosophical* contemplation of the time of Being-in-itself or of Temporality as such, in which nothing happens, from the *Wisdom* that permits us to embrace with a single discursive glance the concrete totality of the completed Universe."[51] But precisely because they are a memory, Action and Desire are consigned to the past and they cannot therefore be reactivated, but only reread (according to the condition of repetition that belongs to the Word-Concept). Whereas historical time is circular, in the sense that it finishes once and for all, that of Science, represented par excellence by Hegelian *Logic* is cyclical, since it is eternally repeated:[52] "thus, arriving at its end it is necessary to *reread* (or rethink) the Book; and this cycle is repeated *eternally*."[53]

The time of the end is the time of truth and the time of repetition, but it is also, above all, the time of homogeneity (a premise expressed by the analogical formula "absence of new information, absence of difference"). The difference between one man and another, but also between man and himself, is both the cause and the result of Desire, and the unhappiness that it generates. The converse of the same principle means that the happiness achieved by the end-realization of Desire will result in homogeneity, as announced in a searing aphorism by Raymond Queneau (who besides Bataille was Kojève's other great "pupil"): "It goes without saying. Put differently: happiness is all the same, but misfortune is always diverse. A run of excellent crops would never go down in history—but poor ones do."[54] This quotation is drawn from the collection of thought with the title *Une histoire modèle* (which, on the question of posthistory, ought to be read in parallel with *The Blue Flowers* [1965], and together with the three novels of "*Les romans de la sagesse*": *Pierrot* [1942], *The Skin of Dreams* [1944], and *The Sunday of Life* [1952], to which Kojève had given his philosophical imprimatur, so to speak).[55] The collection, in fact, opens with the intertwined couplet "history-unhappiness," "end of history-happiness": "If there were no wars or revolutions, there would be no history; there would be no historical material; history would have no object. At the very most, there would be annals. As the proverbs tell us: happy peoples have no history. History is the science of human unhappiness."[56]

Bataille advances this same argument, in a more philosophically developed manner, in identifying both the leveling effect created by the end of all war and the direct link between completion and homogeneity in posthistorical man: "if we speak here of a new man, the only novelty that he enjoys will be that of arranging the entirety of humanity on the plane of a sort of completion. It is easy to specify the point at which this alignment is proposed. It is a question of a culture undoubtedly susceptible to diversifications, but they would vary only quantitatively, lacking any real qualitative distinctions."[57] At this point, however, Bataille continues his commentary on Kojève's commentary with a phrase that, semantically, goes beyond what Kojève had intended. This will mark the point where Bataille overturns the commentary's reasoning and thus takes his distance from Kojève's reading of Hegel[58]—at first uncertainly, then later ever more sharply—departing, above all, from its neutral, declarative tone:

> The culture capable of managing this fundamental homogeneity, and the mutual understanding of those who make it up at its various levels, is a technical culture. The worker does not possess the knowledge of the engineer, but the value of this knowledge is not lost on him in the way that the interests of a surrealist writer might be. This is not a question of a new scale of superior values, nor a systematic contempt for disinterested values; rather it is a matter of reinforcing that which draws men together and suppressing that which separates them. This amounts to a reversal of the movement that has guided man until now. Beginning from this point, each individual can see humanity in himself, within that which makes him the same as others, whereas we founded our humanity on the values that distinguished us.[59]

The culture of which Bataille speaks is not his own, despite it being the culture of his time (or of his non-time, his non-history). Without rushing to the (anti-Hegelian) outcome of his discussion, these references to the "technical" and the "worker" can be considered through another author of the *finis historiae*, so as to clarify Bataille's position by comparison. Before naming that author—he too charged with history and legend—one last useful note on Kojève's understanding of posthistorical homogeneity:[60] whereas on the philosophical plane this is a question of the culmination of Hegel's *Logic*, on the temporal plane Kojève reads the Napoleonic Empire as the first sign of the "homogenous and universal" State, which has by now been realized by the "planetary" convergence of American capitalism and Soviet socialism. "From a certain point of view we can also say that the United States has already reached the final stage of Marxist 'communism,' given that almost all the members of its 'classless society' can now avail themselves of anything they wish, without for that reason working more than they would like."[61]

The author with whom Bataille can usefully be compared, Ernst Jünger, unites this theme of the universal State with the end of history so that the two form a single conceptual figure. It is surprising that the evident rapport that connects Jünger to French philosophy of a Kojèvian stripe (and a Nietzschean vocation) has been systematically ignored by the critical literature on both sides. It is nonetheless patently clear that Jünger's theses on the resolution of the Russian-American antagonism in a new, unitary superstatal formation show strong connections with those of Kojève and Bataille.[62] What Jünger adds in particular is a deepened analysis of the qualitative leap this unification involves; a leap represented by power's transition from being a static symbol (the palace, the throne, but also the crown and scepter) to a dynamic one (space travel, for example). This itself expresses a passage from a phase in which symbolic rank is founded on real power, to one in which it is instead real power that is founded on the rank of the symbol.[63]

In reality, however, the expression "passage of phase" does not give the precise measure of the event. Nor should we speak of a catastrophic shift, really, since no catastrophe—at least as far back as our references can take us—has ever modified the specific structure of man, whereas this is what now seems to be the case. This fact renders historico-political notions like "peace," "war," and "tradition" wholly inadequate to the task of describing the change that is taking place, since the change also affects the originary substratum from which history and politics first emerged into light. This event, which is even more fundamental than the foundational phenomena to which we have been accustomed, is precisely the exhaustion of history. Jünger dedicated an entire book, *An der Zeitmauer*, to the phenomenology of this event, indeed opening his book with the contention that "the edifice of history begins to rend."[64] His metaphor for the situation of contemporary man is, in a temporal idiom, a year that closes the decade, and together the century and the millennium; and in a spatial one "a border-dweller, who with a single step could leave his room, and at the same time his house and even his country."[65] In this sense, Jünger likens man's situation to that of Herodotus, who looked out from the world of myth onto the world of history. Just as Herodotus diverted his gaze from the night of myth to fix it upon the dawning glimmer of history, so we are thrown out of the glare that until yesterday blinded us and into a new night, thick with dark omens.

However, cautions Jünger, we must be careful not to misunderstand this point. The end of the historical world does not bring about the grand return of myth; it is analogical, not symmetrical, with the transition Herodotus was to experience. While the end of history may in fact foster mythical elements, this can only be a partial resumption of myth that takes effect at history's points of fracture—the wounds that riddle the dying body of a history incapable of reconstituting its old force. For the return of myth to be possible, it would take a night as deep as the one from which Herodotus broke his gaze. But this night does not arrive. The darkening of the day is not in itself the reappearance of the original night:

> That mythical powers today cannot return to rule, to affect us convincingly on the personal and material level, depends on a condition of the light. After dawn breaks with Herodotus, there is no longer a night in the old sense. At the light of historical consciousness, the old images become more faint, more delicate. They reveal themselves only to the degree that consciousness weakens, as in a dream, in sleep and in creative ecstasy, or else in times of upheaval. But stepping out of the historical field is in no way a matter of a diminished consciousness; on the contrary, the critical faculties continually increase. That alone speaks against a return of the mythical.[66]

The observation in the final words of this passage marks out the distance that separates Jünger from Kojève (and Hegel). Whereas for Kojève, as we have seen, the circularity that unites beginning and end clearly precludes a new beginning, Jünger's end—because it is not identical with its (mythical) beginning and is therefore not entirely circular—does enable things to begin anew. To be clear, however, it is not that the figure of circularity is wholly absent from Jünger's account, but it is always understood—through the image of the bronze serpent biting its own tail—as the greatest risk to which we are exposed, the risk we must overcome with a decision that, at a certain point, breaks the serpent's coil.[67] This decision is constrained in two ways. It must repeat every time the "knot" reforms (that is, perpetually), and it can take place only when the present is truly exhausted. Jünger alludes to the second of these conditions when he warns that "the pillars of Hercules have to crumble within us before the new Garden of the Hesperides can appear,"[68] and "the dew falls on the grass when the night is darkest."[69] Ours is a constitutively ambivalent condition. That is why, in the crepuscular light reflected by the wall of time, it can be adjudged close to catastrophe—but at the same time, *precisely for that reason*, the bringer of new hope. For Jünger as it was for Broch, the zero-point, the *Nullpunkt*, is both the Nothing and the absolutely Other. The end of the night is the beginning of the dawn. The danger is the salvation.

Given this ambivalent principle, by which nihilism bears within itself the seed of its own overcoming, how is it configured in Jünger's thought in particular? Is it still in its final, nihilistic phase, or has it already arrived at a point beyond itself? It is not easy to give a clear answer to this question, which was posed most radically by Heidegger.[70] Let us say that in Jünger two currents of meaning, or two "gazes," follow each other in time (but perhaps more precisely, alternate and overlap): one, mythical and activist, located squarely within the "power of the void," and another that is antinihilistic (at least in its intention, if not necessarily in fact). The theme of the end of history acts as the hidden transition from one to the other. It is not that the first of these currents, at least as it appears in the book on the Worker [*Arbeiter*], relies on any kind of historicism that is later overcome. Rather, more profoundly, history itself and as such is considered nonexistent—or better, it exists only as the epiphenomenal projection of an eternal elemental substance "that in a miraculous way keeps the world alive"[71] (this is what enables the fundamental optimism of Jünger's entire view—even in its moments of catastrophism).

Jünger will rely on this substance in framing all of his questions, beginning with the foundational figure of the Worker. What changes, along the course of Jünger's output, in line with his increasingly complicated understanding of the essence of technology, is way that this substance inflects the relation between the subject and the form in which the subject appears historically. In the case of the Worker, the relation between *Worker* and *Work*, "technician" and "technology," necessarily models the former in the image of the latter, since "everywhere man falls under the jurisdiction of technology, he sees himself confronted with an inevitable either/or. There remains only one choice: either accept technology's strange instruments and speak its language, or drown."[72] The opportunity for salvation that technology provides is thus not to be attained by its overcoming, but rather its "perfection."[73] Technology's destruction of old values constitutes and *constructs* new figures, new types, and new orders. This is why the subject it "mobilizes"[74] is not only inherently nihilistic, but nihilistic in an active, heroic, and *political* way. Although it is therefore true that it is technology that dominates this political phase, it is exactly technology's "dominance" that inflects its ubiquity in terms that are, in the final analysis, political: the terms of the will to power. "The destructive phase is followed by a real and visible order, and it will come when a race comes to power that can speak the new language not as a purely intellectual instrument—a means of progress, utility, commodity—but as an elementary language."[75]

It is this immediate relation between worker and work, technology and politics, subject and will, that falters in Jünger's postwar works. With time, Jünger takes his distance from the "mythology of the modern"[76] of his early writings; a process that can be seen in his transition from the conceptual category of "completion" toward that of "overcoming." While his nihilism remains, retaining its status as the horizon of our time, it now seems subjected to an urge to "rupture" that forces its inherent fate to the surface—almost as if nihilism's inner Void were divided into two parts, each of which attempts the elimination of the other. The fact that in Jünger all opposition to the void arises from within the void itself signifies his rejection of any nostalgia or any backward retreat (which would necessarily lapse into what Heidegger called "reactive nihilism"). On the contrary, Jünger, identifying any "calm" as merely the "the eye of the storm," ties any possibility of salvation to a passage through a painful ordeal.

The necessity of this sacrifice, which had already been anticipated in 1934's *Über den Schmerz* (*On Pain*), is central to *Über die Linie*, which opens with a reference to none other than the sacrifice of Dostoyevsky's Raskolnikov. This is perhaps where Jünger is closest to an impolitical trajectory. Once he has overcome every kind of activist optimism for the production of new orders, the only remaining means of escape is a crossing of the negative. No ocean appears, no mountain peak rises, to oppose the sandy expanse of negativity's desert—only the oases that it itself produces and nourishes, "gardens to which the Leviathan does not have access, so it paces furiously around them."[77] The constructive "political" will to power, which had animated the *destructio* associated with the Worker and rendered it productive, is thus succeeded by the impolitical silence of oases withdrawn from the sovereign's gaze. Freedom is by now to be found outside of history; in those who observe its rubble with unmoving detachment, and in the spiritual-material unity of the Undifferentiated. This is what Schmitt meant when he ruled out the possibility that Jünger "exalts the solution offered by a blow of the sword."[78] As he wrote of Jünger, "his last word is not an 'either-or' but an 'equally-as-much-as;' a mutual encounter, a tentative knock at the door, an exchange and a balancing, the return to the Eternal within time and a reference to 'hidden answers that the Orient can offer us.' "[79] Schmitt's reference to the Orient—the Occident's *un*-chosen—is a reference to the Spirit of the Earth, which the East still harbors. But it is also a cipher of the impossibility of the decision, and with it a bond that not even Alexander's flaming sword can truly sever if it does not wish to smother the very breath of Life at the same time. The truth of Life lies in the Undivided that inhabits the spirit of the Earth, and the way of this spirit is not the negation of differences but their copresencing. This is why Jünger characterizes the passage from the Father's Apollonian, "decided" order to the Mother's chthonic and undifferentiated one as a taking leave of political monotheism (a monotheism of the political), and at the same time, an impolitical wait for "new gods."[80]

This break with political theology, however, does not achieve the escape from nihilism for which it was designed. Jünger's impolitical remains firmly rooted within the confines of nihilism, and moreover it remains within those confines precisely to the extent that it tries to overcome them. According to Heidegger, the aim of overcoming is inherently complicit with the appropriative nature of the "project," and it is thus precisely the *project* of "overcoming" (*Überwindung*) that welds Jünger to the Nietzschean metaphysics of the will to power. For Heidegger, the element of salvation cannot be understood as opposing the thing that it saves *from*—nor even as something separate from it. This is what Heidegger means when, despite strongly sharing his motivations, he imputes Jünger with the use of a medical-therapeutic paradigm. He does so not merely because nihilism is "incurable," but because the very idea of "cure" is intrinsically nihilistic: "The essence of nihilism is neither curable nor incurable. It is that which is without salvation, but precisely for that reason it bears within it a unique reference to that which is saved."[81]

This distance between Jünger and Heidegger also separates Jünger from Bataille. In that case, too, the difference is not a matter of the variety of "salvation" but rather that salvation's purpose. For Jünger, pain, the negative, and sacrifice are all made to work toward salvation, as we can see in his idea that one accumulates "credit" by undertaking acts of sacrifice: "Malaise depends so much more on things that are lacking than on those that exist. By this logic, this malaise is unavoidable, because it attests to a need that goes beyond every increase in comfort and power, and which must be satisfied. This means that the losses outstrip the gains: and that we are therefore creditors. Something has been sacrificed, there has been a devotion, for which the corresponding sum has not yet been paid out."[82] It is exactly this credit, this "investment," that nihilistically invalidates the renunciation of "growth" or "earnings" to which Jünger entrusts the escape from nihilism.

This is evidently a question of the *subjectum*—which in Jünger remains in healthy credit, and is if anything reinforced by abstinence and deprivation (albeit while being subjected to the cure of immobility, withdrawal, and passivity). We could say the same of *Eumeswil*'s "anarch," the figure that more than any other resembles Bataille's sovereign—but who can be radically distinguished from that sovereign by exactly this kind of solid subjectivity. The anarch, too, comes to light in the "surfeit of a late era,"[83] when "the historical material has consumed itself"[84] and "the catalogue of possibilities seems exhausted."[85] For him, too, "beyond history" means "beyond the will": he is the man of Substance, not the Will. It is his vantage at the final border, from which the rubble of history can be observed with an archival meticulousness, which liberates him from politics and the judgments on value that it involves. But the freedom that distinguishes the anarch from both the "anarchist" and the "forest fleer" is what reinforces his subjective identity, making him the "master of himself": "The difference is that the forest fleer has been expelled from society, while the anarch has expelled society from himself. He is and remains his own master in all circumstances."[86] His is an impolitical "absence," but it is impolitical in a nihilistic, self-empowering way—just as the sovereignty he exercises is also self-empowering and nihilistic: "he is sovereign. He therefore behaves as a neutral power vis-à-vis state and society."[87] He addresses himself not to the disruption or decentering of his nature as a subject, but to the ever-stronger reaffirmation of its centrality:[88] "Each person is the center of the world, and his unconditional freedom creates the gap in which respect and self-respect balance out."[89]

It is true, therefore, that the anarch's "style" is to keep his distance, but only because that distance is a function of centrality: "The anarch recognizes himself as the middle."[90] Thus, occupying the centre with a solar fixity ("Man should be not the sun's friend, but the sun itself"[91]), he may renounce the other in his perfect self-sufficiency: "His own measure is enough for him; freedom is not his goal; it is his property."[92] And although he is described as neither individualist nor solipsistic, the anarch is in fact fully compatible with the tradition of possessive individualism—even and especially in the "prison" of his isolation: "In this way, the prison becomes an island, a refuge of free will, a property."[93] In fact, his property is none other than this "free will," which wills freedom insofar as it means power [*potenza*], and power insofar as it guarantees the will. In this, the anarch is very close to Stirner's Unique, if not entirely identical. He does not concern himself with the truth, but only because he may freely dispense it himself: " 'Truth? None of my business.' It remains his own property. He does not accept it, he does not want to serve it; instead, he disposes of it freely."[94] He does not strive for power, since he detests politics: "he dashes neither after nor ahead of it, because he possesses it and enjoys it in his self-awareness."[95] His power instead comes from his own subjectivity, enriched and augmented by the conclusion of history: it is the power of one who intentionally avoids power. Thus, the reason he does not *will* power is because if he were to do so he would occupy, bring to an end, or "fill in" a will whose power lies in being a void within which it can infinitely pursue itself.

POWER OR EXISTENCE

Bataille, however, inhabits a different void. In fact, it could be said that the antinihilistic critique of the will to power is the main differentiating category of the *finis historiae* as a conceptual paradigm—not only within its Hegelian-Kojèvian strand, but also as it appears in Jünger's notion of "overcoming." In "La limite de l'utile," Bataille devotes a brief section on war to Jünger's term, in which he recovers and develops his own "limitless" conception of war through Jünger's words (as Roger Caillois was to do in his work on the mystique of war).[96] In war, the passions are unleashed with intensity never before reached—not even in revolutions, which are still constrained, "limited," by their utilitarian ends. War—unlike peace, which is marked by the non-consumption of energies and by the exclusion of the useless—is the only thing that liberates society from its productive bonds, working instead toward the unproductive consumption of exorbitant energies, sacrificing them without remainder. According to Bataille, Jünger was the one who best directed his gaze at war's ecstatic, sacrificial reality. "I wish to show that there is an equivalence between *war, ritual sacrifice* and the *mystic[al] life*: it is all the same game of 'ecstasies' and 'terrors' in which man is joined to the play of the heavens. But war is so often betrayed: its glories and its disgust are concealed. This is why I will cite Jünger, who leaves nothing out."[97]

Yet it is exactly the "blood tie" between war and sacrifice[98] (which Jünger does not avoid but rather graphically represents) that brings out certain appreciable differences between these two phenomena, and also, implicitly, between the two authors. The first of these differences has to do with the question of "reality." Whereas war is allocated to the register of real action, religious sacrifice is regarded as merely symbolic. This unreality, however, is what gives sacrifice an intensity, an interiority, a "deepening," that is impossible for war. It is true that military holocausts have a concrete quality that religious ones lack; that they respond to religious fictions with their gift of an effective truth. But is it precisely that truth—the aim of victory over the enemy—that restrains military battle from bringing about the exposition of the self to the other that for Bataille is the very meaning of sacrifice. This is a question of the relationship to death, and to the life that death bears. Whereas for the soldier—Jünger's "Front Soldier"—this relation is something random, for the one who sacrifices, bent over their victim, it is destiny itself: "The soldier is content to say: 'there is death. You confront it without thinking. You laugh at it.' The man of sacrifice assigns to death a greater destiny. For him, 'there is death' is no simple protest, unpleasant or not, because there *must* be death."[99]

It is this *knowing* and *desiring* death that makes the man of sacrifice the man of tragedy. In revealing the tragic character of existence, he can do what the soldier cannot: create a human being through the only phrase that makes him human: "You are tragedy."[100] Whereas war is something one necessarily seeks to win, sacrifice "is the effect of a violent need to lose. And as such it threatens above all he who sacrifices."[101] There is nothing real about this exercise whatsoever; it remains a pure fiction. Yet whereas Jünger's Front Soldier kills or is killed in a game that remains individual to the end, the sacrificial fiction has the capacity to allow the other—or others *in common*—to feel the vertigo of its act of death: "the life of the single individual is lost within a reality much more vast, just as the wave that breaks is lost, plunging again into the flows that envelop it."[102] This is the ground-without-ground of the entire debate. Whereas war, even with all its upheavals of existence, is still a figure of the will to power (give in order to get back, kill in order to be victorious), sacrifice is the place, the only place for Bataille, where that power is extended to the point of losing itself and changing from the will to power into the will to loss; the loss of will.

It is widely known that Bataille's critique of the nihilistic will to power appears most explicitly in his Nietzschean works. These texts are in fact doubly Nietzschean, since they both speak *of* Nietzsche, and speak through or *from within* Nietzsche. This duality was Bataille's acrobatic means of overcoming an apparently insurmountable problem: how to handle a thought that cannot be accounted for in the usual registers of interpretation and "realization"? Nietzsche is impossible to interpret, because his defining feature is precisely that his withdrawal from meaning confounds any kind of hermeneutics. Yet it is all the more unthinkable to try and "realize" his thought, since it contains no theory of action[103]—and is even provocatively posed as a theory (or better, a practice) of inaction. Although we cannot retrace Bataille's entire relation to Nietzsche here, we can nonetheless identify this as the point that requires the most attention as far as our fundamental problem is concerned: Nietzsche, philosopher of inaction, is *the* philosopher of the impolitical. But this claim is complex enough that we should take it one step at a time (complex enough, and also contradictory enough: the "truest" Nietzsche lies in his contradiction with himself). That Bataille protested the instrumentalization of Nietzsche by both the right and the left is all too well known. The problem, he suggests, is that the movement of Nietzschean thought is a "labyrinth"[104] that disrupts any topology of left and right; and with it the "various possible foundations of current political positions."[105] This is why it is irreparably mistaken to situate Nietzsche's thought in a "homeland" (as even certain great interpreters such as Levinas have done),[106] thus grounding it in an holistic community of soil and blood. The condition of Nietzschean thought is rather its deracination of any homeland, a being without homeland (a *Kinderland* as opposed to a *Vaterland*). Indeed, the passage where Bataille's Nietzschean "overcoming" of the political is perhaps declared with the most force has the title "We Who Are Homeless": "The passionate and tumultuous movement that forms life, that responds to its demand for the strange, the new, the lost, sometimes appears to be carried along by political action—but that is only a matter of a brief illusion. Life's movement can only be merged with the limited movements of political formations in clearly defined conditions; in other conditions, it goes far beyond them, precisely into the region to which Nietzsche's attention was drawn."[107]

The only interpreter to have underlined Nietzsche's radically impolitical character was Karl Jaspers, to whom Bataille refers with a long quotation. For Jaspers, Nietzsche's thought is distinguished by the absence of any limiting definition of the political that marks the work of other political thinkers. This limitation, continues Jaspers, characterizes both Machiavellian "power" and the Hegelian "system." Nietzsche stands outside of both, in that his perspective embraces the very condition of man, but without resorting to any principle that tries to be all-encompassing:

> He envisages the decisive origin of political events without becoming methodically absorbed in specific concrete realities of political activity as they are revealed daily in the struggle of powers and personalities. He hopes to generate a movement that will quicken the ultimate grounds of humanity's being, and he wishes through his thinking to impel those who hear and understand him to enter into this movement. Still he does not limit or define the content of this movement politically, ethnologically, or sociologically. Rather, as he sees it, that which underlies and determines all judgment is provided by an attitude directed upon the whole of *being*. It is no longer mere politics but philosophy, on the basis of which, within the wealth of possibilities but without rational principle, opposing and contradictory ways can be tried solely under the guidance of the idea of saving and advancing humanity's being.[108]

It is not easy to unravel in just a few words the complex knot that Jaspers ties with the strands of Nietzsche's thought. What must be emphasized is the connection between the beginning and the end of the foregoing passage: the inquiry into the "decisive origin of political events" and the attempt at (or the temptation of) "opposing and contradictory ways" that arise from the "wealth of possibilities" (which even here are opposed to the power of the real). This is the precise point where the impolitical's difference from the political is reversed because of its radicality in Nietzsche's thought: that difference is inverted on its own ground, such that it puts into question the *limit* that unites by dividing and divides by uniting. In other words, this is the point where the limit becomes understood as the principle of *sharing* (*condividere*). The situation recalls a passage from *On Nietzsche* that elaborates the impolitical criterion of inaction through Jaspers's notion of the "complete man":

> Even if it is true that, as it is usually understood, a man of action cannot be complete man, complete man nonetheless retains the possibility of acting. Provided however, that such action is reduced to appropriately human (or reasonable) principles and ends. Complete man cannot be transcended (that is, subdued) by action, since it would lose its totality. Nor can it transcend action (submit it to its ends), since in this way it would define itself as a motive, and would enter into and be annihilated by the mechanism of motivation. It is important to distinguish between the world of motives on the one hand, that is, things making sense (rational), and the (senseless) world of non-sense on the other. Each of us sometimes belongs to one, sometimes to the other. We can consciously and clearly distinguish what is connected only in ignorance. Reason for me is limited only by itself. If we act, we stray outside the motivation of equity and a rational order of acts. Between the two worlds only a single relationship is possible: action has to be *rationally* limited by a principle of freedom.
>
> The rest is silence.[109]

Here we are able to see that the "transgression" of the "classical" distinction between the political and the impolitical that Bataille's Nietzsche brings about is actually a double transgression (and we should not lose sight of the paradox that Bataille is the most radical interpreter of this distinction, and *precisely for that reason* the most unfaithful one). That transgression works through Bataille's transposition of the binary division between political and impolitical into a split between the "world of motives" and the "world of nonsense." This is already a considerable displacement, because the world of nonsense cannot correspond to the world of the impolitical since the "impolitical" in fact *produces* sense (albeit negatively). Yet this displacement is made even more poignant by a second "transgression," which involves the bar dividing these "two worlds" (assuming there really are two and not just one, "limited" only by its "not being everything"—remembering that "reason . . . is limited only by itself . . . the rest is silence"). It involves the "principle of freedom," which naturally belongs to the impolitical "world" of silence but which Bataille partially transfers to that of "political reason." Freedom, born from the originary co-belonging of philosophy and politics, is precisely the path that crosses both the political and the impolitical (and for that reason, it is also the path of their overlapping—their "sharing," in the sense we have already described). A citation from Bataille's book on sovereignty will make this point: "Nietzsche demanded freedom and was conscious of a breakdown that goes with it. Freedom is, first of all, a political reality: in this case, it corresponds to the oppression of one class by another. (It can also be the occasion of a philosophical chatter, as if the metaphysical question concerning it did not immediately call for the silence of unknowing.) But beyond politics and the domain of efficacious action, freedom signifies a sovereign attitude in the domain of sensible values (I can act in order to be free but the action immediately deprives me of the freedom that I have to respond to passion)."[110]

The opposition here between "efficacious action" and "sovereign attitude" is identical to that which appears in many of Bataille's other texts, where sovereignty is contrasted with power [*potenza*]. As is well known, Bataille imputes to Nietzsche's interpreters, and in some ways to Nietzsche himself, a confusion between power and sovereignty. Power is the mode of action that is directed toward an end, and for Bataille it is therefore the opposite of sovereignty, which is sovereign precisely because of its absence of ends. Here, too, we must be cautious, as things are not as simple as they seem. Consider, again, Bataille's later work on Sovereignty, and in particular the passage where he identifies the error of placing an emphasis on power where Nietzsche had explicitly placed it on sovereignty. The two are "not the same thing" explains Bataille: "sovereignty requires power perhaps, but the pursuit of power reduces man to action, which is a means; it is the contrary of sovereignty."[111] Here the sovereignty/power opposition is anything but symmetrical: Power is not sovereignty—it is rather its opposite—but sovereignty nonetheless requires power. This complication refers us back to the question of decision that we have already considered. Like decision, "power" is a "political" term that Bataille considers acceptable (or even necessary) to the constitution of sovereignty, only if it undergoes a change of semantic register that rids it of any nihilistic inflection.

We find ourselves, by now, on a terrain that has not merely shifted away from the usual partitions and oppositions used by the "impolitical authors"—it has been altogether transformed. Whereas, despite everything, the work of those authors still concerned knowledge, it is now precisely knowledge as such that is called into question—including and especially knowledge as power. In fact, standing opposed to power as the will to knowledge, prediction, or calculation, Bataille's sovereign power is essentially the will to *chance.* It is the power *of* chance: "Nietzsche expressed the principle of open-ended play where *occurrence exceeds the given.* 'Why,' said Zarathustra, 'should the lion become a child?' A child is innocence and forgetfulness, a new beginning and game, a wheel turning on itself, a first impulse, the sacred 'yes.' The will to power is the lion: but isn't the child the will to chance?"[112] The distinctions that Bataille finds in Nietzsche—not oppositions, but rather their destruction—are so intertwined that they preclude all possibility of a simple, binary logic. The child symbolizes the Yes, the absolute affirmation of the game of chance, but that Yes is above all "sacred." This amounts to a warning, on Bataille's part, not to fall into an ingenuously antimetaphysical reading of Nietzsche's thought. The critique of metaphysical foundations implied by Nietzsche's perspective as a whole—and above all by the famous formula of the death of God—in no sense produces an "Enlightened" end to the sacred. Such a reading would only repeat the nihilism that was at work in the metaphysical foundation (or worse, amplify it in the same expansionist way as the will to power, which wants to be everything). For this reason, says Bataille, "Nietzsche is the atheist who bothers about God, because he once recognized that, not existing, the place that God left vacant laid all things open to destruction."[113] This is exactly what Jean Wahl meant, too, when he said (regarding Jaspers's *Nietzsche*) that Nietzsche philosophized "in the presence of the absence of the divinity" and that "the thought of the absence of God does not suppress within him God's creative instinct."[114] In Nietzsche, the critique of the divine does not amount to a secularization: "Never does he cease to attempt the immense undertaking—represented by Socrates and the moral, Christianity and God—of organizing all the discordant possibilities of the human being in a single stroke."

This is Bataille's undertaking, too. For Bataille, to hold in a single grasp "all the conflicting possibilities of the human being"[115] means to understand, as Nietzsche had before him, the "paradoxical impossibility of yielding in either direction."[116] The risks that lie in "either direction" can be discovered through the authors we have considered up to this point. The first is the Weilian Presupposition, which preserves the Other, the Different, in the form of silence. The very essence of the impolitical belongs to this presupposition: namely, the fact that it cannot be reduced to that which exists. The second risk is Hegelo-Kojèvian Completion. What is completed in the master-slave dialectic, by contrast, is the political Principle [*principio*],[117] understood as the *End* of the political. This risk involves a metaphysical circularity that is self-founding precisely because it eliminates any presupposed Alterity:[118] specifically, an Absolute knowledge that excludes the possibility of anything external to it (rendering such a thing *im*possible), being for that very reason the highest will to power.

It is precisely on the ground of this impossibility that Bataille's "mole" excavates. His is not a frontal critique—as Derrida has perhaps most clearly underlined—but a destructuration that creates a state of ambiguity by using Hegel's own "tricks," his own "cards," against him. Bataille is perfectly aware that Hegelian thought cannot be logically refuted. For that reason, instead of attacking it directly, he lies in wait for a moment when the completion of the discourse moves it out from under the complete control of logic. This moment is precisely the *finis historiae*, whose phenomenology Bataille accepts but whose outcomes he overturns. "I grant (as a likely supposition)," refines Bataille in his letter of reply to Kojève (who had accused him of coming to believe in his own tricks, like quite the sorcerer's apprentice)—"that from now on history is ended . . ."[119] But this very admission will be the key to Bataille's reversal of the discourse of Completion in order to relaunch it and reorient it toward the future (or better, the possibility of its transcendence): "However, I picture things differently," he continues. "It certainly doesn't seem impossible that, in some very distant time, everything will begin again."[120] The possibility that completion might lead to a new beginning arises, for Bataille, through a reference to his own life that exceeds the Hegelian dialectic in a single stroke: "I imagine that my life—or, better yet, its aborting, the open wound that is my life—constitutes all by itself the refutation of Hegel's closed system."[121] Bataille understands his life in terms of a negativity without use (*sans emploi*); a pure negative that cannot be made to function in the interests of a new positive. It by being just such a negative that the End can generate—or can itself *be*—a new beginning: "Leaping is life. Settling the score is death. And if history stops, I die. Or . . . Beyond settling the score, is there some new kind of leap? If history is over, is there a leap outside of time as I keep on shouting '*Time is out of joint.*' "[122] It is at this moment that "thought taken to the limit of thought requires the sacrifice, or death, of thought. To my mind, this is the meaning of the work and life of Nietzsche"[123] (this citation is drawn from the section titled "The thought of Nietzsche, that of Hegel, and my own"). "Nietzsche is to Hegel as a bird that breaks its shell is to one who happily absorbs its inner substance":[124] one who extracts from completion the vital possibility of beginning.

This beginning is Nietzsche's "gift": "The resumption of life in the moment."[125] The instant is the time that overhangs [*residua*] the end of time; the only sovereign time, time that has been withdrawn from the restricted economy of duration (which cannot be the time of loss), the time of *chance*: "The combination of an exceeding love and the desire to lose (actually the continuous state of this loss) IS TIME AND IS CHANCE—though this obviously represents a rather rare situation."[126] But we must think through this prospect with care. The overturning of time (or the end of time) in the instant must not be considered as a sort of abandonment to insignificance or to the fleeting moment. The instant is valuable insofar as it is *sacred*. As such, this instant resists becoming rather than yielding to it. It is an acceptance of time, but it is also time's redemption. This is why, in Bataille's Nietzsche, the critique of the Presupposition does not wholly resolve into a praise of the *saeculum*. Certainly, against every faith in a transcendent God, the apparent, the contingent, the event, are real. But they are real insofar as they are themselves divine. They are steeped in time, yet they transcend it.

Bataille's notion of "eternal return" is charged with this same ambivalence (an ambivalence typical of all of Bataille's concepts, as we have seen). It too is torn from its usual lexicon and transplanted into the semantics of the instant:

> In this sense I think the idea of the eternal return should be reversed. It is not a promise of infinite and lacerating repetitions: it is what makes

moments caught up in the immanence of return suddenly appear as ends. In every system, don't forget, these moments are viewed and given as means. Every moral system proclaims that "each moment of life ought to be motivated." Return unmotivates the moment and frees life of ends—thus, above all, it destroys it. Return is the mode of drama, the mask of complete man, a human desert wherein each moment is unmotivated.[127]

The instant's unmotivated quality, here, is closely connected to the "immanence" of the return—which is immanent because it breaks the linearity of Christian time and the uniqueness that time gives to its events. What before was unique is now resolved into infinite repetitions. However, as Bataille is quick to warn, this alone does not express the true sense of eternal return, because it accounts only for the element of "return" and not also its "eternality." The return is above all Eternal,[128] as Shestov had made clear in an account of Nietzsche that had strongly informed Bataille's reading.[129] Eternal, too, is the instant that it grasps. Eternity is what abducts the instant from the world of means; redeeming it from the flow of becoming—without, however, "abstracting" it from that flow. Eternity breaks the serpent's coil with a decision that is grounded not in the will to power, but in precisely the opening of the eternity of the instant. This is why eternity's decision can live alongside necessity. Indeed, *chance* is nothing but the felicitous side of the *Amor Fati*; a love of what there already is and an affirmation of its immutable possibility. *Amor Fati* and *chance*, Necessity and Decision. The Will to what has already been and will return in the future, because it is suspended in the Eternity of the Instant—suspended in its dwelling *in* the becoming *beyond* the Instant. In this way, the world is suspended in its *immanent transcendence*. "Nietzsche's philosophy, Jaspers tells us"—this is Jean Wahl—"is essentially the affirmation of the world as pure immanence." But "Nietzsche is shaken, lacerated, by the idea of this transcendence that he denies . . . When it is radical, the *no* can, by its force, in its frenzy, transform into a *yes*, and nihilism, the nihilism of the strong and no longer that of the weak, can be transformed into a positive philosophy."[130]

Considering now this relation between immanence and transcendence, yet again we find ourselves confronted with a relation that cannot be constructed as a binary opposition. Bataille does not simply oppose immanence to transcendence; he does not nihilistically annul the act of transcending.

Transcendence is, rather, the empty light against which the fullness of immanence appears in silhouette: "Oh summit of all that is comic! Bound as we are, to flee the emptiness (insignificance) of infinite immanence, insanely dedicating ourselves to the lie of transcendence! But in its dementia this lie lights up immanent immensity. An immensity now no longer a pure nonsense or a pure emptiness, it is the foundation of full being, a true foundation before which the vanity of transcendence dissipates. We wouldn't ever have known transcendence (for us it could not have been—and this may be the only way it can exist for itself) if we hadn't first constructed it and then rejected it, torn it down. (Will you be able to follow me this far?)."[131] It is putting transcendence to death that illuminates immanence. But what this really illuminates is that immanence must continually transcend *itself*, internally. Immanence is constituted—not only surrounded—by the cut that separates it from what it is *not*, from its *own* difference from itself. Without this transcendence—which no longer refers to a super-essential substantive entity but precisely to that entity's death—immanence would be made absolute, and that would restore the metaphysical identity that the entirety of Bataille's thought aims to contest.

THE RAPTURE AT NUMANTIA

Bataille's thought should therefore not be understood as moving toward absolute immanence. This is confirmed by his critique of secularization, which, through its Nietzschean lens, leads to his reading of the Modern. Framing this critique requires us to reconstruct the dialectic of the "sacred"; the rich theoretical locus where the three directors of the Collège de Sociologie (Bataille, Leiris, and Caillois) would encounter and reckon with each other, following in the footsteps of the great anthropo-sociology of Mauss,[132] Otto,[133] and Durkheim[134] (but also K. T. Preuss,[135] to say nothing of Freudian analysis). We will see later what it is that radically separates the three directors. What is common to all three is the partition between the "sacred" and the "profane" on the one hand (which, to a certain degree, can be attributed to the distinction between the "heterogeneous" and "homogeneous"), and between the sacred "pure" (*droit*) and the sacred "impure" (*gauche*) on the other.[136] What is most important about these binary oppositions, besides their semantic plurivocity, is that they are complementary, as explained in

Caillois's book *Man and the Sacred*, which offers the most reliable "syntax"[137] of the forms of the sacred. This complementarity means that just as the antithesis between the sacred and the profane is really a scheme of endless interchange between the two terms (each being the reverse of the other), so too the opposition between "pure" and "impure" is a kind of pendulum that perpetually transforms the former term into the latter and vice versa.

Although they therefore appear to the external observer as two separate and opposing poles—one that attracts, fascinates, and bewitches, and another that repels, disgusts, and terrorizes—these terms are two sides of the same coin, as shown by the etymological ambivalence of both the Greek term ἄγος and the Roman *sacer*. Just as constitutively ambiguous are the Polynesian *tapu*, Malay *pamali*, Dakota *wakan*, and Japanese *kami*; with each term expressing both *souillure* and *sainteté*, *fascinans* and *tremendum*.[138] This logic is particularly important, because Bataille needs it in order to be able to posit the law of historico-social development as the transformation of the low heterogeneous (impure) into the high heterogeneous (pure) by means of an originary sacral nucleus. In fact for Bataille the most potent sacralizing device, and therefore device of social cohesion, is a crime: the putting to death of the king. One such crime in particular dominates the occidental imaginary, namely the Crucifixion. It is crime that generates sacred things that are "*gauches et intouchables*," and it is crime that transforms them, in turn, into a force that is just as sacred, but "*droit et glorieuse*"—and itself vulnerable to the threat of a fresh, subsequent crime.[139]

This mechanism of socio-sacral recharge is, however, not eternal. At a point coinciding approximately with modernity, it becomes blocked and threatens to seize up. Yet, although this may be a result of the modern, for Bataille its roots are sunk well into the past, into the time of Christian experience. It is the Crucifixion itself, the archetype of the royal crime, that initiated the secularizing path leading to modern desacralization—although rather than the end of the sacred, we ought to speak instead of the end of the tragic. The first step along this path is the Christian tendency to identify no longer with the criminal, but with the victim of crime, which is already an initial crumbling of the original "spirit of tragedy." But its more profound cause is the expansion of tragedy's direct alternative: power [*potere*]. Despite also being generated from the sacral nucleus, power ends up paralyzing the social dialectic, eventually arriving at the total abolition of crime, which power replaces with its own threats. This will result in the gradual neutralization of conflict. Modern individualism, with the loss of cohesion that it brings, but also with its contradictory tendency to mass homogeneity, is the fruit of this desacralization. All attempts to recreate the minimum of cohesion that is necessary for the reproduction of the social are responses to this state of affairs: from the technico-administrative approach, which contorts the political to fit the intrinsically depoliticizing and nonconflictual dynamics of representative democracy; to the bureaucratic-military, which reacts to the loss of the social bond by forcing social integration.

With the appearance of the "fascist" solution, the dialectic of the sacred is finally presented in its full phenomenology, which essentially has three different embodiments. First, the man of tragedy—the bearer of existence in all its most irreducibly conflictual dimensions, who may be compared on one hand with the secularized "man of law and discourse" (who eliminates conflict), and on the other with military man, who exteriorizes conflict by expelling it from himself and onto the enemy.[140] Bataille dedicated an important and innovative essay to the analysis of fascism, published in *Critique Sociale* (not without some hesitation of a sovereign nature), which anticipated the theses he later developed in his articles in *Acéphale*. Fascism is positioned midway between the communal *theatrum* of tragedy and the representative *theatrum* of democracy. Whereas the latter decomposes the social into its individuals, fascism reproposes a new form of forced cohesion (fascism's etymology also indicates *union*, *concentration*), and Bataille's analysis works against the features of this forced cohesion in a particularly penetrating manner. Put briefly, his contention is that whereas the cohesion achieved by the decapitation of the sovereign was revolutionary, fascist cohesion is political-theological in nature. Indeed fascism is, for Bataille, the highest form of political theology.

Bataille makes his claim concerning political theology on the basis that fascism intertwines the homogenous with the heterogeneous and elevates the outcome of this intertwining to a state *value*. Careful attention is required here. The same intertwining was already apparent in the monarchical form of imperative, which "poses the *having to be* of *homogenous* existences in *heterogeneous* existence."[141] But fascism makes a qualitative leap, in this regard, by bringing the unification of military and religious power, upon which the classical imperative rests, to its extreme completion. "It thus presents itself from the outset as an accomplished concentration,"[142] in the sense that fascism enables both "qualities derived from the introjected *homogeneity*, such as duty, discipline, and obedience, and qualities derived from the essential heterogeneity: imperative violence and the positioning of the chief as the transcendent object of collective affectivity."[143] This fusion, however, has a dominant element, and that element is religion—not its theologico-political aspect, therefore, but the truly politico-*theological* one: "The chief as such is in fact only the emanation of a principle which is none other than that of the glorious existence of a nation raised to the value of a divine force. . . . Incarnated in the person of the chief (in Germany, the properly religious term, prophet, has sometimes been used), the nation thus plays the same role that Allah, incarnated in the person of Mahomet or the Khalif, plays for Islam."[144] Like Islam, fascism is therefore a supreme force for concentration. Yet, differently from Islam, it is not an abstract or absolute concentration; rather it is produced by and in turn productive of the state—*its* state. For this reason, fascism is political theology brought to the level of the state: it is a *state* theology.[145]

It is from this anti–political-theological perspective that Bataille plays Nietzsche—the proliferation and dispossession that Nietzschean experience represents—against fascism's "monocephalic" nature:

> Democracy rests on a neutralization of relatively free and weak antagonisms; it excludes all explosive condensation. Monocephalic society is the result of the free play of the natural laws of man, but it is always a secondary formation, it represents a crushing atrophy and sterility of existence.
>
> The only society full of life and force, the only free society, *is the bi- or poly-cephalic* society that gives the fundamental antagonisms of life a constant explosive outlet, but one limited to the richest forms.
>
> The duality or multiplicity of heads tends to achieve in the same movement the *acephalic* character of existence, because the very principle of the head is the reduction to unity, the *reduction* of the world to God.[146]

These passages are particularly important because they mark one of the most significant moments in Bataille's transition from a political to an impolitical dimension.[147] The common polemic target, in both idioms, is the *reductio ad unum* of fascist political theology. Yet Bataille's response to this monocephalic society seems to be to propose a structure that is bi- or polycephalic, and at the same time *acephalic* (meaning the elimination of the head altogether). The most peculiar thing is that this dual possibility—a political (polycephalic) possibility *or* an impolitical (acephalic) one—is in fact offered as a copresence. Thus the dissolution of the subject, in the acephalic case, is understood as the alternative to the political but also its extreme consequence. The political, for its part, is declared to be not merely insufficient to meet its own aim, but also contradictory to it—as demonstrated by the failure of all revolutions, which are "regularly followed by the reconstitution of the social structure and its head."[148] This is why it would be extremely reductive to interpret these pages of *Acéphale* as purely anarcho-libertarian. The head that must fall is not just that of the king-father, as in Freud's parable in *Totem and Taboo* (though this must surely have been present in Bataille's imagination), but also, and above all, one's own. For this reason, as we have already seen in the cases of Broch, Canetti and Weil, the only possible line of flight from political monotheism is an impolitical one. What separates Bataille from these authors, however, is his elision (or veiling, perhaps) of the border between the political and the impolitical, which can be defined thus: pushed to the extreme limit—the severance of its own head, the *acephalic* condition—the impolitical rediscovers a political *configuration* and recognizes (or imagines) an originary point prior to its "break" with the political. Such a point remains thoroughly unrepresentable, but its unrepresentability itself can be represented. Certainly, it can be represented only in its radical unrelation to all modes of presence, but represented nonetheless.

This representation of the unrepresentable is what Bataille calls "community." It is no coincidence that community appears in Bataille's work (or assumes greater weight within it) precisely when that work's properly political dimension is exhausted and it opens, in a vertiginous deepening, to the impolitical reflection that is inherent in his work on Nietzsche. For Bataille, Nietzsche-Dionysus not only evokes community, it *is* a community: "My life with Nietzsche as a companion is a community. My book is this community."[149] In order to consider this community, we need to turn a final gaze on the dramatic break between Bataille and the other two directors of the Collège less than two years after its foundation (November 1937–June 1939). Bataille's disagreement with Leiris concerns not so much the nature of the sacred as its "use," which for Leiris oscillates between a subjective, autobiographical-narrative register, and a purely descriptive, taxonomic one, which classifies events according to criteria elaborated methodologically. Bataille's position, on the other hand—which gives a sense of why Leiris accused him of heterodoxy[150]—tends to move away ever further from the sociological notion of the sacred, becoming increasingly disposed to an existential sense of the term, even in the Collège years. The sacred, for Bataille, is existential in the literal sense that the sacred is what puts existence into play by inscribing it within the necessity of a death in common.[151] From this point of view, the conception of the sacred closest to Bataille's experience is that of Colette Peignot ("Laure"), who anchors the sacred to two related elements: "the notion of death," and "sharing with others."[152] These two elements are tightly intertwined in the sense that what is "shared with others," what creates community, is death.

This community constituted the primary object of the activity of the Collège. We could even say the Collège itself was the impossible community, the community destined to failure, that its members would attempt to think.[153] On this question, too, they did so in ever more divergent ways. Whereas the notion of the sacred distinguished Bataille from Leiris, it was the thought of community that radically separated him from Caillois. The two otherwise shared no shortage of affinities (as each would publicly acknowledge):[154] Above all, each attributed importance to instinctive, emotional, and irrational factors in sociopolitical behavior, which situated both authors in an eccentric position with regard to the traditional left-right oppositions of the political spectrum. It was also this factor that led each to an encounter with the theme of community as the only possible form in which the sacred could be reactivated in the era of its steady disappearance. Nonetheless, this same theme would cause their paths to diverge—more so, perhaps, than they themselves were aware. It is true that from the very beginning, like Bataille, Caillois understood the term community as antithetical to both "de facto communities (the fact being geographical or racial) that made up the fascist regimes, but also on the other hand, to what can be called de facto absences of any community, that is to say, democracies."[155] However, the conviction that the enemy must be fought on his own ground—a conviction also shared by Bataille—makes Caillois's conception of community at once elitist[156] and Unitarian. Accordingly, his catch-cry of not stopping at "profanation" but rather pushing to "make sacred" what is common[157] ends up in an invitation to "*sursocialization*"[158] that is directly opposed to Bataille's "acephalic."

Whereas the acephalic is defined on the basis of the lack that it brings into being, the constitution of Caillois's elective community appears as strong, substantial, and unitary. So much so that it can be compared with the Society of Jesus, which is to say, an active monastic order, or even a paramilitary unit of "determined and lucid" men.[159] What is critical here is not only that this community is a unitary elite, but also that it is marked by a fundamental activism. Indeed, the "aggressiveness" that "lies in the will to boundless expansion that is inherent in any idea clearly grasped by the intellect"[160] will, in *Le mythe et l'homme*, become something concrete—through the call to an "orthodoxy . . . clothed with an imperative attraction and . . . instantly capable of mobilizing it"[161]—thus signaling Caillois's transition from the level of "observation" to that of "decision," from the "indicative" level to the "imperative," from "conception" to "execution."[162] As is suggested by the appearance of the term "mobilization" (along with certain other factors), here we are not far from the active nihilism of the early Jünger,[163] which Caillois absorbed through the influence of Sorel[164] and the teachings of Dumézil.[165] As a whole, his polemic against the left[166] (which, incapable of wresting Varuna away from the right, aligns itself ever more with Mitra), tends to develop not only a more realistic account of power, in which it is not legality that founds power but power that creates legality, but even a vague apologia for power. It is thus unsurprising that Caillois's debate with Bataille would erupt on the question of the will to power, and its opposition to the "will to tragedy": "In other words"—this is Bataille speaking; in place of Caillois, but *against* him—"*power* is what escapes the tragedy required by the 'overall movement' animating human community—but it escapes tragedy specifically by diverting the forces requiring it to its own benefit."[167]

These words enable us to bring Bataille's new position on power into focus. He is not in principle hostile to power, but he is radically averse to any power that would function to the detriment of a communitarian energy—which is to say, nihilistically. Against this "active" sense of power, Bataille responds with the "passive" power of tragedy; understood as a passion, or suffering, that puts existences "in common" on the basis of what it unceasingly takes away from them. This is what enables him to distinguish between communities that are "formed to act" and those "formed to exist."[168] In this regard, Caillois's distance and difference from Bataille is clearly expressed in this passage from *The Winter Wind*:

Just as there exists a primitive, irreducible experience of *self* constituting the basic dynamic of anarchic individualism, the same sort of existential, inalienable basis of collective effort must be brought to light. In no case can the latter take for its affective foundation some given that is entirely retrospective, such as something decisive in a de facto manner—race or language, historical territory or tradition, on which the existence of nations depends and which feeds patriotism. . . . A social nucleus of the kind in question must be based on elements of an entirely different nature. A common will to carry out the same work already implies the elective affinities that alone are able to direct the aggregation of a community.[169]

Bataille's conception of community is formed in direct opposition to this model. For Caillois it is the "common will to carry out the same work" that connects the individual experience of the self to an enterprise "in common" (not to use the semantically overloaded term "communitarian"). Bataille, on the other hand, denies the community any parallel with the sphere of the individual precisely because of its *absence of task*. It is this absence—according to Jean-Luc Nancy, who has written the most philosophically convincing work on this theme[170]—that situates the experience of community at an equal distance from both the individualist and communist traditions. As we know, Bataille considered communism to be not only the most important political experience of his time, but also the only one capable of definitively "concluding" it. It is this "finality" that makes communism, for Bataille, the sign of an entropic rationality that subjects not only life, but also life's transcendence in death, to a principle of equivalence. From this point of view, then, communism signals the death of death: that is, the end of the effective alterity of death, given that life is rendered wholly immanent to itself.[171]

This life's immanence is absolute. (In fact, the Absolute, as that which has no relations beyond itself, with what is outside of it, is immanence *as such*.) It is the result of a (humanist) conception of man as the producer of his own essence in the form of his work, and of society itself as the common work of man. Such a *productive* humanism marks the culture of the individual (an atom containing the reason and meaning of its own existence, thus giving rise to inalienable rights), as well as the communitarian tradition (in both of its versions: the premodern *Gemeinschaft*, and the rational community of post-Enlightenment and post-Kantian ends—for example, in Habermas).[172] In each of these cases, the community that is nostalgically longed for—be it in the past or in the future—is the immanent community of absolute presence to itself; a closed cosmos in which any member can identify with any other through everyone's common identification with the community. It is this identification—or the immanent completeness that it induces—that shields its members from what would otherwise erode their individual "absoluteness": their mortal finitude. Death does not perturb humanist man (whether individualist or communist) because he is already dead: dead to the possibility of his transcendence, and, at the same time, excluded from death by his belonging to an organism that cannot die as such.

Contrary to this tradition, whose various strands are united by their exorcism of death (and, correspondingly, their absolutization of work), Bataille's *communauté de coeur* is above all a community *of* death: "Seeing his fellow man die, the living can no longer subsist except *outside himself*. . . . Each of us is from then on crushed by the tightness of his persona and loses himself as much as he can in the community of his kind. This is why the life in common must be lived *at the level of death*. The destiny of a great number of private lives is smallness. But a community can only endure at the level of intensity of death; it decomposes when it lacks the particular grandeur of danger."[173] For Bataille, it is death that liberates the community from its immanence to itself; but in a way that is entirely unlike traditional transcendence (which requires an external higher being). The community does not transcend its members through a collective hypostasis that redeems their finitude through its immortality. On the contrary, a community is the means by which that finitude can become constitutive of the beings who, in their difference, compose it. They compose a community not through a bond (as Caillois had intended), but through an *alterity in common*, an alterity that is *shared*. As such, what is shared is not a presence, but an absence of being, in the sense that my lack can be empowered only by a lack in the other (the other *as* lack):[174] "The beyond of my being is first of all nothingness. This is the absence I discern in laceration and in painful feelings of lack: it reveals the presence of another person. Such a presence, however, is fully disclosed only when the other similarly leans over the edge of nothingness or falls into it (dies). 'Communication' only takes place between two people who risk themselves, each lacerated and suspended, perched atop a common nothingness."[175]

This reasoning makes plain why the Bataillian community is opposed to any theory of intersubjectivity. In order to be intersubjective, a community—or even simply the communicative sphere, any multiple or dual relation—must bind its subjects in a way that excludes the "other" in principle. For Bataille, on the other hand, as we have seen, it is exactly the presence of the other—the presence, that is, of absence, difference, distinction—that creates community. The formation of intersubjectivity, moreover, requires the presence of subjects: subjects who are present to each other, but even before that, present to themselves. Yet, the condition of community is the rupture of subjective identity (the *ipse*, but also the *alter ego*). It is not formed by a series of subjects, but by those subjects' exposure to the loss of subjectivity. What is shared is precisely the loss that turns the subject—with its inevitably appropriative intention—into simple existence. Community is, therefore, an existence in which finitude is shared—*partagée*. Or we could even say: a *partage* of existences. If there is a subject of community (in the sense of an *origin* for community), it is *partage*: the exposure-appearance [*l'exposition-comparition*] that is the destiny of any being withdrawn from presence. "'Communication' cannot proceed from one full and intact individual to another. It requires individuals whose separate existence in themselves is risked, placed at the limit of death and nothingness; the moral pinnacle is a moment of risk taking, it is a being suspended beyond oneself, at the limit of nothingness."[176]

Seen from this point of view, it could be said that community is not exactly the opposition between self and other, so much as the achievement of making the two come to overlap. The other *is* the self, once its identity as a subject is shared [*partagé*]. Or it is the "self's" transcendence of itself: not an external transcendence, but immanence's resistance to itself—*immanence's* transcendence. This interiorization of alterity is what makes intersubjectivity impossible, along with any notion whatsoever of recognition or representation. We have already seen how death is the specific place [*luogo*] of community, but we can be more precise about this: what precipitates community is the relation between the death of the other and the possibility of one's own death. This relation, however, does not take the form of "recognition"—not only because what is sought in the other is not their (or one's own) identity, but their (or one's own) fracture, but also because there is nothing recognizable in the death of another. Death is rather precisely the Unrecognizable; it cannot be made into a knowledge [*conoscenza*] of the self and of others. Death belongs only to the individual (or perhaps the individual belongs only to death), in the sense that it is a *part* of him that cannot be divided up among others. And yet, community is precisely this dividing up. It is a kind of dividing up, though, that does not identify parts or draw them together; rather, it infinitely distances them. I cannot recognize myself in the death of the other that associates [*accomuna*] me with him (in withdrawing me from his presence), this much is clear. Yet neither can that other: The other who dies is no more capable of affirming or appropriating his own death; in fact, he dies within exactly this impossibility, within his unbridgeable distance from his own death. He dies within the impossibility of dying consciously, of living the moment of his own death. It is this impossibility, therefore, this solitude—the solitude of what is most "proper" to him, the *definitive* "proper"—and not death in itself, that is shared by a community. Community is therefore the sharing of the impossibility of dying one's *own* death. This is why community is, in a specific sense, impossible. It is thus always an impossible community—the community of impossible commonality. Nothing about this community is representable (not even its distance, its *being* distance); neither can it be made present. If this were not so, and something about this community were representable, if the community conceded a single one of its parts to representation, it would disappear (into absolute immanence or absolute transcendence). In this sense, community is truly the extreme figure of the impolitical: uncommunicable, and irreducible to a common *place*.

Bataille, however, does not content himself with this fact. His entire work seems to strain toward the violation of what is prohibited, which is its only possible criterion of success. It thus seeks to communicate this commonality that cannot be communicated, to represent the unrepresentable. Or we could say that Bataille tries to deny identity *even to the impolitical*, by subjecting it to the internal process of transcendence that forces it to overturn at its own threshold and return to its *own* difference (its difference from itself). Thus Bataille's own idea of community is excluded from any attempt at "definition"—given the fixity and absoluteness that that would involve. It is as if the impolitical were pushed beyond itself by the restlessness of its own negative. However, this "beyond" refers not to whatever lies past its outer borders, but rather the penetration by those borders of its internal void, opening the impolitical to a sovereign *affirmation*.[177] Such an affirmation is not the result of a crisis of the negative, or its weakening, but is a consequence of its absolute radicality. The affirmation *is* that radical negativity. "Affirmation and the passion of negative thought," reads the title of a text on Bataille, in which Blanchot names this power-passion, this "*nonpower that is not simply the negation of power*":[178] "For thought, the limit-experience represents something *like* a new origin. What it offers to thought is the essential gift, the prodigality of affirmation; an affirmation, for the first time, that is not a product (the result of a double negation), and that thereby escapes all the movements, oppositions and reversals of dialectical reason, which, having completed itself before this affirmation, can no longer reserve a role for it under its reign. This event is hard to circumscribe. The interior experience affirms; it is pure affirmation and it does nothing but affirm. It does not even affirm itself, for then it would be subordinate to itself: it rather affirms affirmation."[179]

This affirmation that "affirms more than can be affirmed," this "more" that affirms "only by an excess of affirmation," or that affirms "without anything being affirmed" (in the end "finally affirming nothing"),[180] is for Bataille the destiny (*not* the task) of community. There is a text by Bataille—entrusted to the pages of *Acéphale*—that has the force to conclude this chapter, and this book. It expresses both the foundering of representation, and, at the same time, the representation of that foundering. The text is "the performance [*répresentation*] of *Numantia*," which discusses Cervantes's play about the "merciless war carried out by the Roman general Scipio against the Numantines in revolt who, besieged and exhausted, kill each other rather than surrender."[181] The unrepresentable object of representation is therefore the decision for a death in common; a community that is *decided* in death. In two ways, this decision is situated at the limit—and thus at the origin—of the impolitical. First, in the sense of an opposition between the city, the *civitas*, of the political (Rome), and what that city leaves at its margins, destroying and unrealizing what it cannot allow to remain, except in the night time of presence: "Just as the Romans, commanded by the implacable authority of a leader, as associated with the glory of the sun, in the same way the Numantines, WITHOUT A LEADER, WITHOUT A HEAD, are located in the region of the Night and of the Earth, in the region haunted by the phantoms of the Tragedy-Mother."[182] The tragedy at Numantia is opaque to Rome's sun. But this opacity—this absence of light—is itself the "image," the "expression," the affirmation of a blinding "everything": "and insofar as agony and death have entered the city, this city becomes the image of everything in this world that can demand a total love; insofar as this city dies, all the nostalgia for the lost world can now be expressed by the single name, NUMANTIA."[183] The fact that that world is lost, that its only connection is to the unreality of a pure *name*, vindicates the restless negativity "without use" of the impolitical. This lost world is the void [*nulla*] of the political; the empty, devastated space within which the impolitical's negativity is thrown into sharp relief.

All of this addresses only the first side of the question, the fact of death, and not yet that death's being "in *common*." This commonality, more than death itself, is the impossible object of representation:

> The tragedy of Numantia is great because in it one is confronted not only with the death of a certain number of men, but with the entry of death into the entire city: it is not individuals who are dying, but an entire people. That must be disconcerting, and in principle it must make *Numantia* inaccessible, because the game destiny plays with men can only appear to most of them clothed in the brilliant colors of individual existence. Moreover, what is currently in the air—if one is speaking of collective existence—is the poorest thing one can imagine, and no representation can be more disconcerting than one that presents death as the fundamental object of the *communal* activity of men, death and not food or the production of the means of production.[184]

The most unrepresentable aspect of the *réprésentation* of Numantia is the commonality—and for that reason, despite all evidence to the contrary, the *politicality*—of its impoliticality. Indeed, the "passion" that its performance generated, on the scorched earth of another death in common, was a "political" passion: "*Numantia*, in fact, took on for those present at the spectacle a meaning that had to do neither with individual drama nor with national feeling, but with political passion. This was made possible by the war in Spain. That is an obvious paradox, and it is possible that such a confusion is as lacking in importance as the confusion of the inhabitants of Saragossa, who presented the tragedy during a siege. *Numantia*, today, has been performed not only in Paris, but in Spain, in burned-out churches, without any other decor than the traces of the fire, and without any other actors than red militiamen."[185] The *mark* left by the impolitical tragedy of Numantia (the tragedy of the impolitical) is a political one, just as the destiny of its political passion is impolitical. How, wonders Bataille at the conclusion of his text, can we conceive of this unknowable nexus, this identity *of* differences? How can we listen with a political ear to what lies outside of all political opposition, outside of the political, outside of any conflict between opposing *parties*? The answer—which is, in reality, a question—depends on the existence of a thought that is capable of taking "what is generally accepted in the opposite way":

> Nevertheless, a reality exists which, behind this facade, is in contact with the most powerful secrets of existence; anyone who wants to enter this reality need only take in the opposite way what is generally accepted. If the image of *Numantia* expresses the grandeur of a people struggling against oppression by the powerful, it reveals at the same time that the struggle currently engaged in most often lacks any grandeur: the antifascist movement, if it is compared to *Numantia*, appears to be an empty mob, a vast decomposition of men linked only by what they refuse.[186]

Beyond this refusal, a space for *affirmation* opens. It is uninhabited; indeed, it is uninhabitable. But bound to this affirmation as if by an invisible thread, bound to its extreme "Yes," there is another affirmation—albeit one that the impolitical cannot yet make: "There is only illusion and comfort in admiring *Numantia* because one sees in it an expression of the current struggle. But tragedy confronts the world of politics with an evident truth: the battle joined will only take on a meaning and will only be effective to the extent that fascist wretchedness comes face to face with something other than troubled negation—namely, the heartfelt community of which *Numantia* is the image."[187]

NOTES

PREFACE TO THE ITALIAN EDITION OF 1999

1. Massimo Cacciari, "L'impolitico nietzscheano," in *Il libro del filosofo*, ed. Marina Beer and Maurizio Ciampa (Rome: Savelli, 1978), 104–120.

2. Some useful considerations on the nature of Mann's "unpolitical" are set out in Loretta Monti, "Thomas Mann e le 'Categorie dell'impolitico' di Roberto Esposito," *Filosofia Politica* 13, no. 1 (1999): 143–158.

3. For an essential reference on the category of the impolitical, albeit by an author apparently distant from its semantic idiom, see the particularly good essay by Silvana Borutti, "Wittgenstein impolitico?" in *Wittgenstein politico* (Milan: Feltrinelli, 2000), 127–152.

4. It seems to me that notwithstanding its attempt to clarify the term, Julien Freund's *Politique et impolitique* (Paris: Sirey, 1987) adds to the confusion over the meaning of the impolitical.

5. From a wide range of possible examples, I refer to Eugenio Scalfari's editorial "Poteri forti, idee deboli," *La Repubblica*, July 21, 1996. Scalfari returns to the argument, from a different perspective, in a longer article also published in *La Repubblica* on April 23, 1997, on the Adelphi edition of Mann's *Reflections of a Nonpolitical Man.*

6. See Roberto Esposito, "Poesia e comunità in René Char," *Micromega* 2 (1998): 13–27.

7. See Dolf Sternberger, *Drei Wurzeln der Politik* (Frankfurt: Insel Verlag, 1978), particularly at 310. Sternberger's text thematizes the genesis of the impolitical, but without clearly distinguishing it from the antipolitical.

8. Thomas Mann, *Reflections of a Nonpolitical Man*, trans. Walter D. Morris (New York: F. Ungar, 1983), 303.

9. See the timely reconstruction by Pier Paolo Portinaro in "Antipolitica o fine della politica?" *Teoria Politica* 4, no. 1 (1998): 121–137.

10. For example, Hella Mandt, "Antipolitik," *Zeitschrift für Politik* 34, no. 4 (1987): 383–395.

11. As is the case for György Konrád, *Antipolitik: Mitteleuropäische Meditationen* (Frankfurt: Suhrkamp, 1985).

12. I borrow here the expression coined by Alessandro Pizzorno, *Le radici della politica assoluta e altri saggi* (Milan: Feltrinelli, 1993).

13. On this point, see the observations made by Giuseppe Cantarano, who conveniently frames the genesis and development of impolitical thought within the Italian philosophical debate at large. Giuseppe Cantarano, *Immagini del nulla: La filosofia italiana contemporanea* (Milan: Mondadori, 1998), in particular 159.

14. In this regard, see Jean-Luc Nancy, *A Finite Thinking*, ed. Simon Sparks (Stanford: Stanford University Press, 2003) and Roberto Esposito, "La 'fine della politica,'" *Micromega* 1 (1994): 147–164.

15. A "gnostic" reading of the impolitical as "negative political theology" can be found in Franco Cassano, "Le regole dell'impolitico," *Rinascita* (May 27, 1989), 16–17; and, in a different way, in Alessandro Dal Lago, "La forza dell'impolitico," *L'Unità* (January 7, 1989), 17.

16. On the anti-political-theological character of the impolitical, see also Francesco Garritano, "L'impolitico," in Francesco Garritano, *Questioni di legge: Valore ed etica in Pierre Klossowski* (Milan: Jaca Book, 1996).

17. See Eric Voegelin, "The Political Religions," in *Modernity without Restraint* (Columbia: University of Missouri Press, 2000), 19–74.

18. I am referring to Peterson's *Monotheism as a Political Problem*, in Erik Peterson, *Theological Tractates*, trans. Michael J. Hollerich (Stanford: Stanford University Press, 2011).

19. For this reading of Schmitt's political theology, see Carlo Galli's indispensable book *Genealogia della politica: Carl Schmitt a la crisi del pensiero politico moderno* (Bologna: Il Mulino, 1996), in particular at 333.

20. Jacob Taubes, *The Political Theology of Paul*, trans. Dana Hollander (Stanford: Stanford University Press, 2004).

21. For similar interpretations of Barth and Bonhoeffer, see Roberto Esposito, *Nove pensieri sulla politica* (Bologna: Il Mulino, 1993), 78–83 and 137–157.

22. On this difference between impolitical registers, see my introduction to Roberto Esposito, ed., *Oltre la politica: Antologia del pensiero "impolitico"* (Milan: Mondadori, 1996), 1–26.

23. See Massimo Cacciari and Roberto Esposito, "Politica e pensiero," *Leggere* 7 (1988), 14–19.

24. Ibid., 19.

25. Carlo Galli, "Review of *Nove pensieri sulla politica* by Roberto Esposito," *Filosofia Politica* 1 (1994), 154–156.

26. Biagio de Giovanni, "Politica e filosofia," *Rivista di Filosofia* 88, no. 1 (1997): 59–78, at 59. De Giovanni had already made a critical intervention on the question of the impolitical in "Il colore della disperazione," *Micromega* 2 (1989): 231–237.

27. De Giovanni, *Politica e filosofia*, 59–78, at 66.

28. In this regard, see Fabrizio di Stefano, "Review of *Oltre la politica: Antologia del pensiero 'impolitico,'* ed. Roberto Esposito," *Filosofia Politica* 11, no. 1 (1997): 143–146.

29. An original proposition of the *Begriffsgeschichte* is formulated in Giuseppe Duso, "Storia concettuale come filosofia politica," *Filosofia Politica* 11, no. 3 (1997): 393–426.

30. The reference is to Reiner Schürmann, *Heidegger on Being and Acting: From Principles to Anarchy*, trans. Christine-Marie Gros (Bloomington: Indiana University Press, 1987); and Reiner Schürmann, *Broken Hegemonies*, trans. Reginald Lilley (Bloomington: Indiana University Press, 2003).

31. This is the still-current core of Gerhard Ritter's 1948 book *Die Dämonie der Macht*, published in English as *The Corrupting Influence of Power* (Hadleigh: Tower Bridge Publications, 1952).

32. Massimo Cacciari rightly argues this in *Dell'inizio* (Milan: Adelphi, 1990), especially at 408.

33. For this interpretation of Weil, and more generally on the problem of the origin, I refer to my own book *L'origine della politica: Hannah Arendt o Simone Weil?* (Rome: Donzelli, 1996).

34. [The Italian word *ritratto* also means "portrait," and in this passage Esposito thus foregrounds a paradox of visibility and invisibility, presence and absence.]

35. I allude to Philippe Lacoue-Labarthe and Jean-Luc Nancy, eds., *Le retrait du politique* (Paris: Galilée, 1983).

36. "L'impolitico," in Collettivo 33, *Per l'emancipazione: Critica della normalità* (Naples: Cronopio, 1997), 23–26, at 24.

37. Ibid., 25.

38. Roberto Esposito, *Communitas: The Origin and Destiny of Community*, trans. Timothy Campbell (Stanford: Stanford University Press, 2010).

39. Beginning with the foundational text by Jean-Luc Nancy, *The Inoperative Community*, trans. Peter Connor, Lisa Garbus, Michael Holland, and Simona Sawhney (Minneapolis: University of Minnesota Press, 1991).

40. Jacques Derrida, *Politics of Friendship*, trans. George Collins (London: Verso, 1997).

41. The first five issues of *Acéphale* (1936–39), the review founded by Bataille, were published in Italian as *La congiura sacra* with an introduction by Roberto Esposito and a dossier of unpublished texts compiled by Marina Galletti. Georges Bataille, *La congiura sacra*, trans. Fabrizio Di Stefano and Riccardo Garbetta (Turin: Bollati Boringhieri, 1997).

42. Maurizio Ferraris, "Il filosofo desidera morire? Dall'impolitico all'altro che è in noi," *Aut Aut* 231 (1989): 87–98, at 91.

43. Ibid., 92.

44. This is precisely the theme, and the task, of *Communitas: The Origin and Destiny of Community.*

INTRODUCTION: AN IMPOLITICAL DEPARTURE

1. Erik Peterson, *Theological Tractates*, trans. Michael J. Hollerich (Stanford: Stanford University Press, 2011), 69.

2. [In addition to the two English senses of the word "terms" that are relevant here (the vocabulary of the political lexicon, and the conditions of an accord), the Italian word *termini* implies spatial and temporal endpoints more strongly than does its English equivalent.]

3. [Esposito's punctuation of the Italian word for sharing [*condivisione*] draws attention to an internal contrast and connection between its elements, *con* (with) and *divisione* (dividing or splitting), thus emphasizing sharing as sharing-*with*.]

1. AT THE LIMITS OF THE POLITICAL

1. Romano Guardini, *The Lord*, trans. Elinor Castendyk Briefs (South Bend, Ind.: Gateway Editions, 1954), 175, 206.

2. Rudolf Bultmann, *Das Verhältnis der Urchristlichen Christusbotschaft zum Historischen Jesus* (Heidelberg: C. Winter, 1960), republished in Rudolf Bultmann, *Exegetica* (Tübingen: Mohr, 1967), 445–469, 452–453.

3. Romano Guardini, *The Humanity of Christ: Contributions to a Psychology of Jesus*, trans. Ronald Walls (London: Burns & Oates, 1964), 38.

4. Karl Adam, *The Christ of Faith: The Christology of the Church*, trans. Joyce Crick (New York: New American Library, 1957).

5. Hans Urs von Balthasar, *Romano Guardini: Reform from the Source*, trans. Albert K. Wimmer and D. C. Schindler (San Francisco: Ignatius Press, 2010), 95.

6. Guardini, *The Lord*, 212.

7. Ibid., 211.

8. Cf. Romano Guardini, *Unterscheidung des Christlichen: Gesammelte Studien, 1923–1963*, ed. Hans Waltmann (Mainz: Matthias-Grünewald-Verlag, 1963), 334–335.

9. Romano Guardini, *Religiöse Gestalten in Dostojewskis Werk* (Leipzig: Hegner, 1939), 164, 162.

10. Ibid.

11. *Renouveau* is Tommissen's expression. Piet Tommissen, "Carl Schmitt e il 'Renouveau' cattolico nella Germania degli anni venti," *Storia e Politica* 14, no. 4 (1975): 481–500. See Wust's "Die Rückkehr aus dem Exil," *Kölnische Volkszeitung* (May 1924),

collected in Peter Wust, *Gestalten und Gedanken/Die Rückkehr aus dem Exil* (Münster: Regensberg, 1965).

12. Peter Lippert, *Vom Gesetz und von der Liebe* (Munich: Verlag "Ars sacra," J. Müller, 1932); Theodor Haecker, *Wahrheit und Leben: Ein Vortrag* (Hellerau: Hegner, 1930).

13. I allude here to Friedrich Wilhelm Förster, *Autorität und Freiheit: Betrachtungen zum Kulturproblem der Kirche* (Munich: J. Kösel, 1910).

14. Max Bondy, "Jugendbewegung und Katholizismus," *Die Schildgenossen* 2, no. 1 (1921): 44–56.

15. Romano Guardini, "Katholische Religion und Jugendbewegung," *Die Schildgenossen* 2, no. 2 (1921): 96–110, 97.

16. Romano Guardini, *Sorge um den Menschen* (Würzburg: Werkbund Verlag, 1962), 88.

17. Ibid., 91.

18. Ibid., 93.

19. Ibid., 94.

20. Ibid., 94–95.

21. Herman Hefele, *Der Katholizismus in Deutschland* (Darmstadt: O. Reichl, 1919); Hermann Platz, *Geistige Kämpfe im Modernen Frankreich* (Munich: J. Kösel & F. Pustet, 1922); Ildefons Herwegen, *Kirche und Seele: Die Seelenhaltung des Mysterienkultes und ihr Wandel im Mittelalter* (Münster in Westfal: Aschendorff, 1928).

22. Georg Moenius, *Italienische Reise* (Freiburg im Breisgau: Herder, 1925).

23. See Georg Moenius's introduction to Henri Massis, *Verteidigung des Abendlandes*, trans. Georg Moenius (Hellerau: Jakob Hegner, 1930), 11–12.

24. Johann Peter Steffes, *Die Staatsauffassung der Moderne: Auf der Grundlage der Kulturphilosophischen Zeitidee* (Freiburg: Herder, 1925), 4–5. "Every life, and above all the free life of the spirit, requires formation and education in order to preserve and develop itself. This can be achieved only with the purposeful arrangement of all the basic elements making up the content and matter of life. These, however, are in no sense to be found only within the subject, within the living being. Life, in fact—even in its lowest manifestations, vegetable and sensate—consists in an exchange of forces occurring between subject and object, between the living being and the environment. Life preserves itself through a process of give and take; as long as it remains within the currents of life as a whole, in the conditions correct for its species. Every life is presented, so to speak, as a sum of universal and particular forces. Only in the grand nexus of total life can there be a single life. Division, separation are not life; they are death."

25. Massis, *Verteidigung des Abendlandes*, 37.

26. Herman Hefele, "Die Römische Wirklichkeit," in *Wiederbegegnung von Kirche und Kultur in Deutschland*, ed. Max Ettlinger, Philipp Funk, and Friedrich Fuchs

(Munich: Kösel & Pustet, 1927), 195–206; Massis, *Verteidigung des Abendlandes*, 18. Moenius refers directly to the opening words of Schmitt's book: "There is an anti-Roman temper that has nourished the struggle against popery, Jesuitism and clericalism with a host of religious and political forces, that has impelled European history for centuries." Carl Schmitt, *Roman Catholicism and Political Form*, trans. G. L. Ulmen (Westport, Conn.: Greenwood Press, 1996).

27. Ibid., 32, 3.

28. Ibid., 7.

29. Ibid., 11.

30. Ibid., 18–19.

31. See Carl Schmitt, *Political Theology: Four Chapters on the Concept of Sovereignty*, trans. George Schwab (Cambridge, Mass.: MIT Press, 1985).

32. Schmitt, *Roman Catholicism and Political Form*, 17.

33. Romano Guardini, "Vom Wesen Katholischer Weltanschauung," now in Guardini, *Unterscheidung des Christlichen*, 13–33.

34. Romano Guardini, *Letters from Lake Como: Explorations in Technology and the Human Race*, trans. Geoffrey William Bromiley (Grand Rapids, Mich.: W. B. Eerdmans, 1994), 10 (second letter). "Carl Schmitt in his brilliant book on romantic Catholicism (I read it on the journey here) has rightly seen that the longing for untouched nature is itself a product of culture originating in the over-artificiality of existence."

35. Guardini, *Unterscheidung des Christlichen*, 14, 19.

36. Guardini, *The Lord*, 156.

37. Guardini, *Unterscheidung des Christlichen*, 23–24.

38. Ibid., 24.

39. Ibid., 31.

40. Ibid., 30.

41. See, e.g., Adolf von Harnack, *Die Aufgabe der Theologischen Facultäten und die Allgemeine Religionsgeschichte* (Giessen: T. Ricker, 1901); Peter Lippert, *Die Weltanschauung des Katholizismus* (Leipzig: Verlag Emmanuel Reinicke, 1927); Friedrich Heiler, *Der Katholizismus: Seine Idee und Seine Erscheinung* (Munich: E. Reinhardt, 1923); Karl Adam, *The Spirit of Catholicism*, trans. Dom Justin McCann (London: Sheed & Ward, 1969).

42. The idea that Roman Catholicism is characterized by its directionality "from on high" is also underlined by Erich Przywara, "Römische Katholizität—all-Christliche Ökumenizität," in *Gott in Welt. Festgabe für K. Rahner*, ed. Johannes Baptist Metz et al. (Freiburg: Herder, 1964), 524–528.

43. Guardini, *Unterscheidung des Christlichen*, 31.

44. Ibid.

45. Romano Guardini, *Der Gegensatz: Versuche zu einer Philosophie des Lebendig Konkreten* (Mainz: Matthias-Grünewald-Verlag, 1955). The theoretical nucleus

for this work was already contained in Romano Guardini, *Gegensatz und Gegensätze: Entwurf Eines Systems der Typenlehre* (Freiburg: Caritas-Dr., 1914).

46. Emmanuel Mounier's "Contraires et contradictoires ou de la discorde" is a 1929 text.

47. In order to understand the intensity of Przywara's rapport with Guardini, it is enough to note the continual reference to his work in both volumes of *Ringen der Gegenwart: Gesammelte Aufsätze 1922–1927* (Augsburg: B. Filser-Verlag, 1929).

48. Adam, *The Christ of Faith: The Christology of the Church.*

49. I allude to Paul Roubiczek, *Thinking in Opposites: An Investigation of the Nature of Man as Revealed by the Nature of Thinking* (Boston: Beacon Press, 1952).

50. Unlike Barth, Emil Brunner does not give these oppositional dialectics the sense of an absolute antithesis, but rather that of a correlation, which gives rise to the "bipolar" titles of many of his works: see Emil Brunner and Karl Barth, *Natural Theology: Comprising "Nature and Grace" by Emil Brunner and the Reply "no!" by Karl Barth*, trans. Peter Fraenkel (Eugene, Ore.: Wipf and Stock, 2002); Emil Brunner, *Revelation and Reason: The Christian Doctrine of Faith and Knowledge*, trans. Olive Wyon (Philadelphia: Westminster Press, 1946); Emil Brunner, *God and Man: Four Essays on the Nature of Personality*, trans. David Cairns (London: Student Christian Movement Press, 1936); Emil Brunner, *Philosophie und Offenbarung* (Tübingen: J. C. B. Mohr, 1925).

51. In Tillich, too, the opposing poles always have a point of encounter. See Paul Tillich, *Systematic Theology* (Chicago: University of Chicago Press, 1951). From volume 1, see in particular 60–66, 168–204; and in volume 2, 13–16, 19ff.

52. Carl Schmitt, *Political Romanticism*, trans. Guy Oakes (Cambridge, Mass.: MIT Press, 1986), 75ff.

53. Guardini, *Der Gegensatz*, 127.

54. Ibid., 240.

55. Among those who assigned a relevant role to Catholicism in Schmitt's formation, see George Schwab, *The Challenge of the Exception: An Introduction to the Political Ideas of Carl Schmitt between 1921 and 1936* (New York: Greenwood Press, 1989). Schwab traces Schmitt's anti-Semitism in the years of the regime to its Catholic roots.

56. Schmitt, *Roman Catholicism and Political Form*, 26.

57. Ibid., 25.

58. Ibid., 21.

59. A point helpfully underlined by Carlo Galli in the introduction to the Italian edition of *Political Romanticism*. Carl Schmitt, *Romanticismo politico*, trans. Carlo Galli (Milan: Giuffrè, 1981).

60. Schmitt's "The Age of Neutralizations and Depoliticizations" (1929), trans. Matthias Konzen and John P. McCormick, in Carl Schmitt, *The Concept of the*

Political: Expanded Edition, trans. George Schwab (Chicago: University of Chicago Press, 2007).

61. Ibid., 94–95.

62. Romano Guardini, *The End of the Modern World*, trans. Joseph Theman, Herbert Burke, and Elinor Castendyk Briefs (Wilmington, Del.: ISI Books, 1998).

63. Ibid., 51.

64. Ibid., 59.

65. Ibid., 70.

66. Ibid., 63.

67. Guardini, *Letters from Lake Como*, 83 (ninth letter); Guardini, *Sorge um den Menschen*, 57.

68. Elinor C. Briefs's 1961 English translation of *Die Macht* is now in Guardini, *The End of the Modern World*. See also "Der unvollständige Mensch und die Macht" and "Das Phänomen der Macht" both in Guardini, *Sorge um den Menschen*.

69. Guardini, *The End of the Modern World*, 154.

70. The theme of the relation between technology and power arises frequently in the German Catholic culture of the time. Consider Friedrich Dessauer, *Philosophie der Technik: Das Problem der Realisierung* (Bonn: F. Cohen, 1927). See also Friedrich Dessauer, *Technische Kultur? Sechs Essays* (Munich: Kösel, 1908); and Friedrich Dessauer, *Streit um die Technik* (Frankfurt am Main: Knecht, 1956). Further, on the power-technology relation, or rather that between power, life, and technology, see also Eberhard Zschimmer, *Philosophie der Technik* (Berlin: E. S. Mittler, 1917); and above all Eberhard Zschimmer, *Technik und Idealismus* (Jena: Verl. der Jenaer Volksbuchhandlung, 1920), in argument with Jakob Schwadt.

71. Guardini, *The End of the Modern World*, 122.

72. Ibid., 131–148.

73. Ibid., 133.

74. Guardini, *Sorge um den Menschen*, 58.

75. Guardini, *The End of the Modern World*, 133.

76. Ibid., 91.

77. Ibid., 199.

78. Ibid., 184.

79. Guardini, *Letters from Lake Como*, 35 (fifth letter).

80. Guardini, *The End of the Modern World*, 200.

81. [The phrase Esposito cites, which appears at page 197 of the Italian translation of Guardini's *Das Ende der Neuzeit*, does not appear in the English translation.]

82. The relation of this theme of risk [*Wagnis*] or *insecuritas* to Wust's problematic is very clear. It is well known that for Wust, man's typical situation as an intermediate [*Zwischenwesen*] between the world of nature and that of the spirit necessarily exposes him to risk, which is to say, to continual decisions whose outcomes cannot be certain. In any case such a necessarily risky decision does not imply the absolute

voluntarism of irrationalism [*Entscheidungsirrazionalismus*], so much as the boldness of wisdom [*Wagnis der Weisheit*]. See in particular "Die 'Insecuritas humana' und das Wagnis des Entscheidungsirrationalismus" in Peter Wust, *Ungewissheit und Wagnis* (Salzburg: A. Pustet, 1937), 271–288.

83. Guardini, *The End of the Modern World*, 189.

84. Ibid.

85. Ibid., 201–202.

86. Carl Schmitt, *The Nomos of the Earth in the International Law of the Jus Publicum Europaeum*, trans. G. L. Ulmen (New York: Telos Press, 2003).

87. Guardini, *Sorge um den Menschen*, 268–269 (concerning the discussion entitled "Europe: Reality and Task" held after the conferral of the *Praemium erasmianum* in Brussels on April 28, 1962).

88. Jacques Maritain, *The Things That Are Not Caesar's: A Translation of Primauté du Spirituel*, trans. J. F. Scanlan (London: Sheed and Ward, 1932). As regards Europe, Maritain argues precisely against Belloc, that is, against the confusion of Latinity and Catholicism, or Occidentalism and Catholicism.

89. Henri Massis, *Defence of the West*, trans. F. S. Flint (New York: Harcourt, Brace & Co., 1928); the Belloc text to which Maritain refers is Hilaire Belloc, *Europe and the Faith* (New York: Paulist Press, 1920).

90. Karl Adam, *Two Essays by Karl Adam: Christ and the Western Mind; Love and Belief*, trans. Edward Bullough (New York: Macmillan, 1930).

91. I am thinking not only of Ildefons Herwegen's *Antike, Germanentum und Christentum: Drei Vorlesungen* (Salzburg: A. Pustet, 1932), but also of his *St. Benedict: A Character Study*, trans. P. Nugent (St. Louis: Herder Books, 1924).

92. Massis, *Verteidigung des Abendlandes*, 102–103.

93. Peter Wust, *Crisis in the West*, trans. E. I. Watkin (London: Sheed & Ward, 1931).

94. Romano Guardini, *Der Heilbringer in Mythos, Offenbarung und Politik* (Zürich: Thomas-Verl., 1946), in Guardini, *Unterscheidung des Christlichen*, 411–456.

95. Ibid., 426.

96. Ibid., 428–429.

97. Ibid., 430.

98. Ibid.

99. Ibid., 439.

100. Ibid., 440.

2. THE UNREPRESENTABLE POLIS

1. Eric Voegelin, "Review Essay of *Verfassungslehre*, by Carl Schmitt," in Eric Voegelin, *Selected Book Reviews*, ed. Barry Cooper, trans. Jodi Cockerill (Columbia: University of Missouri Press, 2001), 42–66. Voegelin also devoted a section of

a later book to a critical analysis of Schmitt's thesis ("Carl Schmitt's Concept of the Total State"), in Eric Voegelin, *The Authoritarian State: An Essay on the Problem of the Austrian State*, ed. Gilbert Weiss, trans. Ruth Hein (Columbia: University of Missouri Press, 1999), 58–63. Schmitt would respond in "The State as a Mechanism in Hobbes and Descartes," now the appendix to Carl Schmitt, *The Leviathan in the State Theory of Thomas Hobbes: Meaning and Failure of a Political Symbol*, trans. George Schwab and Erna Hilfstein (Chicago: University of Chicago Press, 2008).

2. Carl Schmitt, *Roman Catholicism and Political Form*, trans. G. L. Ulmen (Westport, Conn.: Greenwood Press, 1996), 3.

3. Ibid., 8.

4. Ibid., 17.

5. Ibid., 20.

6. Voegelin dwells on "noesis" in particular in Eric Voegelin, *Anamnesis: On the Theory of History and Politics*, ed. David Walsh, trans. G. Niemeyer and M. J. Hanak (Columbia: University of Missouri Press, 2002), especially 320–412.

7. See the first three chapters of Eric Voegelin, *The New Science of Politics: An Introduction* (Chicago: University of Chicago Press, 1987).

8. Voegelin, *Selected Book Reviews*, 55–56.

9. On the necessity of an anthropological presupposition for every theory of the state, see Eric Voegelin, *Race and State*, trans. Ruth Hein (Baton Rouge: Louisiana State University Press, 1997), especially 2.

10. Voegelin, *The New Science of Politics*, 69–70.

11. Voegelin, *Selected Book Reviews*, 52.

12. Ibid., 54.

13. See Carl Schmitt, *Constitutional Theory*, trans. Jeffrey Seitzer (Durham, N.C.: Duke University Press, 2008), 239–240: "In the reality of political life, a state can no more forego all structural elements of the principle of identity than one can forego all structural elements of representation. Even when the attempt is made to realize unconditionally an absolute identity, elements and methods of representation remain unavoidable, as on the contrary no representation without images of identity is possible. Both these possibilities, identity and representation, do not exclude one another. They are, rather, only two opposing orientation points for the concrete formation of the political unity. In every state, one or the other is stronger, yet both are part of the political existence of a people."

14. As regards Voegelin's reading of Hobbes, see above all Voegelin, *The New Science of Politics*, 152–161, 178–187. But Voegelin had already devoted a chapter of an earlier work to Hobbes: Eric Voegelin, *Political Religions*, trans. T. J. DiNapoli and E. S. Easterly (Lewiston, Maine: E. Mellen Press, 1986). Both are in Eric Voegelin, *Modernity without Restraint*, ed. Manfred Henningsen (Columbia: University of Missouri Press, 2000).

15. Voegelin, *The New Science of Politics*, 184.

16. Passages like this one leave open the opposite possibility: "The dialectic of the concept is that the invisible is presupposed as absent and nevertheless is simultaneously made present. That is not possible with just any type of being. Indeed, it presupposes a special type of being. Something dead, something inferior or valueless, something lowly cannot be represented. It lacks the enhanced type of being that is capable of an *existence*, of rising into the public being. . . . In representation, by contrast, a higher type of being comes into concrete appearance. The idea of representation rests on a people existing as a political unity, as having a type of being that is higher, further enhanced, and more intense in comparison to the natural existence of some human group living together. If the sense for this peculiarity of political existence erodes and people give priority to other types of existence, the understanding of a concept like representation is also displaced." Schmitt, *Constitutional Theory*, 243.

17. Voegelin's quotation is drawn from his review of *The Origins of Totalitarianism*: Eric Voegelin, "The Origins of Totalitarianism," *Review of Politics* 15, no. 1 (1953): 68–76, 75. This review was published together with Arendt's response and a final counterresponse by Voegelin. See Hannah Arendt, "[The Origins of Totalitarianism]: A Reply," *The Review of Politics* 15, no. 1 (1953): 76–84; Eric Voegelin, "[The Origins of Totalitarianism]: Concluding Remark," *The Review of Politics* 15, no. 1 (1953), 84–85. On the debate between the two, see Elisabeth Young-Bruehl, *Hannah Arendt: For Love of the World* (New Haven: Yale University Press, 1982), 253–55.

18. On this point I refer to my own essay and the bibliography it contains: Roberto Esposito, "Politica e tradizione: Ad Hannah Arendt," *Il Centauro* 13–14 (1985): 97–136.

19. Eric Voegelin, "The Origins of Totalitarianism," *The Review of Politics* 15, no. 1 (1953): 68–76, 74.

20. Ibid., 69.

21. Ibid.

22. Ibid., 75.

23. Arendt, "[*The Origins of Totalitarianism*]: A Reply," 76–84, 77.

24. Ibid., 80.

25. Ibid., 82.

26. Ibid.

27. Ibid.

28. "Configurations of History" in Eric Voegelin, *Published Essays, 1966–1985*, ed. Ellis Sandoz (Baton Rouge: Louisiana State University Press, 1990), 95–114, 96 [emphasis added].

29. See in this regard Eric Voegelin, *From Enlightenment to Revolution*, ed. John H. Hallowell (Durham, N.C.: Duke University Press, 1975), especially 74ff.

30. Carl Schmitt, *Hamlet or Hecuba: The Intrusion of the Time into the Play*, trans. David Pan and Jennifer R. Rust (New York: Telos Press, 2009).

31. See, in this regard, Voegelin's "Wisdom and the Magic of the Extreme," now in Voegelin, *Published Essays, 1966–1985*, 315–375.

32. Now in Voegelin, *Anamnesis*, 312–337, 327.

33. Ibid., 345–373.

34. Ibid., 354–355.

35. On Gnosis in Voegelin, see Gregor Sebba, "History, Modernity and Gnosticism," in *The Philosophy of Order: Essays on History, Consciousness, and Politics*, ed. Peter-Joachim Opitz, Gregor Sebba, and Eric Voegelin (Stuttgart: Klett-Cotta, 1981), 434–488.

36. I have addressed this theme at greater length in Esposito, *Politica e tradizione*, 97–136, 105–111. The most important of Voegelin's texts on this matter are "Ersatz Religion" and "Science, Politics and Gnosticism," both in Voegelin, *Modernity without Restraint*.

37. Voegelin, *The New Science of Politics*, 41.

38. See ibid., 102.

39. Ibid., 85.

40. Ibid., 88.

41. Ibid., 107.

42. Ibid., 182.

43. See Hannah Arendt, *The Human Condition* (Chicago: University of Chicago Press, 1998), 189, and *Between Past and Future: Eight Exercises in Political Thought* (New York: Penguin Books, 2006), 108.

44. On Arendt's reading of revolution, expressed not only in *On Revolution* but also in "Thoughts on Politics and Revolution" in Hannah Arendt, *Crises of the Republic* (New York: Harcourt Brace, 1972); as well as in Hannah Arendt, "Totalitarian Imperialism: Reflections on the Hungarian Revolution," *The Journal of Politics* 20, no. 1 (1958): 5–43; included only in the 1958 Meridian edition of *The Origins of Totalitarianism* (New York: Harcourt Brace Jovanovich, 1976).

45. Hannah Arendt, *On Revolution* (New York: Penguin Books, 2006), 24.

46. Ibid., 17.

47. See in this regard J. Miller, "The Pathos of Novelty: Hannah Arendt's Image of Freedom in the Modern World," in *Hannah Arendt: The Recovery of the Public World*, ed. Melvyn A. Hill (New York: St. Martin's Press, 1979), 177–208.

48. Arendt, *On Revolution*, 32.

49. Ibid., 141.

50. Ibid., 196.

51. Ibid., 205.

52. Ibid., 193.

53. The opposition between seeing and hearing runs though the entire first section ("Thinking") of Hannah Arendt, *The Life of the Mind* (San Diego: Harcourt, 1981); see, for example, 111. As is well known, however, the argument about the Jew-

ish proscription of the image is anything but a given, historiographically speaking. For example, limiting ourselves to a reference directly concerning Arendt, it was contested by Sheldon Wolin, who, when reviewing *The Life of the Mind* for the *New York Review of Books*, maintained the "visionary" and, that is, essentially "imagist" character of Jewish prophecy. Sheldon Wolin, "Stopping to Think," *New York Review of Books* 25, no. 16 (1978), 16–21.

54. Arendt, *On Revolution*, 229.

55. This phrase that Arendt cites (ibid., 233) is Leclerc's, as cited by Albert Soboul, "An Den Ursprüngen der Volkdemokratie: Politische Aspekte der Sansculottendemokratie im Jahre II," in *Beiträge zum neuen Geschichtsbild: Festschrift für Alfred Meusel*, ed. Fritz Klein and Joachim Streisand (Berlin: Rütten & Loening, 1956).

56. The principal passage in Rousseau (*The Social Contract*, III, 15) is this: "Sovereignty can not be represented, for the same reason that it can not be alienated; its essence is the general will, and the will cannot be represented—either it is the general will or it is something else; there is no intermediate possibility." Here Rousseau addresses the (historically disputable) thesis of the "modernity" of representation: "the idea of representation is a modern one; it comes to us from feudal government, from that iniquitous unfair and absurd system under which the human race is degraded and which dishonours the name of man. In the republics and even in the monarchies of the ancient world, the people never had representatives; the very word was unknown." Jean-Jacques Rousseau, *The Social Contract*, trans. Maurice Cranston (Harmondsworth: Penguin, 1968), 141.

57. The passage in Hobbes most explanatory of the unifying character of the representative is in *Leviathan*, XVI: "A Multitude of men, are made *One* Person, when they are by one man, or one Person, Represented; so that it be done with the consent of every one of that Multitude in particular. For it is the *Unity* of the Representer, not the *Unity* of the Represented, that maketh the Person *One*. And it is the Representer that beareth the Person, and but one Person: And *Unity*, cannot otherwise be understood in the Multitude." Thomas Hobbes, *Leviathan* (Harmondsworth: Penguin, 1968), 220.

58. This was precisely Rousseau's thesis, in *The Social Contract*, II, 1: "My argument, then, is that sovereignty, being nothing other than the exercise of the general will, can never be alienated; and that the sovereign, which is simply a collective being, cannot be represented by anyone but itself—power may be delegated, but the will cannot be. . . . The sovereign might say: 'What I want at present is precisely what this man wants, or at least what he says he wants'; but no sovereign could say: 'What this man is going to want tomorrow I too shall want', for it is absurd that anyone should wish to bind himself for the future, and it is a contradiction in terms to say that any human being should wish to consent to something that is the reverse of his own good. If a people promises simply and solely to obey, it dissolves

itself by that very pledge; it ceases to be a people; for once there is a master, there is no longer a sovereign, and the body politic is therefore annihilated." Rousseau, *The Social Contract*, 69–70.

59. Arendt, *On Revolution*, 66.

60. The process of the metamorphosis of the individual within the *unity* of all is already perfectly delineated in Rousseau: *The Social Contract*, II, 7: "Whoever ventures on the enterprise of setting up a people must be ready, shall we say, to change human nature, to transform each individual, who by himself is entirely complete and solitary, into a part of a much greater whole, from which that same individual will then receive, in a sense, his life and his being. . . . So much so, that if each citizen can do nothing whatever except through cooperation with others, and if the acquired power of the whole is equal to, or greater than, the sum of the natural powers of each of the individuals, then we can say that law-making has reached the highest point of perfection." Rousseau, *The Social Contract*, 84–85.

61. Arendt, *On Revolution*, 67.

62. Ibid.

63. Ibid., 68.

64. Ibid., 68–69.

65. Arendt, *Between Past and Future: Eight Exercises in Political Thought*, 150. The essay is "What Is Freedom?"

66. Ibid., 162.

67. Ibid., 157.

68. Ibid., 160. [References omitted.]

69. Arendt, *The Life of the Mind*, 26.

70. Ibid., 141.

71. Ibid., 63.

72. ["I want you to be."]

73. Ibid., 213.

74. Ibid., 199.

75. Ibid., 200.

76. Ibid., 217.

77. These are now gathered, with an important introduction by Ronald Beiner, in Hannah Arendt, *Lectures on Kant's Political Philosophy*, ed. Ronald Beiner (Chicago: University of Chicago Press, 1982).

78. [Used as a noun, the Italian word *fatto* has the dual sense of a fact and a completed deed.]

79. Arendt, *The Life of the Mind*, 216.

80. For example, according to Gadamer, Kant tends to depoliticize "common sense." Hans-Georg Gadamer, *Truth and Method*, trans. Joel C. Weinsheimer and Donald G. Marshall (London: Continuum, 2004).

81. Arendt, *Lectures on Kant's Political Philosophy*, 77.

82. ["The victorious cause pleased the gods, but the defeated one pleases Cato." See Arendt, *The Life of the Mind*, 216.]

83. Hannah Arendt, "Walter Benjamin," in *Men in Dark Times* (New York: Harcourt, Brace & World, 1968), 205–206.

84. [Examples of Arendt's use of this phrase can be found in Arendt, *The Life of the Mind* at 75 and 85, in the first case with an attribution to Heidegger.]

85. Ibid., 85.

86. Ibid., 192.

87. Ibid. Arendt's quotations from Jaspers may be found in Karl Jaspers, *Philosophy (Vol. 2)*, trans. E. B. Ashton (Chicago: University of Chicago Press, 1970), 178–179.

88. Arendt, *The Life of the Mind*, 192.

89. Ibid.

90. Ibid., 181.

91. Ibid.

92. Ibid., 182.

93. Ibid.

94. Ibid., 202–210. The same theme may be found in the preface to *Between Past and Future*, 6–14.

95. Arendt, *The Life of the Mind*, 206.

96. Cicero, *De Republica*, I, 17. ["Never is he more active than when he does nothing, never is he less alone than when he is by himself."]

3. POWER AND SILENCE

1. Hannah Arendt, *The Life of the Mind* (San Diego: Harcourt, 1981), 192.

2. Niccolò Machiavelli, *Discourses on Livy*, trans. Harvey C. Mansfield and Nathan Tarcov (Chicago: University of Chicago Press, 1996), III, 1. "It is a very true thing that all worldly things have a limit to their life; but generally those go the whole course that is ordered for them by heaven, that do not disorder their body but keep it ordered so that either it does not alter or, if it alters, it is for its safety and not to its harm. Because I am speaking of mixed bodies, such as republics and sects, I say that those alterations are for safety that lead them back toward their beginnings. So those are better ordered and have longer life that by means of their orders can often be renewed or indeed that through some accident outside the said order come to the said renewal. And it is a thing clearer than light that these bodies do not last if they do not renew themselves."

3. Hannah Arendt, *Between Past and Future: Eight Exercises in Political Thought* (New York: Penguin Books, 2006), 139. See also Hannah Arendt, *On Revolution* (New York: Penguin Books, 2006), 26–29.

4. Hannah Arendt, *On Violence* (New York: Harcourt, Brace, Jovanovich, 1970), 56.

5. See, naturally, Sigmund Freud, *Totem and Taboo*, trans. James Strachey (London: Routledge and New York, 1960).

6. Hannah Arendt, *The Origins of Totalitarianism* (New York: Harcourt Brace Jovanovich, 1976), 465.

7. Hannah Arendt, *Crises of the Republic* (New York: Harcourt Brace, 1972), 80.

8. Regarding Hermann Broch's texts, I have referred to the multiple-volume edition of his works presented by P. M. Lützeler (Frankfurt: Suhrkamp, 1974–81). I have also considered the Rhein-Verlag edition of Broch's *Gesammelte Werke* (Zürich: Rhein-Verlag, 1953), which remains important, above all because of the valuable introduction to each volume. There are also some unpublished manuscripts held by the "Hermann Broch-Archiv" at Yale University Library, New Haven, Connecticut (which were consulted on microfilm). The text Arendt devoted to Broch appeared as the introduction to volumes 6 and 7 of Broch's *Gesammelte Werke* (*Dichten und Erkennen* and *Erkennen und Handeln*). It appears in English in the collection *Men in Dark Times* (New York: Harcourt, Brace & World, 1968). Arendt's other essays on Broch are "Hermann Broch und der Moderne Roman," *Der Monat* 8–9 (1949): 147–151; "No Longer and Not Yet," *The Nation* (September 14, 1946): 300–302; reprinted in *Essays in Understanding, 1930–1954* (New York: Harcourt, Brace & Co., 1994), and then in *Reflections on Literature and Culture* (Stanford: Stanford University Press, 2007), which also contains a reprint of "The Achievement of Hermann Broch," *The Kenyon Review* 11, no. 3 (1949): 476–483; and finally, "A Writer's Conscience," *Times Literary Supplement* (March 29, 1963), 209–210. As for Broch's essay, "Politik: Ein Kondensat" is in Hermann Broch, *Gesammelte Werke 7: Erkennen und Handeln* (Zürich: Rhein-Verlag, 1955).

9. Hermann Broch, "Politik: Ein Kondensat," 204.

10. The theme of the "metapolitical" recurs frequently in Broch, especially in his letters, and often in connection with an approving stance on the Marxist "return to fundamentals." See, for example, his letter to Abraham Sonne of March 14, 1950, in Hermann Broch, *Gesammelte Werke 8: Briefe von 1929–1951* (Zürich: Rhein-Verlag, 1957), 385.

11. Broch, "Politik: Ein Kondensat," 205.

12. On the slippery question of ancestry, however, we should overlook neither Broch's direct affiliation with Pascal, nor a more remote Gnostic connection. Givone has convincingly underlined Broch's propensity for Gnosticism, above all in *The Death of Virgil*, in "Broch interprete di Virgilio," in Sergio Givone, *Ermeneutica e romanticismo* (Milan: Mursia, 1983), 121–141. Regarding Pascal, whose connection with Gnosticism was noted by Hans Jonas in *The Gnostic Religion: The Message of the Alien God and the Beginnings of Christianity* (Boston: Beacon Press, 1963), I refer particularly to his *pensées* on justice, one of which recalls in an almost literary

fashion certain of Broch's passages on the justice-force nexus: "*Justice, force*: It is just that what is just should be followed (obeyed); it is necessary that what is the strongest should be followed. Justice without force is impotent; force without justice is tyrannical. Justice without force is contradicted, because there are always the wicked; force without justice is denounced. And so it is necessary to put (bring) justice and force together, and to that end let us make that which is just be strong and that which is strong be just. Justice is open to dispute; force which is easily recognisable and beyond dispute. That was force bestowed upon justice; because force has contradicted justice, and has said that it was unjust, and that it was force itself which was just. Thus, being unable to make what is just to be strong we have made what is strong to be just." Blaise Pascal, *Pensées*, trans. W. F. Trotter (London: Dent, 1931).

13. Broch, "Politik: Ein Kondensat," 207.

14. Ibid., 210.

15. Ibid., 211.

16. Ibid.

17. Ibid.

18. Ibid., 212.

19. Ibid., 213.

20. Ibid., 214.

21. On the distinction from Mann's sense of the "unpolitical," Massimo Cacciari's observations are decisive: see his "Nietzsche and the Unpolitical," in Massimo Cacciari, *The Unpolitical: On the Radical Critique of Political Reason*, ed. Alessandro Carrera, trans. Massimo Verdicchio (New York: Fordham University Press, 2009), 92–103.

22. Broch, "Politik: Ein Kondensat," 232. "We can understand the meaning of 'value' only beginning from the negative pole, beginning from death."

23. Ibid., 218.

24. "A democratic theology has therefore to be based on a theory of human rights. However, though we have histories of the development of human rights, there does not exist a real scientific theory, quite simply because the human rights [*sic*] are still a religious concept deriving from the idea that man is an image of God. What we need is a secularization. We have to bring back to earth the absolute that as yet was only in Heaven, and I think that the time is ripe for it. Everywhere in scientific thinking you see that the dialectical absolute had to yield to an empirical and earthly one." Letter to Alvin Johnson of March 17, 1950, in English in the original, in Broch, *Gesammelte Werke 8*, 389–390.

25. Broch, "Politik: Ein Kondensat," 221. Here the Kafkaesque image and metaphor of the blindfold of justice appears.

26. Obviously I am thinking of "Critique of Violence" which can be found in Walter Benjamin, *Reflections: Essays, Aphorisms, Autobiographical Writings*, trans. Edmund Jephcott (New York: Schocken Books, 1986); but see also the fragments in

"Theses on the Philosophy of History" in Walter Benjamin, *Illuminations: Essays and Reflections*, trans. Harry Zohn (New York: Schocken Books, 1986).

27. See Freud's September 1932 response to Einstein's letter of July 30, 1932, concerning war, as part of the series of open letters originally published by the International Institute of Intellectual Cooperation of the League of Nations in Paris. Albert Einstein and Sigmund Freud, *Why War? The Correspondence between Albert Einstein and Sigmund Freud*, trans. Fritz Moellenhoff and Anna Moellenhoff (Chicago: Chicago Institute for Psychoanalysis, 1978).

28. See especially Broch, "Politik: Ein Kondensat," 241, 248–249.

29. On the Benjaminian opposition between justice and law [*diritto*], see Massimo Cacciari's essay "Law and Justice," in *The Unpolitical*, 173–196.

30. See the letter to Arendt of February 21, 1949, in Broch, *Gesammelte Werke 8*, 328–332.

31. Broch, "Politik: Ein Kondensat," 254.

32. Ibid., 254–255.

33. On this point, some further observations are necessary. Benjamin rejected historical mediation as a remedy for violence, because it is itself a bearer of violence. Law's "conservative" character is implicated here. Insofar as its nature is to endure, law belongs to a history that violently suppresses the new, posing itself precisely as the polar opposite of the new to such an extent that it rigidifies into myth. And law's ancient roots are sunk into mythic time, as Benjamin observes in his essay "Fate and Character," which constitutes the necessary complement to "Critique of Violence": "Mistakenly, through confusing itself with the realm of justice, the order of law, which is only a residue of the demonic stage of human existence when legal statutes determined not only men's relationships but also their relation to the gods, has preserved itself long past the time of the victory over the demons." (Benjamin, *Reflections*, 307).

What is the effect of this critique of mediation, rooted in the violent confluence of history and myth, on Benjamin's understanding of the political? Above all it is the rejection of any "theologization" of the political in the Roman Catholic sense. Nowhere in "Critique of Violence" is there a refutation of representation, be it Roman Catholic or Hobbesian-modern, as resounding as that of "Fate and Character." Neither the Catholic-transcendent dimension of Schmitt's language nor his modern-immanent inflection is even minimally present in Benjamin. It is Arendt, if anyone, who Benjamin preempts (besides Broch), but with an incomparable radicality. His critique of representation is essentially a critique of the political, and the political's inability to be positively represented is for Benjamin without exception. He permits neither origin (violence) nor end (redemption) to form a connection between law and Justice. As it is in Broch, the political is consigned to the language of the negative. In fact, it remains in question whether we can even still speak of language here—because it is only beyond language, in a realm that cannot be predicated linguistically (nor historically), that "pure divine violence" gleams; an "unmediated violence" without "bloodshed," that opposes the mythic violence of the law [*diritto*]. This "saving" violence, too, or rather, *especially* this violence, lies within the secret of the impolitical. For this reason it can be experienced in particular events such as revolutionary action or the general strike, but it can never be properly "systematized" as part of a scheme; a "means to an end" that would retranslate it into the terms of mythic violence. Yet this "impolitical" is not without a relation to the political from which it "justly" withdraws. Not only because it continues to be characterized in Benjamin's thought, albeit "silently," by political categories (most glaringly that of "decision"), but above all because of the opposition it demands of the political.

It can fall only to the political to define the impolitical: that is, negatively. And only the political can call to it, though without any hope of a response. It is perhaps to this extreme dialectic (a dialectic of the extreme, not a dialectic of mediation) that an "obscure" passage of the *Theologico-Political Fragment* alludes in naming the relation between the profane and the Messianic as "the precondition of a mystical conception of history, containing a problem that can be represented figuratively." Benjamin elaborates: "If one arrow points to the goal toward which the profane dynamic acts, and another marks the direction of Messianic intensity, then certainly the quest of free humanity for happiness runs counter to the Messianic direction; but just as a force can, through acting, increase another that is acting in the opposite direction, so the order of the profane assists, through being profane, the coming of the Messianic Kingdom. The profane, therefore, although not itself a category of the Kingdom, is a decisive category of its quietest approach" (*Reflections*, 312).

34. On the question of kitsch, see three essays by Broch, "Das Weltbild des Romans" (1933), "Das Böse im Wertsystem der Kunst" (1933), and "Einige Bemerkungen zum Problem des Kitsches (1950), which Lützeler unites under the rubric "Kitsch und Literatur" in the second volume of Hermann Broch, *Schriften zur Literatur* (Frankfurt: Suhrkamp-Taschenbuch-Verlag, 1975), 89–173.

35. The relevant Chamberlain text is Houston Stewart Chamberlain, *Immanuel Kant: Die Persönlichkeit als Einführung in das Werk* (Munich: Bruckmann, 1905).

36. See Hans Vaihinger, *The Philosophy of "As If": A System of the Theoretical, Practical and Religious Fictions of Mankind*, trans. C. K. Ogden (London: Routledge, 2002).

37. "Konstruktion der historischen Wirklichkeit," in Hermann Broch, *Philosophische Schriften 2: Theorie*, ed. Paul Michael Lützeler (Frankfurt: Suhrkamp, 1986).

38. Ibid., 36.

39. The *Offener Briefe* appeared in *Die Rettung* on December 20, 1918, (published in Vienna by Franz Blei and in Paris by Gütersloh, and is in Hermann Broch, "Die

Straße (Offener Brief an Franz Blei)," in *Kommentierte Werkausgabe. 13/1, Briefe 1 (1913–1938): Dokumente und Kommentare zu Leben und Werk*, ed. Paul Michael Lützeler (Frankfurt: Suhrkamp, 1981), 30.

40. Ibid., 33, 30–31.

41. On this point there is a certain parallel with an essay on the multitude written by another German author of the same period. I refer to Kracauer's observations in his article "Das Ornament der Masse," *Frankfurter Zeitung* 9–10 (1927).

42. Broch, "Die Straße (Offener Brief an Franz Blei)," 31.

43. Ibid.

44. Ibid., 32.

45. Ibid., 32–33.

46. Ibid., 33.

47. Ibid., 34.

48. See Othmar Spann, *Der Wahre Staat, Vorlesungen über Abbruch und Neubau der Gesellschaft* (Jena: G. Fischer, 1938).

49. Hermann Broch, "Konstitutionelle Diktatur als demokratisches Rätesystem," in Hermann Broch, *Politische Schriften* (Frankfurt: Suhrkamp, 1978), 11–23.

50. I am essentially thinking of the 1949 piece "Die Demokratie im Zeitalter des Versklavung," in ibid, 110–191. This essay, which begins with the same presuppositions as does "Politik: Ein Kondensat," arrives at the conclusion that what is necessary is a " 'Totalisierung' der Demokratie" (ibid., 161). But see also "Trotzdem: Humane Politik. Verwirklichung einer Utopie" of 1950 in ibid., 364–396.

51. The book to which Broch refers is Paul Schrecker, *Leibniz: Ses idées sur l'organisation des relations internationales* (London: H. Milford, 1937).

52. Broch, *Politische Schriften*, 15.

53. Ibid., 19.

54. Ibid., 22–23.

55. Hermann Broch, "Die Erkenntnistheoretische Bedeutung des Begriffes 'Revolution' und die Wiederbelebung der Hegelschen Dialektik," in *Philosophische Schriften 1. Kritik*, ed. Paul Michael Lützeler (Frankfurt: Suhrkamp, 1977), 257–263. The essay originally appeared in *Prager Presse* in 1922. The Liebert texts are *Vom Geist der Revolution* (Berlin: Pan-Verlag, 1919); and *Wie ist Kritische Philosophie Überhaupt Möglich? Ein Beitrag zur Systematischen Phaenomenologie der Philosophie* (Leipzig: F. Meiner, 1919).

56. Broch, "Theorie der Geschichtsschreibung und der Geschichtsphilosophie," in *Philosophische Schriften 2*, 94–155.

57. Broch, "Die Erkenntnistheoretische Bedeutung des Begriffes 'Revolution,' " 258.

58. Ibid., 260.

59. Ibid.

60. For T. G. Masaryk, see *Die Wissenschaftliche und Philosophische Krise innerhalb des Gegenwärtigen Marxismus* (Vienna: Konegen, 1898), and *Die Philosophischen und Soziologischen Grundlagen des Marxismus* (Vienna: Konegen, 1899).

61. Otto Liebmann, *Kant und die Epigonen* (Stuttgart: Schober, 1865).

62. Hermann Broch, *The Sleepwalkers: A Trilogy*, trans. Willa Muir and Edwin Muir (New York: Vintage International, 1996), 526.

63. Ibid., 448.

64. Broch, "Die Erkenntnistheoretische Bedeutung des Begriffes 'Revolution,'" 258–259.

65. Broch, *The Sleepwalkers: A Trilogy*, 636.

66. Ibid., 636–637.

67. Ibid., 637.

68. Ibid., 645.

69. Ibid.

70. "We shall neither be the first upon those heights / nor the last; no, a few of our kind / will join us continually, and one fine day / we shall say We, we shall / forget the I. And then perhaps / we shall speak thus: . . ." Hermann Broch, *The Guiltless*, trans. Ralph Manheim (Boston: Little, Brown and Company, 1974), 237.

71. Broch, *The Sleepwalkers*, 645–646.

72. Hermann Broch, *The Death of Virgil*, trans. Jean Starr Untermeyer (New York: Vintage Books, 1995), 351.

73. Ibid.

74. Ibid., 352.

75. Ibid.

76. Ibid., 363–364.

77. Ibid., 368.

78. Ibid., 370–371.

79. Ibid., 367.

80. Ibid., 372.

81. Ibid.

82. Ibid., 306.

83. Ibid., 317.

84. Ibid., 367.

85. Ibid., 322.

86. Broch elaborates concepts not dissimilar to these in an essay written immediately after the war: "Die Zweiteilung der Welt" (1947), in *Politische Schriften*, in particular at 278–279, where, beginning with the premise that states are required for the protection of their citizens, he arrives at the conclusion that as a "machine of power" [*Machtmaschine*] the state tends inevitably toward totalitarianism.

87. Broch, *The Death of Virgil*, 366.

88. Ibid., 368.

89. Ibid., 363.

90. Ibid., 48.

91. Ibid., 50.

92. Ibid., 367.

93. Ibid.

94. Ibid., 338.

95. Ibid., 359.

96. Ibid., 364.

97. Ibid., 480–481.

98. Elias Canetti, *The Play of the Eyes*, trans. Joachim Neugroschel (London: Pan, 1991), 31–55.

99. Elias Canetti, *The Conscience of Words*, trans. Joachim Neugroschel (New York: Seabury Press, 1979), 9.

100. Canetti, *The Play of the Eyes*, 33.

101. Ibid., 38.

102. Ibid.

103. Ibid., 38–39.

104. Canetti, *The Conscience of Words*, 5. There Canetti writes, "his first comprehensive opus, the trilogy of novels entitled *The Sleepwalkers*, is the literary realization of his philosophy of history."

105. Ibid., 6.

106. Canetti, *The Play of the Eyes*, 293.

107. Elias Canetti, *The Human Province*, trans. Joachim Neugroschel (London: Picador, 1986), 218.

108. Ibid., 84.

109. Canetti's radio conversation with Adorno is most interesting in this respect. It is found as "Crowds and Power: Conversation with Elias Canetti" in Theodor Adorno, *Can One Live After Auschwitz? A Philosophical Reader*, ed. Rolf Tiedemann, trans. Rodney Livingstone and others (Stanford: Stanford University Press, 2003), 182–201.

110. Canetti, *The Human Province*, 124.

111. In this sense, besides his proximity with Arendt, Canetti also shares something with Benjamin. On this question, see Youssef Ishaghpour, "Variationen über den Selbst-Denker Canetti," *Literatur und Kritik* 18 (1983): 385–393, as well as Furio Jesi, "Composizione e antropologia in Elias Canetti," *Nuovi Argomenti* 42 (1974): 332–354. Jesi's essay should be borne in mind more generally as regards allegory in Canetti's work, which he correctly interprets as being strictly nonrepresentational: "In Canetti, allegory is concerned precisely with itself. It does not represent something other than itself. There is nothing behind it, and precisely because of this fact—because it is utterly un-unmaskable for not even having a mask in the first place—it has an eminently unmasking effect" (336–337).

112. Canetti, *The Human Province*, 26.
113. Ibid., 166.
114. Ibid., 138.
115. Ibid., 105.
116. Ibid., 248.
117. Ibid., 61.
118. Ibid., 55.
119. Ibid., 31.
120. Ibid., 37–38.
121. Ibid., 31.
122. Ibid., 200.
123. Ibid., 126.
124. Elias Canetti, *Auto da Fé*, trans. C. V. Wedgwood (New York: Stein and Day, 1964), 365.
125. Ibid., 372.
126. Ibid., 377.
127. Ibid., 402.
128. Canetti, *The Human Province*, 76.
129. Elias Canetti, *Crowds and Power*, trans. Carol Stewart (New York: Farrar Straus Giroux, 1984), 381.
130. Canetti, *The Human Province*, 190. "I think I have found the key to *Metamorphoses* and inserted it in the lock, but I have not turned the key. The door is shut, one cannot enter. We will have a lot more trouble with it."
131. Canetti, *Crowds and Power*, 110.
132. Ibid., 368.
133. Canetti, *Auto da Fé*, 377–378.
134. Ibid., 398.
135. Canetti, *Crowds and Power*, 465–470.

4. A POLITICS OF ASCESIS

1. Elias Canetti, *The Human Province*, trans. Joachim Neugroschel (London: Picador, 1986), 80.
2. Ibid., 137. Canetti writes: "I want in order that the will be *deviated* from me." From the point of view of this peculiar dialectic, the idol of Canetti's polemics is no longer death as such, but a life absolutely immanent to itself that produces death.
3. Ibid., 101.
4. Ibid., 106.
5. Ibid., 243.
6. Ibid., 69.
7. Ibid., 24.

8. Ibid., 53.

9. Ibid., 245.

10. This is an impotence, however, that is always in a relation with the power that constitutes that impotence's condition of conceivability and existence—as Canetti does not fail to note in his book on Kafka's correspondence with Felice Bauer. Elias Canetti, *Kafka's Other Trial: The Letters to Felice*, trans. Christopher Middleton (London: Penguin Classics, 2012), 94–95. On this subject, see Kafka's letter of November 1, 1920, in Franz Kafka, *Letters to Felice*, ed. Erich Heller and Jürgen Born, trans. James Stern and Elisabeth Duckworth (New York: Schocken Books, 1973), 21: "Just as I am thin, and I am the thinnest person I know (and that's saying something, for I am no stranger to sanatoria), there is also something to me which, in relation to writing, one could call superfluous, superfluous in the sense of overflowing. If there is a higher power that wishes to use me, or does use me, then I am at its mercy, if no more than as a well-prepared instrument. If not, I am nothing, and will suddenly be abandoned in a dreadful void."

11. "Indecisiveness . . . fearfulness, coldness of feeling, detailed description of lovelessness . . ." Canetti, *Kafka's Other Trial*, 32.

12. Ibid., 47.

13. Ibid., 39.

14. Ibid., 37.

15. Ibid., 96. "Standing upright signifies the power of man over beast; but precisely in this most obvious attitude man is exposed, visible, vulnerable. For this power is also guilt, and only on the ground, lying among the animals, can one see the stars, which free one from this terrifying power of man."

16. Ibid., 97. "Confronted as he was with power on all sides, his obduracy sometimes offered him a reprieve. But if it was insufficient, or if it failed him, he trained himself to disappear; here the helpful aspect of his physical thinness is revealed, though often, as we know, he despised it. By means of physical diminution, he withdrew power *from himself*, and thus had less part in it; this asceticism, too, was directed against power."

17. Or even a reduction to wood, as Kafka wrote to Felice in February 1913: "These are the fantasies or the wishes I indulge in when lying sleepless in bed: To be a large piece of wood, and to be pressed against her body by the cook, who with both hands draws the knife toward her along the side of this stiff log (approximately in the region of my hip) and with all her might slices off shavings to light the fire." Kafka, *Letters to Felice*, 201–202.

18. Canetti, *Kafka's Other Trial*, 98.

19. Ibid., 103.

20. Elias Canetti, *The Play of the Eyes*, trans. Joachim Neugroschel (London: Pan, 1991), 206.

21. Ibid., 114.

22. Ibid., 113.

23. Ibid.

24. Ibid., 115. Note also the impressions of Veza Canetti, as helpful as ever: "When she saw him for the first time at the house of the painter Georg Merkel, she said to me: 'He does *not* look like Karl Kraus. How can you say such a thing? A mummy of Karl Krauss, that's what he looks like.' She was referring to his sunken, ascetic look and she was referring also to his silence." (Ibid., 140).

25. Ibid., 136.

26. Ibid., 166.

27. Ibid., 165.

28. Ibid., 166.

29. Ibid., 143.

30. Ibid., 143–144.

31. Ibid., 133.

32. Ibid., 140–141.

33. Ibid., 144.

34. Ibid.

35. Robert Musil, *The Man without Qualities*, trans. Sophie Wilkins and Burton Pike (New York: Vintage International, 1995), 2:1,383.

36. "Science and Perception in Descartes," in Simone Weil, *Formative Writings, 1929–1941*, trans. Dorothy Tuck McFarland and Wilhelmina van Ness (Amherst: University of Massachusetts Press, 1987), 59.

37. On this matter, see Miklós Vetö, *The Religious Metaphysics of Simone Weil*, trans. Joan Dargan (Albany: State University of New York Press, 1994), which is the best monograph on Weil's metaphysics (though it does give perhaps excessive weight to the role of Kantianism in her thought).

38. Simone Weil, *The Notebooks of Simone Weil*, trans. Arthur Wills (New York: G. P. Putnam's Sons, 1956), 1:329.

39. Ibid., 2:335.

40. Ibid., 637.

41. Ibid., 1:24.

42. See "Simone Weil interprete del mondo di oggi," in Augusto Del Noce, *L'epoca della secolarizzazione* (Milan: Giuffrè, 1970), especially 154.

43. See Simone Pétrement, "Sur la religion d'Alain (Avec quelques remarques concernant celle de Simone Weil)," *Revue de Métaphysique et de Morale* 60, no. 3 (1955): 306–330. See also Simone Pétrement, *Simone Weil: A Life*, trans. Raymond Rosenthal (London: Mowbrays, 1976), 436: "'Alain's shortcoming,' she told me, 'is to have rejected pain.'"

44. Pétrement, *Sur la religion d'Alain*, 329.

45. I refer, obviously, to the Heidegger of "The Age of the World Picture," in *The Question Concerning Technology and Other Essays* (New York: Harper & Row, 1977).

46. See Pétrement's references in *Simone Weil: A Life*; but see also Alain Goldschläger, *Simone Weil et Spinoza: Essai d'interpretation* (Sherbrooke: Naaman, 1982), 121.

47. See Simone Pétrement, *La vie de Simone Weil* (Paris: Fayard, 1973), 1:88, 2:173. [Here and elsewhere, the original French references are provided, since the relevant passages do not appear in the English translation.]

48. Weil, *Notebooks*, 2:446.

49. Simone Weil, *Intimations of Christianity among the Ancient Greeks*, ed. and trans. Elisabeth Chase Geissbuhler (London: Routledge and Kegan Paul, 1958), 187. On this, see A. A. Devaux, "Liberté et nécessité selon Simone Weil," *Revue de Théologie et de Philosophie* 1 (1976): 1–11. I would like to thank André Devaux for allowing me to consult important biographical sources on Simone Weil.

50. For example, paragraph 32 of the appendix to Part IV of the *Ethics*: "But human power is very limited and is infinitely surpassed by the power of external causes, and so we do not have absolute power to adapt to our purposes things external to us. However, we shall patiently bear whatever happens to us that is contrary to what is required by consideration of our own advantage, if we are conscious that we have done our duty and that our power was not extensive enough for us to have avoided the said things, and that we are a part of the whole of Nature whose order we follow. If we clearly and distinctly understand this, that part of us which is defined by the understanding, that is, the better part of us, will be fully resigned and will endeavor to persevere in that resignation. For insofar as we understand, we can desire nothing but that which must be, nor, in an absolute sense, can we find contentment in anything but truth. And so insofar as we rightly understand these matters, the endeavor of the better part of us is in harmony with the order of the whole of Nature."

51. This concept had already been established almost word for word in Alain, *Spinoza* (Paris: Gallimard, 1949), 147–148.

52. Weil, *Notebooks*, 1:96.

53. This had already been clearly indicated by Léon Brunschvicg, in *Spinoza et ses contemporains* (Paris: Presses Universitaires de France, 1923), 292–293, which is the other great work on Spinoza, besides Alain's, that Weil had to hand.

54. On the theme of decreation, see Vetö, *The Religious Metaphysics of Simone Weil*. Besides the references to Luria and Vital (through Scholem's works on Jewish mysticism and the Kabbalah), Vetö makes a dual reference to Schelling and Hamman. See also Rolf Kühn, "La décréation: Annotations sur un néologisme philosophique, religieux et littéraire," *Revue d'Histoire et de Philosophie Religieuses* LXV, no. 1 (1985): 45–52.

55. See Jules Lagneau, "Quelques notes sur Spinoza," *Revue de Métaphysique et de Morale* 3, no. 4 (1895): 375–416. Evidence for the fact that Alain considered Lagneau the most profound of the Spinoza specialists can be found in André Canivez,

Jules Lagneau: Essai sur la condition du Professeur de Philosophie jusqu'à la fin du XIXe siècle (Paris: Les Belles Lettres, 1965), 1:382.

56. See Charles Péguy, "Note conjointe sur M. Descartes et la philosophie cartésienne," in *Oeuvres en Prose, 1909–1914* (Paris: Gallimard, 1961), 1385 and 1405. Péguy's use of the term, however, tends in a direction opposed to that of Weil.

57. Maurice Blanchot, *The Book to Come*, trans. Charlotte Mandell (Stanford: Stanford University Press, 2003), 227. [At this page, the English translation of Blanchot's text erroneously renders the verb *décréer*, in relation to poetry's specific operation, as "to decree" rather than "to decreate."]

58. Stanislas Breton, *Foi et raison logique* (Paris: Éditions du Seuil, 1971), 257. By Breton, see also "Les intuitions préchrétiennes de Simone Weil. La meditation platonicienne de la croix," *La passion du Christ et les philosophies* (Teramo: Eco, 1954), 61–80.

59. Paul Ricoeur, *Les incidences théologiques des recherches actuelles concernant le langage* (Paris: Institut Supérieur d'Études Oecuméniques, 1969), 47.

60. Simone Weil, *Waiting for God*, trans. Emma Craufurd (New York: Harper Perennial, 2009), 126.

61. Ibid., 127.

62. See Weil's letter to Joë Bousquet in *Seventy Letters*, trans. Richard Rees (London: Oxford University Press, 1965), 137: "Translators say *in patentia*, but ὑπομένειν is quite another thing. It means to remain where one is, motionless, in expectation, unshaken and unmoved by any external shock." The letter is also found in Simone Weil, *Simone Weil*, ed. Eric O. Springsted (Maryknoll, N.Y.: Orbis Books, 1998).

63. Weil, *Waiting for God*, 128.

64. See Del Noce, *L'epoca della secolarizzazione*.

65. Weil, *Waiting for God*, 62.

66. In English as Simone Weil, *First and Last Notebooks*, trans. Richard Rees (London: Oxford University Press, 1970), 362.

67. Only a fragment of this text has been published, in Simone Weil, *Oeuvres complètes, Tome 1: Premiers écrits philosophiques*, ed. G. Kahn and R. Kühn (Paris: Gallimard, 1988), 316. The passage in question appears in Pétrement, *La vie de Simone Weil*, 1:86.

68. Weil, *The Notebooks of Simone Weil, Volume 1*, 224.

69. On the notion of a "passive state" the obligatory reference is to Fénelon's *Mémoire sur l'état passif*, published as an appendix to Jeanne-Lydie Goré, *La notion d'indifférence chez Fénelon et ses sources* (Paris: Presses Universitaires de France, 1956).

70. Weil, *Notebooks*, 1:124.

71. See Weil's short essay "Le conte des six cygnes dans Grimm," in *Oeuvres Complètes*, 1:58.

72. Ibid., 59.

73. Weil, *Notebooks*, 1:246.

74. In this sense, the title of Dal Lago's otherwise useful essay is misleading: Alessandro Dal Lago, "On the Ethics of Weakness, Simone Weil, and Nihilism," in *Weak Thought*, ed. Gianni Vattimo and Pier Aldo Rovatti, trans. Peter Carravetta (Albany: State University of New York Press, 2013), 111–137.

75. *Bhagavad Gita* IV:13–14.

76. Ibid., XVIII:2.

77. Ibid., II: 47.

78. Weil, *Notebooks*, 1:96.

79. Ibid., 324.

80. Simone Weil, *The Iliad, Or the Poem of Force*, trans. Mary McCarthy (Wallingford: Pendle Hill, 1956). McCarthy's translation was reprinted in 1965. See Simone Weil, "The Iliad, Or the Poem of Force," *Chicago Review* 18, no. 2 (1965): 5–30. It also appears in Weil, *Intimations of Christianity among the Ancient Greeks*

81. Weil, "L'Allemagne en attente," appearing in *La Revolution Prolétarienne* 138 (October 25, 1932) and in *Libres Propos* 10–11 (October 25 and November 25, 1932); in Weil, *Oeuvres complètes* (Paris: Gallimard, 1988), 2:120–137.

82. Ibid., 122–123.

83. Ibid., 126.

84. Ibid., 127.

85. Here Weil's language reaches one of its characteristic climaxes: "Every human group that exercises power does so, not in such a way as to bring happiness to those who are subject to it, but in such a way as to increase that power. . . . If the free play of competition is the final object of production in the hands of the capitalists, its final object in the hands of technicians organized into a state bureaucracy would necessarily be preparation for war." See Simone Weil, "Prospects: Are We Heading for the Proletarian Revolution?" in *Oppression and Liberty* (London: Routledge, 1958), 15.

86. Weil, *Formative Writings, 1929–1941*, 241. These quotations are drawn from the 1933 essay "Reflections on War."

87. Ibid.

88. Ibid., 245.

89. Weil, *Oppression and Liberty*, 62.

90. Ibid.

91. Ibid. Alain's consideration of power was also undertaken in similar terms: see Alain, *Politique* (Paris: Presses Universitaires de France, 1952), 109; but also the entirety of Alain, *Propos sur les pouvoirs: Éléments d'éthique politique* (Paris: Gallimard, 1985).

92. Weil, *Oppression and Liberty*, 62.

93. Ibid., 63–64.

94. Notwithstanding, naturally, that the question of the *imaginatio* in Spinoza is much more complex, as is clearly visible in the first chapter of the *Theological-Political Treatise* for example ("on prophecy"). See Benedict de Spinoza, *Theological-Political Treatise*, trans. Michael Silverthorne and Jonathan Israel (Cambridge: Cambridge University Press, 2007).

95. Weil, *Oppression and Liberty*, 64.

96. Also in ibid.

97. "Let us not start another Trojan War." Weil's essay was published in English as "The Power of Words," in Simone Weil, *Selected Essays, 1934–1943*, ed. and trans. Richard Rees (London: Oxford University Press, 1962), also in Simone Weil, *Simone Weil: An Anthology*, ed. Siân Miles (New York: Grove Press, 1986).

98. Weil, *Oppression and Liberty*, 131: "When it seems that a sanguinary struggle replaces one system by another, this struggle is in reality the crowning point of a transformation that is already more than half accomplished, and brings to power a category of men who already more than half possessed that power."

99. From "Meditation on Obedience and Liberty," in ibid., 135.

100. "The Power of Words," in Weil, *Simone Weil: An Anthology*, 230.

101. Ibid., 233.

102. Weil, *Oppression and Liberty*, 137–138.

103. Simone Weil, *Oeuvres complètes* (Paris: Editions Gallimard, 1997), 6.2:434. [The equivalent passage in the English translation renders the term *côtoyer* without the sense of "bordering" that it acquires in Esposito's reading. It may however be found in Weil, *The Notebooks of Simone Weil, Volume 1*, 311.]

104. Weil, *Waiting for God*, 4.

105. Ibid., 89.

106. Simone Weil, *Gravity and Grace*, trans. Emma Crawford and Mario von der Ruhr (London: Routledge, 2002), 60.

107. Weil, *Notebooks*, 1:296.

108. Weil, *Gravity and Grace*, 165.

109. No less partisan, however, are the accounts of Weil's anti-Judaism by certain critics—for example Paul Giniewski in *Simone Weil: Ou, la haine de soi* (Paris: Berg International, 1978). On this question, Lévinas is more careful and balanced. See his essay "Simone Weil against the Bible," in Emmanuel Lévinas, *Difficult Freedom: Essays on Judaism*, trans. Seán Hand (Baltimore: Johns Hopkins University Press, 1990).

110. See Pétrement, *La vie de Simone Weil*, 2:302.

111. Simone Weil, *Letter to a Priest*, trans. A. F. Wills (London: Routledge & Kegan Paul, 1953), 16. [Translation modified.]

112. Ibid., 64.

113. Weil, *Gravity and Grace*, 160.

114. Simone Weil, "The Great Beast: Reflections on the Origins of Hitlerism," in *Selected Essays*, 89–144.

115. Simone Weil, *The Need for Roots*, trans. Arthur Wills (London: Routledge, 2002), 265.

116. Ibid., 268.

117. Ibid., 238.

118. Note that Canetti shares not only Weil's dislike of the Romans but also her political-theological reading of the relation between Rome and Christianity. See Canetti, *The Human Province*, 27–29.

119. Weil, *The Need for Roots*, 269.

120. Ibid., 272.

121. Ibid., 2. [Translation modified.]

122. Originally titled "La personalité humaine, le juste et l'injuste," and better known as "La personne et le sacré," this essay appears in English as "Human Personality" in Weil, *Selected Essays*, 9–34; in Simone Weil, *Two Moral Essays*, ed. Ronald Hathaway (Wallingford: Pendle Hill Publications, 1981); and most recently in Weil, *Simone Weil: An Anthology*, 49–78, from which this quotation is drawn at 61.

123. Simone Weil, *On the Abolition of all Political Parties*, trans. Simon Leys (Collingwood: Black, 2013).

124. Weil, *Simone Weil: An Anthology*, 61.

125. Ibid.

126. It should be noted on this matter that on the whole, Weil and Mounier were on good terms, as Weil was with all the *Esprit* group. On this, see the three letters preserved within Weil's manuscripts, one of which was published by Géraldi Leroy: Simone Weil, "Lettre à Emmanuel Mounier (1937)," *Cahiers Simone Weil* 4 (1984): 315–319; see also Mounier's "Simone Weil: L'enracinement," *Esprit* 163 (1950): 172–174.

127. Weil, *The Need for Roots*, 272. The full passage from Maritain reads: "The human person possesses rights because of the very fact that it is a person, a whole, master of itself and of its acts, and which consequently is not merely a means to an end, but an end, an end which much be treated as such. The dignity of the human person? The expression means nothing if it does not signify that by virtue of natural law, the human person has the right to be respected, is the subject of rights, possesses rights." And he continues, by way of a typically political-theological "analogical" logic: "In the last analysis, as every creature acts only by virtue of its Principle, which is the Pure Act; as every authority worthy of the name (that is to say, just) is binding in conscience only by virtue of the Principle of beings, which is pure Wisdom; so too every right possessed by man is possessed only by virtue of the right possessed by God, which is pure Justice, to see the order of his wisdom in beings respected, obeyed and loved by every intelligence." See Jacques Maritain, *The Rights of Man and Natural Law*, trans. Doris C. Anson (London: Geoffrey Bles/The Centenary Press, 1944), 37–38. See also the letters exchanged by Weil and Maritain

between July and August 1942: Simone Weil and Jacques Maritain, "Un échange de lettres entre Simone Weil et Jacques Maritain," *Cahiers Simone Weil* 3, no. 2 (1980): 68–74, where at 69 in the first letter, there is perhaps a cutting, argumentative jibe on Weil's part, albeit within the broader context of a mutual respect: "Christian dogma has always attracted me for its beauty; and this attraction has only grown as days and years go by, to the point of having become an attachment—an attachment out of love, and not an assertion."

128. It should not go unobserved that Denis de Rougemont binds the ambit of rights to the individual, as opposed to the personalist tradition which binds it to the person. See his *Politique de la personne* (Paris: Je sers, 1946), 54. But it is perhaps Rougement's anti-idolatrous stance that offers the closest connection with Weil, visible in his critique of theopolitical "idols," at 104.

129. Weil, "Human Personality," in *Simone Weil: An Anthology*, 55.

130. Ibid., 54.

131. Weil, *The Need for Roots*, 2–3.

132. Ibid., 4.

133. Ibid., 279.

134. Ibid., 215. [Translation modified.]

135. Ibid., 237.

136. Ibid., 281.

137. Ibid., 282.

138. Simone Weil, "Remarques sur le nouveau projet de constitution," in *Écrits de Londres et dernières lettres* (Paris: Gallimard, 1957), 86.

139. Weil, *The Need for Roots*, 286.

140. Ibid., 287.

5. THE COMMUNITY OF DEATH

1. Georges Bataille, "La victoire militaire et la banqueroute de la morale qui maudit," in *Oeuvres complètes* (Paris: Gallimard, 1970–), 11:532–549.

2. Bataille's essay "Le problem de l'état," published in 1933 in *La Critique Sociale*, is in ibid., 1:332–336. But the text perhaps semantically closest to the "political" Weil remains "En attendant la grève générale," in *Oeuvres complètes*, 2:256–263.

3. See Simone Pétrement, *Simone Weil: A Life*, trans. Raymond Rosenthal (London: Mowbrays, 1976), 208.

4. See Georges Bataille, "André Malraux," originally in *La Critique Sociale* (1933), in *Oeuvres complètes* 1:372–375.

5. Pétrement, *Simone Weil*, 210.

6. Georges Bataille, *Blue of Noon*, trans. Harry Mathews (London: Marion Boyars, 1986), 34.

7. Ibid., 19.

8. Ibid., 94–95.

9. Bataille, "La victoire militaire," 536–537.

10. Ibid., 537.

11. Ibid., 539.

12. Simone Weil, *Gravity and Grace*, trans. Emma Crawford and Mario von der Ruhr (London: Routledge, 2002), 109–113.

13. Simone Weil, *The Notebooks of Simone Weil*, trans. Arthur Wills (New York: G. P. Putnam's Sons, 1956), 1:151.

14. Ibid., 238.

15. Weil, *Gravity and Grace*, 98.

16. Ibid., 97.

17. Ibid., 70–71.

18. Ibid., 77.

19. Ibid., 75. [Translation modified.]

20. Weil, *Notebooks*, 2:431.

21. Georges Bataille, *Inner Experience*, trans. Leslie Anne Boldt (Albany: State University of New York Press, 1988), 131.

22. Bataille, "La victoire militaire," 539.

23. From "Affirmation (desire, affliction)," in Maurice Blanchot, *The Infinite Conversation*, trans. Susan Hanson (Minneapolis: University of Minnesota Press, 1993), 108.

24. Weil, *Notebooks*, 2:334–335. "The past—it forms part of the reality of this world, but a reality absolutely beyond our reach, toward which we are unable to make a single step, toward which all we are able to do is to turn ourselves so that an emanation from it may come to us. For this reason it is the image *par excellence* of eternal, supernatural reality."

25. Sartre's essay "A New Mystic" is found in Jean-Paul Sartre, *Critical Essays (Situations I)*, trans. Chris Turner (London: Seagull Books, 2010).

26. Bataille, *Inner Experience*, 3.

27. Bataille, "La victoire militaire," 546. "Weil herself knew that the truth of Christianity was not the public good, but that which was revealed by its mystics. She allowed herself to be seduced by the performance of 'good works'; nevertheless, she attested to evil like a mystic. Beyond Weil's 'good works' there was undoubtedly within her a prevailing attraction to evil and the disruption of the order of things brought about by misfortune."

28. Bataille, *Inner Experience*, 23.

29. Ibid.

30. Ibid., 113–114.

31. Ibid., 9.

32. Ibid., 53.

33. Ibid., 54.

34. Ibid., 27.

35. Ibid., 6.

36. Ibid., 8.

37. Jacques Derrida, "From Restricted to General Economy: A Hegelianism without Reserve," in *Writing and Difference*, trans. Alan Bass (Chicago: University of Chicago Press, 1978), 251–277, 259.

38. Ibid., 272.

39. Bataille, *Inner Experience*, 26.

40. Ibid., 26.

41. This is the epigraph that appears on the initial page of the book. See ibid., xxx.

42. Alexandre Kojève, *Introduction à la lecture de Hegel: Leçons sur la phénoménologie de l'esprit, professées de 1933 à 1939 à l'École des Hautes-Études*, ed. Raymond Queneau (Paris: Gallimard, 1947). [A partial translation also appears in English: Alexandre Kojève, *Introduction to the Reading of Hegel: Lectures on the Phenomenology of Spirit*, ed. Harold Bloom, trans. James H. Nichols Jr. (New York: Basic Books, 1969). Since the lectures to which Esposito refers do not appear in the English edition, all references to this text are to the original.]

43. Georges Bataille, "Hegel, l'homme et l'histoire," in *Oeuvres complètes*, 12:349–369, at 359. The essay originally appeared in 1956 in *Le monde nouveau paru*.

44. Georges Bataille, "Hegel, Death and Sacrifice," *Yale French Studies* 78 (1990): 9–28, at 9–10.

45. Ibid., 10.

46. Ibid.

47. Ibid., 12.

48. Kojève, *Introduction à la lecture de Hegel*, 392.

49. Ibid., 392.

50. Ibid., 419.

51. Alexandre Kojève, "Les romans de la sagesse," *Critique* 60 (1952): 387–397, at 396. (Concerning Queneau's three novels *Pierrot mon ami*, *Loin de Rueil*, and *Le dimanche de la vie*.)

52. See Kojève's comments on this question in the introduction to Alexandre Kojève, *Essai d'une histoire raisonnée de la philosophie païenne (Vol. I)* (Paris: Gallimard, 1968), 3:88–89.

53. Kojève, *Introduction à la lecture de Hegel*, 393.

54. Raymond Queneau, *Une histoire modèle* (Paris: Gallimard, 1966), 15.

55. See Kojève, *Les romans de la sagesse*, 387–397. For a literary and biographical reconstruction of Kojève's lectures, see Raymond Queneau, "Premières confrontations avec Hegel," *Critique* 19, nos. 195–196 (1963): 694–700.

56. Queneau, *Une histoire modèle*, 9.

57. Bataille, "Hegel, l'homme et l'histoire," 363–364.

58. The distance that Kojève felt from Bataille—albeit within the context of their very distinctive common motivation—is attested by numerous letters, two of which are partially reproduced by Giorgio Agamben in *Language and Death: The Place of Negativity* (Minneapolis: University of Minnesota Press, 1991), 49–53.

59. Bataille, "Hegel, l'homme et l'histoire," 364.

60. On this theme see Alexandre Kojève, "The Latest New World," *Parallax* 3, no. 1 (1997): 23–27, as well as Alexandre Kojève, "L'entretien avec Gilles Lapouge," *La Quinzaine Litteraire* 3 (1968): 18–20.

61. This passage comes from the note to the first edition, inserted in the second (1962) edition on page 434 of Kojève, *Introduction à la lecture de Hegel*, appearing on page 436.

62. See above all Ernst Jünger, *Der Weltstaat: Organismus und Organisation* (Stuttgart: Klett, 1960), in *Sämtliche Werke* (Stuttgart: Klett-Cotta, 1980), 7:481–526.

63. Ibid., 493–495.

64. Ernst Jünger, *An der Zeitmauer* (Stuttgart: Ernst Klett Verlag, 1959), 13.

65. Ibid., 88.

66. Ibid., 106–107.

67. On the question of decision, it is thus no coincidence that its necessity (and its risk) is evoked in Jünger's *Strahlungen*, in a discussion with Carl Schmitt: Ernst Jünger, "Strahlungen 1," in *Sämlichte Werke*, 2:265: "At the Trocadéro, walking along the right bank of the Seine, discussing the situation. For C.S. the real issue is that certain strata begin to dislodge from the human aggregate and sediment themselves below the zone of free will, just as animals are fallen masks of the human image. The human is expelling a new zoological order from itself, and the true and proper danger of this process is becoming involved in it. I added that this ossification process is already described in the Old Testament by the symbol of the bronze serpent. That which today is technology, was then the law."

68. Jünger, *An der Zeitmauer*, 111.

69. Ibid., 129.

70. Martin Heidegger, "Über 'Die Linie,'" in *Freundschaftliche Begegnungen Festschrift für Ernst Jünger zum 60. Geburtstag* (Frankfurt: Klostermann, 1955), 9–45. It is well known that Heidegger's text was conceived in response to Jünger's essay, "Über die Linie (Betrachtungen zur Zeit)," appearing originally in *Anteile: Martin Heidegger zum 60. Geburtstag* (Frankfurt: Klostermann, 1951), in Jünger, *Sämtliche Werke*, 7:237–280.

71. Ernst Jünger, *Der Gordische Knoten* (Frankfurt: Klostermann, 1953), 146.

72. Ernst Jünger, *Der Arbeiter: Herrschaft und Gestalt* (Hamburg: Hanseatische Verlagsanstalt, 1932), in *Sämtliche Werke* (Stuttgart: Klett-Cotta, 1981), 8:170.

73. I allude to the title of the opportune book by Jünger's brother, Friedrich Georg, *Die Perfektion der Technik* (Frankfurt: Klostermann, 1946). The book was actually written in 1939 with the more perspicuous title *Illusion der Technik*.

74. Ernst Jünger, "Total Mobilization," in *The Heidegger Controversy: A Critical Reader*, ed. Richard Wolin (Cambridge, Mass.: MIT Press, 1993).

75. Jünger, *Der Arbeiter*, 173.

76. This is Ferruccio Masini's expression: "Ernst Junger: Dall' 'Arbeiter' all' 'anarcha,'" *Il Mulino* 34, no. 301 (1985): 787–801, at 797.

77. Jünger, "Über die Linie," 273.

78. Carl Schmitt, "Die Geschichtliche Struktur des Heutigen Welt-Gegensatzes von Ost und West," in *Freundschaftliche Begegnungen Festschrift für Ernst Jünger*, 136. Schmitt's essay originally appeared in *Merkur* in 1953.

79. Ibid., 137.

80. See Jünger's interview with Gilles Lapouge, "Ernst Jünger: 'Nous entrons dans l'ere du verseau,'" *La Quinzaine Littéraire* 319, no. 16 (February 1980): 5–6, at 6.

81. Heidegger, "Über 'Die Linie,'" 9–45, at 11.

82. Jünger, *An der Zeitmauer*, 188.

83. Ernst Jünger, *Eumeswil*, trans. Joachim Neugroschel (New York: Marsilio Publishers, 1993), 73.

84. Ibid., 50.

85. Ibid., 73.

86. Ibid., 147.

87. Ibid., 249.

88. See Jünger's own affirmations on the matter in Julien Hervier, *The Details of Time: Conversations with Ernst Jünger*, trans. Joachim Neugroschel (New York: Marsilio Publishers, 1995), 81–83.

89. Jünger, *Eumeswil*, 259.

90. Ibid., 280.

91. Ibid., 253.

92. Ibid., 280.

93. Ibid., 279.

94. Ibid., 332.

95. Ibid., 334.

96. Roger Caillois, *Bellone ou la pente de la guerre* (Paris: Nizet-Renaissance du Livre, 1963), 179–180.

97. Georges Bataille, "La limite de l'utile," in *Oeuvres complètes*, 7:181–280, at 251. The text to which Bataille refers is Ernst Jünger, *Der Kampf als Inneres Erlebnis* (Berlin: E. S. Mittler, 1922), which was translated into French with the title *La guerre, notre mère*.

98. See also Georges Bataille, *Theory of Religion*, trans. Robert Hurley (New York: Zone Books, 1989), 57–61.

99. Georges Bataille, "Le Sacrifice" in *Oeuvres complètes*, 2:238–243, at 238.

100. Ibid., 239.

101. Bataille, "La limite de l'utile," 257.

102. Ibid., 259.

103. We ought to recall that Bataille was particularly concerned to withdraw Nietzsche from the "posthumous" shadow of Carl Schmitt (who, incidentally, was not well-known to Bataille). See "Nietzsche and the Fascists," in Georges Bataille, *Visions of Excess: Selected Writings, 1927–1939*, trans. Allan Stoekl, Carl R. Lovitt, and Donald M. Leslie (Minneapolis: University of Minnesota Press, 1985), 189: "National Socialism is less romantic and more Maurrassian than is sometimes imagined, and one must not forget that Rosenberg is its ideological expression closest to Nietzsche; the jurist Carl Schmidt (*sic!*), who incarnates it just as a much as does Rosenberg, is very close to Charles Maurras and, with a Catholic background, has always been alien to the influence of Nietzsche."

104. Ibid., 187.

105. Ibid., 184.

106. The article to which Bataille alludes (also in ibid., 192–193) is Emmanuel Levinas, "Reflections on the Philosophy of Hitlerism," *Critical Inquiry* 17 (1990): 62–71.

107. Bataille, *Visions of Excess*, 193.

108. Karl Jaspers, *Nietzsche: An Introduction to the Understanding of His Philosophical Activity*, trans. Charles F. Wallraff and Frederick J. Schmitz (Tucson: University of Arizona Press, 1965), 252–253.

109. Georges Bataille, *On Nietzsche*, trans. Bruce Boone (London: Continuum, 2004), xxx.

110. Georges Bataille, *The Accursed Share, Volumes 2 & 3*, trans. Robert Hurley (New York: Zone Books, 1991), 409.

111. Ibid., 384.

112. Bataille, *On Nietzsche*, 145.

113. Bataille, *The Accursed Share*, 409.

114. Jean Wahl, "Nietzsche et la mort de Dieu. Note à propos du 'Nietzsche' de Jaspers," *Acéphale* 2 (1937): 22–23.

115. Bataille, *The Accursed Share*, 410.

116. Ibid., 409.

117. [The Italian word *principio* can and in this case does encompass the English words "principle" and "principal" (in the sense of first, initial, or beginning).]

118. Bataille, *Inner Experience*, 81.

119. Bataille's letter to Kojève, dated December 6, 1937, is in Georges Bataille, *Oeuvres complètes*, 5:369–371, at 369 and in Denis Hollier's volume on the College of Sociology. It appears in English translation in Denis Hollier, ed., *The College of Sociology (1937–39)*, trans. Betsy Wing (Minneapolis: University of Minnesota Press, 1988), 89–93, at 90.

120. Ibid.

121. Ibid.

122. Bataille, *On Nietzsche*, 79.

123. Bataille, *The Accursed Share*, 370.

124. I am citing from Denis Hollier, "De l'au-delà de Hegel à l'absence de Nietzsche," in *Bataille*, ed. Philippe Sollers (Cerisy: Centre Culturel de Cerisy La Salle, 1973), 75–96.

125. Bataille, *The Accursed Share*, 371.

126. Bataille, *On Nietzsche*, 125.

127. Ibid., xxix.

128. See in this regard Klossowski's commentary on Löwith's *Nietzsche*: Pierre Klossowski, "Löwith's 'Nietzsche (Nietzsches Philosophie der ewigen Wiederkunft des Gleichen,'" *Acephale* 2 (1937): 30. [Karl Löwith, *Nietzsche's Philosophy of the Eternal Recurrence of the Same*, trans. J. Harvey Lomax (Berkeley: University of California Press, 1997).] On this topic in Klossowski, see also "L'expérience de la mort de Dieu chez Nietzsche et la nostalgie d'une expérience authentique chez Georges Bataille," in Pierre Klossowski, *Sade Mon Prochain* (Paris: Éditions du Seuil, 1947), particularly from 174. [The original French reference is provided since the essay in question does not appear in the English translation. Pierre Klossowski, *Sade My Neighbor*, trans. Alphonso Lingis (Evanston, Ill.: Northwestern University Press, 1991).]

129. See Lev Shestov, *La philosophie de la tragédie: Dostoïewsky et Nietzsche*, trans. Boris de Schloezer (Paris: J. Schiffrin, 1926). An important (and distinctive) affirmation by Bataille himself is found in Georges Bataille, *Oeuvres complètes*, 8:563.

130. Wahl, "Nietzsche et la mort de Dieu," 22–23.

131. Bataille, *On Nietzsche*, 156.

132. The principal reference here is obviously Marcel Mauss, *The Gift*, trans. Ian Cunnison (London: Cohen & West, 1966); based on Bronislaw Malinowski, *Argonauts of the Western Pacific: An Account of Native Enterprise and Adventure in the Archipelagoes of Melanesian New Guinea* (New York: Dutton, 1961).

133. Recall that *Das Heilige* was translated in France in 1929 with the title *Le sacré*. Rudolf Otto, *Le sacré: L'élément non rationnel dans l'idée du divin et sa relation avec le rationnel*, trans. André Jundt (Paris: Payot, 1969).

134. See in particular Durkheim's *The Elementary Forms of Religious Life* (New York: Free Press, 1995).

135. Of the elements found in K. T. Preuss's essay "Der Ursprung der Religion und Kunst," published in *Globus* 86 (1904) and 87 (1905), the one that recurs with the most intensity and frequency in Bataille (as it does also in Leiris and Caillois) is the relation between the sacred and the excretory functions.

136. See particularly Bataille's two papers on "Attraction and Repulsion" (presented Saturday, January 22 and Saturday, February 5, 1938), in Hollier, *The College of Sociology (1937–39)*, 103–124.

137. Roger Caillois, *Man and the Sacred*, trans. Meyer Barash (Chicago: University of Illinois Press, 2001), 13.

138. Ibid., 35–36.

139. See the essay "Power," delivered by Bataille at the College on Saturday, February 19, 1938, in place of an ill Caillois: Hollier, *The College of Sociology (1937–39)*, 125–136.

140. See the paper delivered by Bataille at the College, again in place of Caillois, on March 19, 1938, with the title "Brotherhoods, Orders, Secret Societies, Churches," in ibid., 147.

141. Georges Bataille, "The Psychological Structure of Fascism," *New German Critique* 16 (1979): 64–87, at 75.

142. Ibid., 81.

143. Ibid.

144. Ibid.

145. Ibid., 83.

146. Bataille, *Visions of Excess*, 199. The quotation is drawn from "Propositions on Fascism," originally published in *Acéphale* in 1937, in Bataille, *Oeuvres complètes*, 1:467–470.

147. On Bataille and the political, in addition to Jacqueline Risset, ed., *Georges Bataille: Il politico e il sacro* (Napoli: Liguori, 1987); see also Francis Marmande, *Georges Bataille politique* (Lyon: Presses Universitaires de Lyon, 1985); as well as the less recent Denis Hollier, *Against Architecture: The Writings of Georges Bataille*, trans. Betsy Wing (Cambridge, Mass.: MIT Press, 1989).

148. Bataille, *Visions of Excess*, 199.

149. Bataille, *On Nietzsche*, 9.

150. The other objection Leiris leveled against Bataille was that he wanted to found an order before having defined a doctrine. See Leiris's letter to Bataille of July 3, 1939, in Hollier, *The College of Sociology (1937–39)*, 355.

151. See above all Georges Bataille, "Le sacré," *Cahiers d'Art* 1–4 (1939): 47–50, in Bataille, *Oeuvres complètes*, 1:559–563.

152. Laure, *Laure: The Collected Writings*, trans. Jeanine Herman (San Francisco: City Lights Books, 1995), 44.

153. See the appraisal of the Collège given by Bataille on Tuesday, July 4, 1939. Hollier, *The College of Sociology (1937–39)*, 333–341.

154. See Caillois in *Man and the Sacred*, 15, and Bataille in *The Accursed Share*, 438–439.

155. Hollier, *The College of Sociology (1937–39)*, 73.

156. There is a reference specifically to the elite as a condition of the formation of sects in Roger Caillois, *Instincts et société: Essais de sociologie contemporaine* (Genève: Gonthier, 1964), 111.

157. See Roger Caillois, "The Winter Wind," in Hollier, *The College of Sociology (1937–39)*, 36.

158. Ibid., 36, 401. Hollier's note attributes the neologism to Caillois's text "Poisons sacrés, ivresses divines," published in April 1937 in *Cahiers du Sud*.

159. Roger Caillois, "La hierarchie des etres," *Les Volontaires* 5 (1939): 317–326, at 323.

160. Roger Caillois, "Aggressiveness as a Value," originally published in *L'Ordre Nouveau* in 1937, is now in Roger Caillois, *The Edge of Surrealism: A Roger Caillois Reader*, ed. Claudine Frank, trans. Claudine Frank and Camille Naish (Durham, N.C.: Duke University Press, 2003), 163.

161. Roger Caillois, *Le mythe et l'homme* (Paris: Gallimard, 1938), 181–182.

162. Ibid., 11–12.

163. Caillois cites Jünger more than once concerning the theme of "War and the Sacred," for example in Caillois, *Man and the Sacred*, 168–173. But an implicit reference to a post-*histoire* horizon can also be found in another of his texts: *Pierres* (Paris: Gallimard, 1966).

164. There is an approving reference to Sorel in a note by Caillois in the *Nouvelle Revue Française* in April 1936.

165. The entire "myth" of the *Acephale* is constructed in close relation not only to Freud's *Totem and Taboo*, but also patricide in Georges Dumézil's *Ouranos-Varuna: Étude de mythologie comparée indo-europééne* (Paris: Adrien-Maisonneuve, 1934). Caillois was to publish an intervention concerning this book in *Cahiers du Sud*, June 1935.

166. See the polemic by Caillois published in the *Nouvelle Revue Française* in October 1937, concerning Léon Blum's book *L'exercice du pouvoir*. The Dumézil reference is to Georges Dumézil, *Mitra-Varuna: An Essay on Two Indo-European Representations of Sovereignty*, trans. Derek Coltman (New York: Zone Books, 1988).

167. Bataille, "Power," in Hollier, *The College of Sociology (1937–39)*, 132.

168. Bataille, "Brotherhoods, Orders, Secret Societies, Churches," in ibid., 154.

169. Caillois, "The Winter Wind," in ibid., 37.

170. Jean-Luc Nancy, *The Inoperative Community*, trans. Peter Connor, Lisa Garbus, Michael Holland, and Simona Sawhney (Minneapolis: University of Minnesota Press, 1991). The pages that follow here owe much to Nancy's work—which Giorgio Agamben has also addressed, for example in "Bataille and the Paradox of Sovereignty," in Risset, *Georges Bataille*, 115–119. [A broadly similar text now appears in Giorgio Agamben, *Homo Sacer: Sovereign Power and Bare Life*, trans. Daniel Heller-Roazen (Stanford: Stanford University Press, 1998), 112–115.]

171. In this sense, the pages of the second, third and fourth parts of Bataille's book on sovereignty are critically decisive (see Bataille, *The Accursed Share*).

172. On this matter, we can only regard as wholly misplaced that part of Habermas's *Philosophical Discourse of Modernity* that concerns Bataille. The problem Habermas poses, how to explain Stalinism's conversion into sovereignty, is in no way the Bataillian question. See Jürgen Habermas, *The Philosophical Discourse of*

Modernity: Twelve Lectures, trans. Frederick Lawrence (Cambridge, Mass.: MIT Press, 1987), 211–237, especially at 234.

173. Bataille, "La limite de l'utile," 181–280, at 245–246.

174. Pages of rare intensity were written on this theme by Maurice Blanchot, in the first part of *The Unavowable Community*, trans. Pierre Joris (Barrytown, N.Y.: Station Hill Press, 1988).

175. Bataille, *On Nietzsche*, 21.

176. Ibid., 19.

177. This is what Derrida means when he cautions that "sovereignty is not neutral, even if it neutralizes, *in its discourse*, all the contradictions and all the oppositions of classical logic. Neutralization is produced within knowledge and within the syntax of writing, but it is related to a sovereign and transgressive affirmation." Derrida, *From Restricted to General Economy*, 274.

178. Blanchot, *The Infinite Conversation*, 208.

179. Ibid., 208–209.

180. Ibid., 209.

181. This quotation, which appears in the "Nietzschean Chronicle," in Bataille, *Visions of Excess*, 212, comes from the stage directions accompanying the text.

182. Ibid., 207. The specifically Roman character of the principle of the political, and the role of the command function ("imperium"), were signaled by Heidegger in his 1942–43 course on Parmenides, where he wrote: "We think the 'political' as Romans, i.e., imperially." See Martin Heidegger, *Parmenides*, trans. André Schuwer and Richard Rojcewicz (Bloomington: Indiana University Press, 1992), 43.

183. Bataille, *Visions of Excess*, 207–208.

184. Ibid., 208.

185. Ibid., 209.

186. Ibid.

187. Ibid., 209–210.

COMMONALITIES

Timothy C. Campbell, series editor

Roberto Esposito, *Terms of the Political: Community, Immunity, Biopolitics.* Translated by Rhiannon Noel Welch. Introduction by Vanessa Lemm.

Maurizio Ferraris, *Documentality: Why It Is Necessary to Leave Traces.* Translated by Richard Davies.

Dimitris Vardoulakis, *Sovereignty and Its Other: Toward the Dejustification of Violence.*

Anne Emmanuelle Berger, *The Queer Turn in Feminism: Identities, Sexualities, and the Theater of Gender.* Translated by Catherine Porter.

James D. Lilley, *Common Things: Romance and the Aesthetics of Belonging in Atlantic Modernity.*

Jean-Luc Nancy, *Identity: Fragments, Frankness.* Translated by François Raffoul.

Miguel Vatter, *Between Form and Event: Machiavelli's Theory of Political Freedom.*

Miguel Vatter, *The Republic of the Living: Biopolitics and the Critique of Civil Society.*

Maurizio Ferraris, *Where Are You? An Ontology of the Cell Phone.* Translated by Sarah De Sanctis.

Irving Goh, *The Reject: Community, Politics, and Religion after the Subject.*

Kevin Attell, *Giorgio Agamben: Beyond the Threshold of Deconstruction.*

J. Hillis Miller, *Communities in Fiction.*

Remo Bodei, *The Life of Things, the Love of Things.* Translated by Murtha Baca.

Gabriela Basterra, *The Subject of Freedom: Kant, Levinas.*

Roberto Esposito, *Categories of the Impolitical.* Translated by Connal Parsley.